THEN & NOW

CHESTER COUNTY

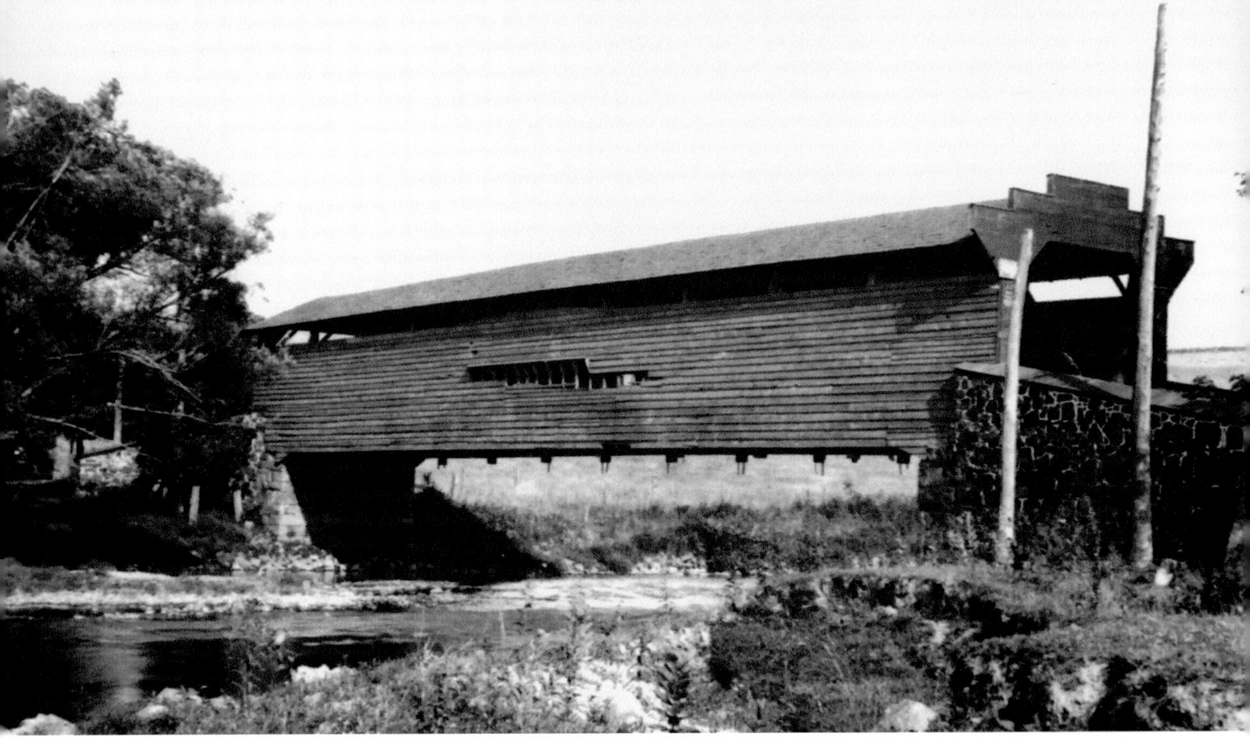

Sheeder-Hall Bridge, on Hollow Road north of Birchrunville, is Chester County's oldest covered bridge. Built in 1850, the 100-foot span crosses French Creek with the total length of the bridge at 116 feet. The name honors two prominent local families. The Halls operated a farm on the West Vincent side while the Sheeder family operated a paper mill a half-mile upstream from the bridge in East Vincent Township.

THEN & NOW

CHESTER COUNTY

Chester County Historical Society
with the Chester County Camera Club

ARCADIA
PUBLISHING

ISBN 978-0-7385-3661-3

Published by Arcadia Publishing,
Charleston, South Carolina

Printed in the United States of America

Library of Congress Catalog Card Number: 2004107293

For all general information, contact Arcadia Publishing:
Telephone 843-853-2070
Fax 843-853-0044
E-mail sales@arcadiapublishing.com
For customer service and orders:
Toll-free 1-888-313-2665

Visit us on the Internet at www.arcadiapublishing.com

To the photographers, past and present, who have documented our Chester County landscape.

Contents

Acknowledgments 6

Introduction 7

1. New Uses for Old Structures 9

2. Things That Aren't There Anymore 35

3. Places That Have Been Preserved 53

4. Places That Have Changed 75

Acknowledgments

The Chester County Historical Society (CCHS) thanks everyone who made this project and publication possible. Co-author Ray Doyle is to be lauded for his dedication and technical expertise.

The Chester County Camera Club volunteers jumped into this project with fabulous results. Each photographer is credited with taking photographs on the following pages: Emilie McI. Barber 50, 65; Ernest B. Bogusch 14, 45; Timothy Brennan 18, 92, 93; Stephanie Clist 49, 96; Patricia M. Danzon 82; Laura Densmore 34, 54, 55; Robert H. Diefenbacher 62, 63; Ray Doyle 15, 33, 39, 51, 59, 71, 76, 89, 90; Steve Fredrick 16, 78, 83, 84, 85; Seán Gallagher 21; Bill Hein 26; Eileen M. Hogan 20, 27, 30, 46, 74; Ed Huberty 19, 56, 67; Michelle M. Hughes 52, 80; Cris Staley Hutchinson 37, 77; A. Lybrand Hutton 66; John Koskulitz 32, 48, 69; William B. Matakas Jr. 88; Robert McCook 10, 11, 13, 36, 95; Mary Painter 68, 81; Dorothy Brinton Parker 24, 61; Vince Piotti 17, 28, 44; Carol Frost Poling 29, 57, 58, 73, 79; Lillian Reiss 25, 94; Sally Riddle 40, 41, 70, 72; Geoffrey Ruth 42; Daniel J. Williams 22, 31, 43; Gordon J. Wissinger 47, 86, 87; and Mark W. Wlaz 23, 60, 64.

We are grateful to the private property owners who graciously gave permission to photograph their homes and businesses, especially John Baird and Mary Brooks, who coordinated the Westtown School students photograph.

The historical society is grateful to the lenders who provided images necessary for this project: Larry Drennen Sr., Larry Drennen Jr., Chris Drennen, Eugene DiOrio, Millard McComsey, Frank March, Dennis Park, Wanda McGlinchey-Ryan, Harry Walters Jr., and the West Nottingham Historical Commission.

CCHS appreciates the project advisors who generously gave of their time and knowledge. They are John Bradley, Sandy Brannan, William and Rosalind Brewster, Charles and Jane Brosius, Francis G. Brown, Estelle Cremers, Eugene DiOrio, Lois Donovan, Dr. Faye Doyle, Mary Dugan, East Goshen Historical Commission, Lois and Richard Farmer, Dorothy Freese, C. Herbert Fry, Robert Garrett, Roger and Carol Grigson, Joann Grosso, Jim Guthrie, Katherine Harlan, Fran Jackson, Margaret Brosius Jones, Dr. Henry Jordan, Joseph Lordi, Thomas Marshall, Vivian Miller, Nancy Mohr, Hervey Painter, Rosemary Philips, Celeste Reiffer, Barbara Rutz, Mary Sproat, and Eric Wilson. Chris Densmore of Friends Historical Library and David Shields of Brandywine Conservancy provided essential information.

We are thankful for the eager helpfulness of interns Huyen Ta and Rose Marie Jacobs for research, Heidi Benedict for editorial assistance, and Tim Manni and Ed Huberty for scanning.

I appreciate the assistance of CCHS staff Ellen Endslow, Barbara Jobe, Diane and Laurie Rofini, and the support of the CCHS Board of Trustees, especially board chairman John Diffey and board member Bruce Mowday.

—Pamela C. Powell
Chester County Historical Society

Introduction

This book is an ambitious project undertaken by the Chester County Historical Society to document the changes in the use of our land. Chester County is the fastest developing county in the commonwealth of Pennsylvania. How we have used the land tells the history of the evolution of our county from the agriculture and industries of the 19th century to the specialty agriculture and service industries of today. Through this process, the landscape has been transformed. Some significant historical structures have disappeared, while others have been restored and used for different purposes.

In order to undertake the project we have asked these questions: What areas show the greatest changes? What areas show little change? How have changes in our economy, transportation systems, and lifestyle brought about these changes?

Advisors from all parts of the county provided input. These people generously shared their knowledge and memories out of love for the county. Many of them serve on historic commissions and area historical societies and act as township planners, librarians, or area historians. They suggested places they thought were most important to the people of each township or borough. These places were, and some still are, significant due to their economic importance, their role in the life of the community, their value as landmarks that we identify with the county, or simply as places that have generated fond memories.

Research information was then gathered from the resources of the Chester County Historical Society library. Historical property atlases, newspaper articles, business records, and personal accounts proved invaluable. Wills, deeds, and road papers provided necessary facts from the Chester County Archives. Many hours were spent poring over the historical society's collection of more than 80,000 photographs, and images were located of places that were identified as significant to the county's past. What has become of those places today? More hours in the car circumnavigating the county revealed sites that made interesting comparisons.

The possible sites included 18th-century mills that ground flour during the Revolutionary era and mills that made paper and textiles during the Industrial Revolution. There were iron furnaces and foundries that made cannons and steel for bridges. There were networks of railroads that took farmers' goods to market, connecting dairy farms, creameries, stock farms, and orchards to points beyond. There were schools, churches, lyceums, Granges, fire companies, and organizations serving as the backbone of our community. There were picnic grounds, fairgrounds, and movie theaters that provided entertainment. All of these elements have made our county the unique place that it is and have endeared it to generations.

But what about the places that are important to us today as economic or social centers? Could we locate historical images of the places that have since become the major employers of today—Vanguard, Shared Medical Systems, or QVC? What about sites like the Exton Mall or Route 202? For some of these locations we simply have no historical documentation because the site may have been a farmer's field that was not considered a good subject for a photograph in years gone by.

Individuals offered the historical society a number of key images to use for this project. Without the kind generosity of these lenders, essential sites could not have been included. Although the historical society's photograph collection offers a fine representation of most parts of the county, some areas require further collecting. The major part of the collection has been built on the donations of thoughtful people who wanted to preserve the visual memory of the county.

After a substantial number of sites were identified, it was time to begin the photography. The Chester County Camera Club, under former club president Bob Diefenbacher, stepped up to the challenge of undertaking this project. The energy and enthusiasm of the club members was overwhelming. The photographers were willing to drive many miles in early-morning hours to find obscure places. They climbed through bushes, drove down gravel roads, and were good humored through it all. In the process they met some interesting people, saw new parts of the county, and learned more about its history.

Technical difficulties had to be surmounted in re-photographing the sites seen in the historical images. The first consideration was that the historical photographs were taken with equipment and materials that are very different from what is used today. Many of the historical photographers used highly adjustable view cameras with lenses that are of a different focal length from what we now use. They used glass-plate negatives with a very slow ASA rating. All of these elements produced sharp, fine-grained prints. The historical prints themselves are of a great variety of processes—albumen prints, cyanotypes, platinum prints, and early silver gelatin developing-out papers.

Rather than try to duplicate these views exactly, our photographers reinterpreted the sites, using their modern equipment. They used a variety of 35-millimeter cameras and lenses, but all used slow-speed black-and-white film. Sometimes it was impossible to get exactly the same view as in the historical photograph due to the growth of trees or the highways or buildings that have recently appeared. When this was the case, they photographed the subject from a new perspective. How does an old building relate to super highways or other structures that have been built around it? What story does the landscape have to tell? What is the use of that site now? If an old building has been removed, what is there now? How quickly we forget what was on a site before!

Altogether, the images our photographers have created document our county as it is today for the researchers of tomorrow. The results have indeed been gratifying. As our landscape evolves, it is the Chester County Historical Society's mission to document that transformation and preserve the images of the past for future residents.

The Chester County Chamber of Business and Industry, on Paoli Pike in East Goshen Township, is a good example of an old structure that has found a new use. Previously, it was a farm where generations of the Garrett family lived. More recently it was used as an experimental farm for a pharmaceutical company.

Chapter 1
NEW USES FOR OLD STRUCTURES

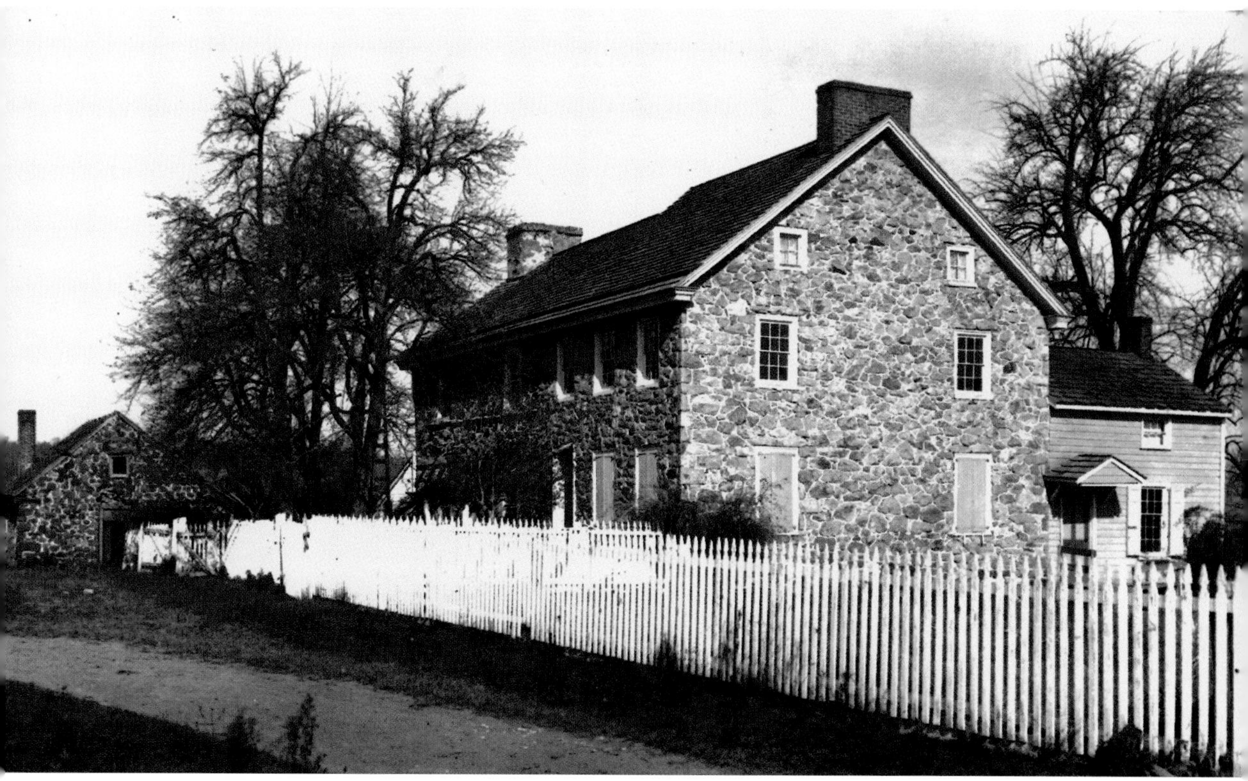

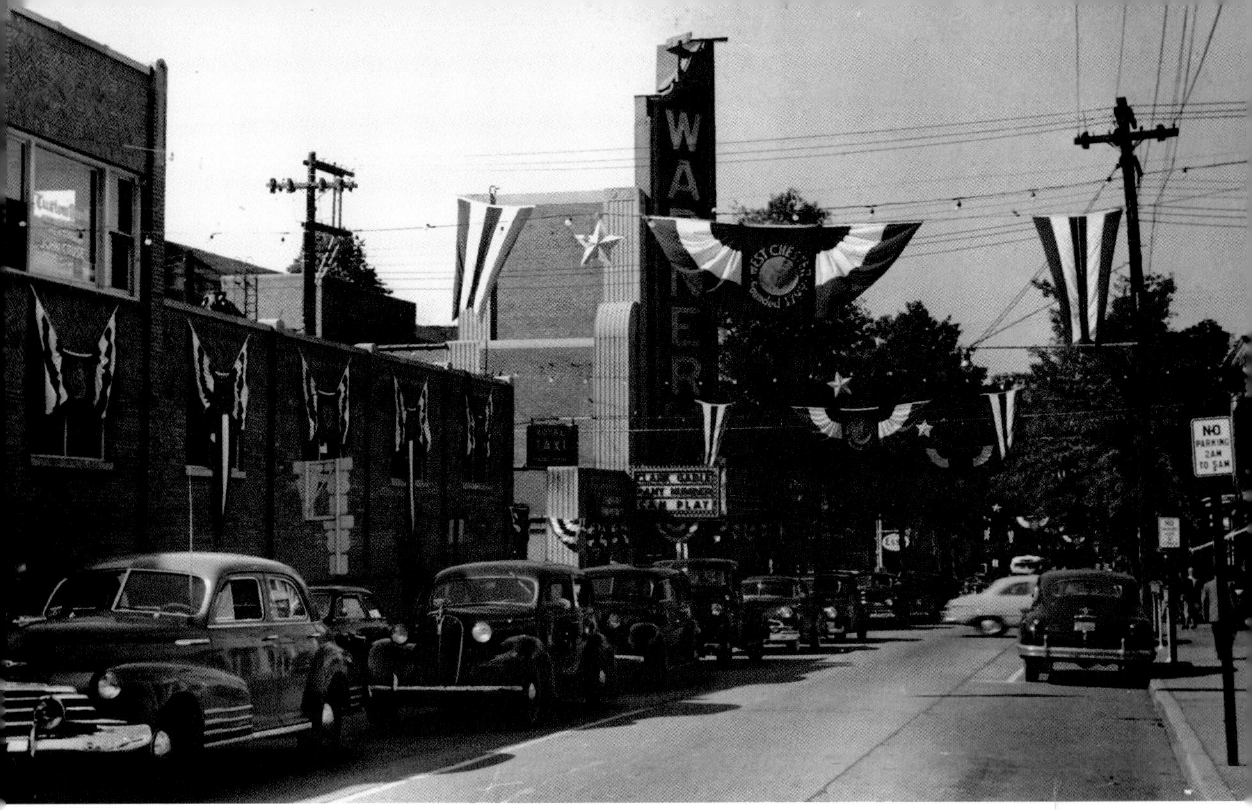

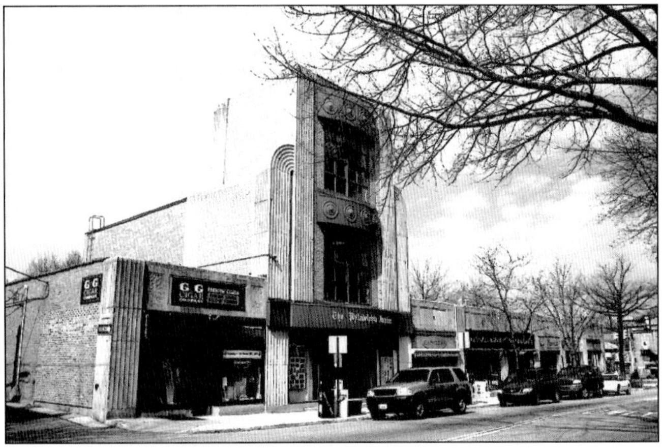

The lavish Warner Theater in West Chester opened on November 14, 1930. The first film shown was *The Life of the Party,* an all-talking Technicolor comedy starring wisecracking Winnie Lightner. Featured live on stage that evening was the singing and dancing of child star Davey Lee. It was one of the last theaters built directly by Hollywood to market its films. The theater closed in May 1984. On the final evening's bill was Woody Allen's *Broadway Danny Rose.* Efforts made to preserve the building intact failed and demolition took place in late 1986, leaving only the Art Deco façade and lobby areas in place. Today, the remaining portion of the building houses the Chester County offices of the Philadelphia Inquirer.

Philip M. Sharples, a practical machinist, first came in contact with a cream separator when a customer asked him to install the equipment on his farm. Sharples became a distributor for the Swedish-made DeLaval Separators and, after making some improvements on the design, patented his own model in 1883. The Sharples Separator became a popular cream separator distributed worldwide. By the early 20th century, the Sharples Separator Company became the largest employer in West Chester, employing more than 500 workers and producing more than 200 machines a week. The factory complex occupied two entire city blocks convenient to the railroad. The company was forced to close during the Great Depression in 1934. The

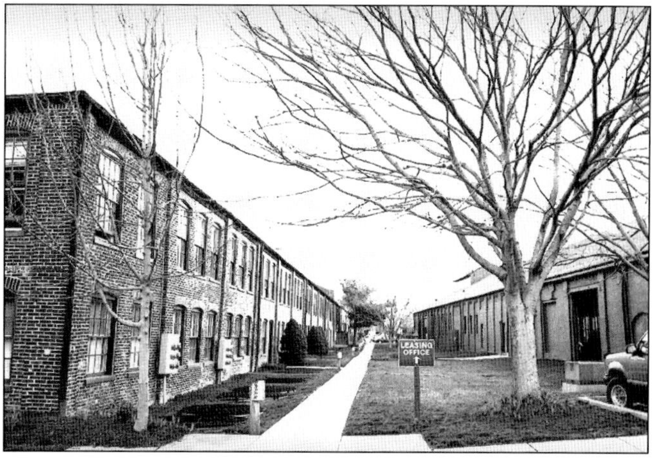

Esco Cabinet Company took over the buildings in 1939, manufacturing refrigerators and freezers until 1969. After sitting vacant for many years, the buildings were converted into luxury apartments in 1989.

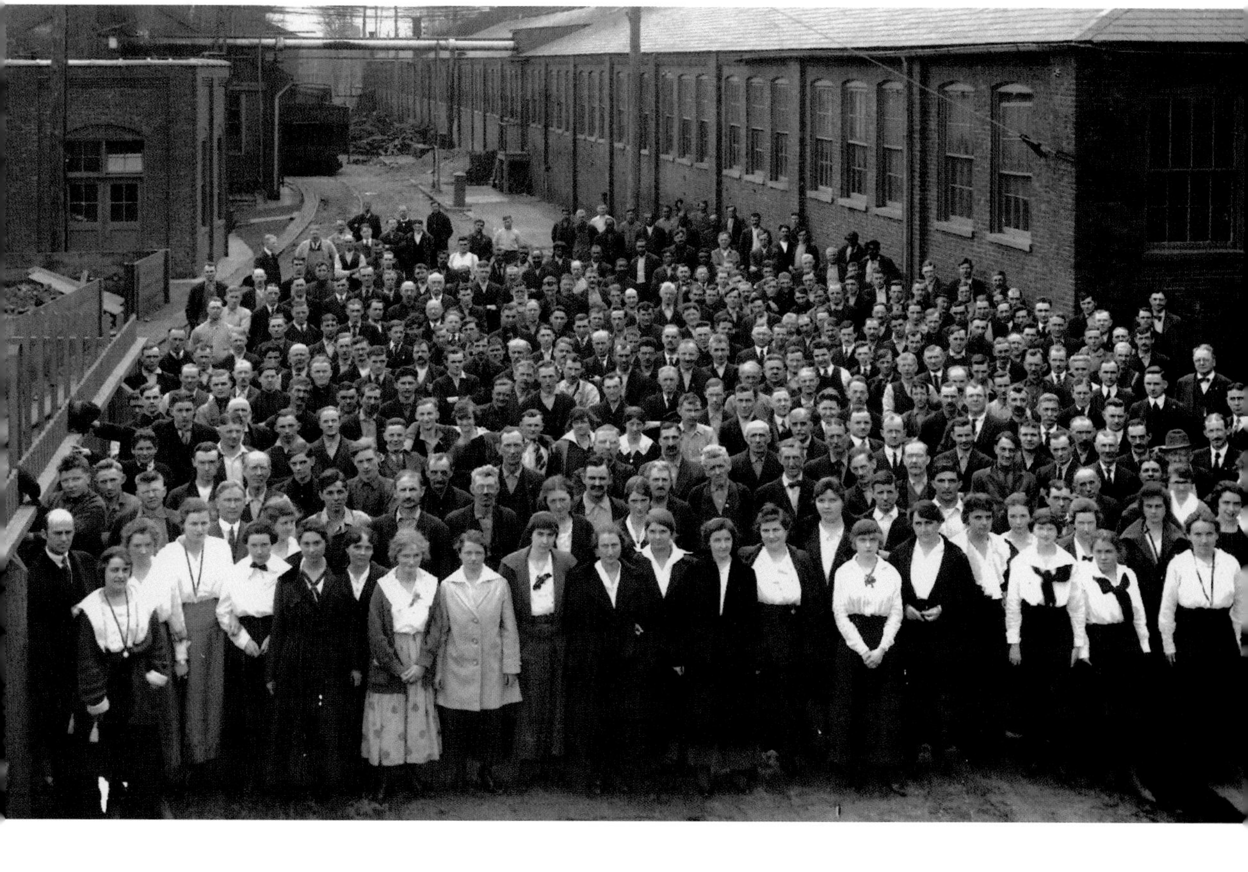

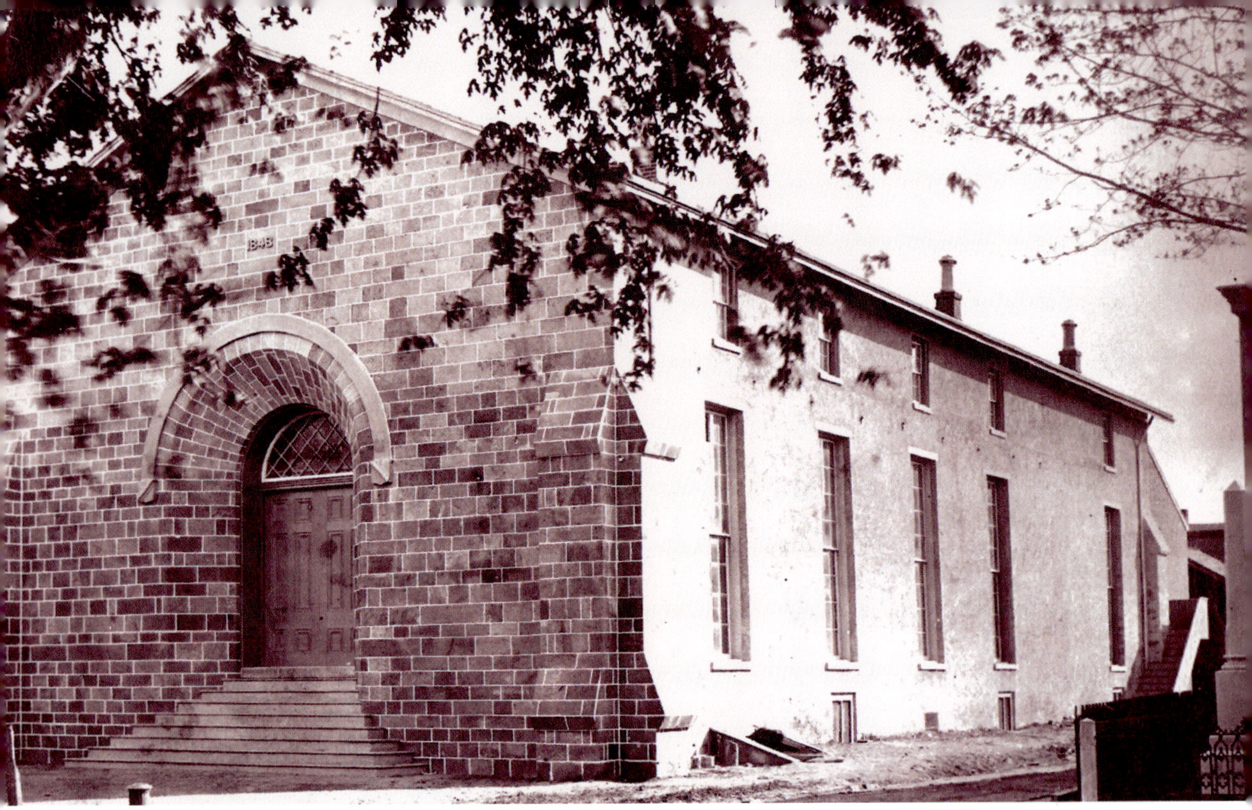

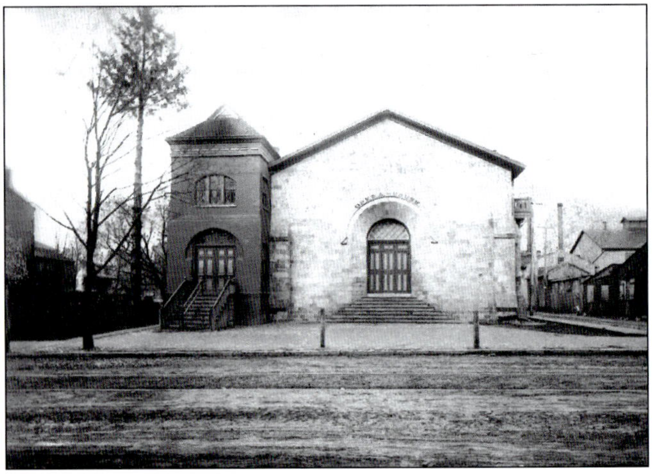

The Norman-style building of serpentine stone designed by Thomas U. Walter has seen a great variety of uses. Originally constructed in 1848 as the home of the Chester County Horticultural Society, the site hosted agricultural displays and was used as a lecture hall. In 1852, it was the site of the first Pennsylvania woman's rights convention. In 1880, the agricultural society sold its hall to entrepreneur Uriah Hunt Painter, who refurbished it as an opera house. He added a stage area to the back of the building, a second story, and a staircase tower. The opera house featured everything from Buffalo Bill's Wild West Show to recitals by Madam Louise Homer and speeches by Frederick Douglass.

After remodeling the building, Painter's widow gave the hall to the McCall Post of the Grand Army of the Republic (GAR) in 1904 and renamed it Memorial Hall. It was to be used until the last Civil War veteran died and was then to be given to the Chester County Historical Society. This did not occur until 1939. The historical society did extensive remodeling on Memorial Hall and opened the building to the public in 1942. The historical society restored the building to its appearance as Horticultural Hall and expanded its quarters in 1995 to include the old YMCA building next-door. It houses a museum and library and hosts an active schedule of public programs for children and adults.

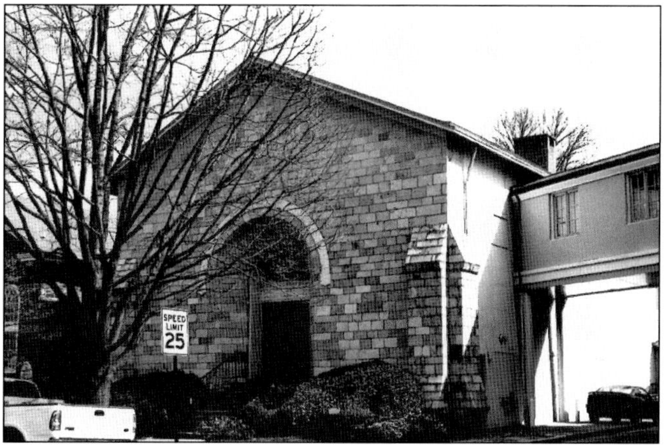

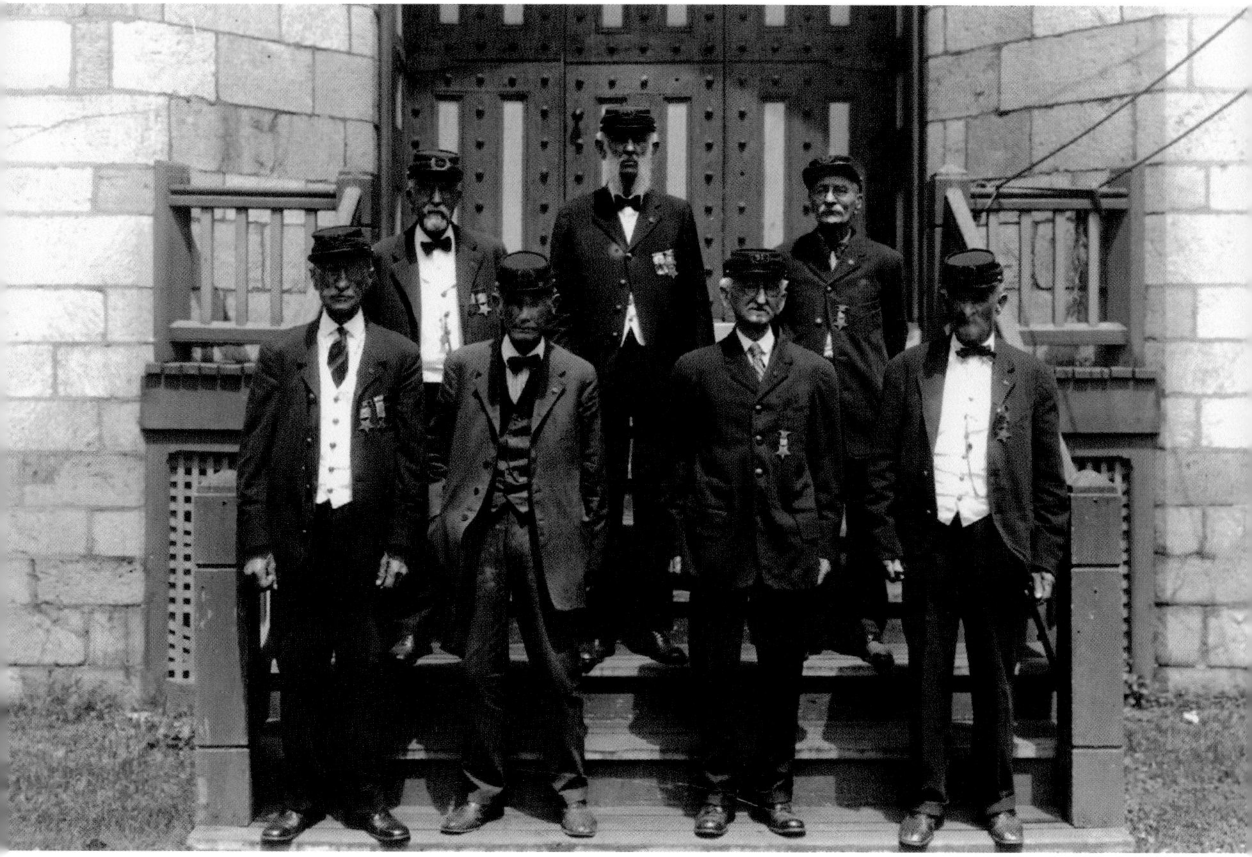

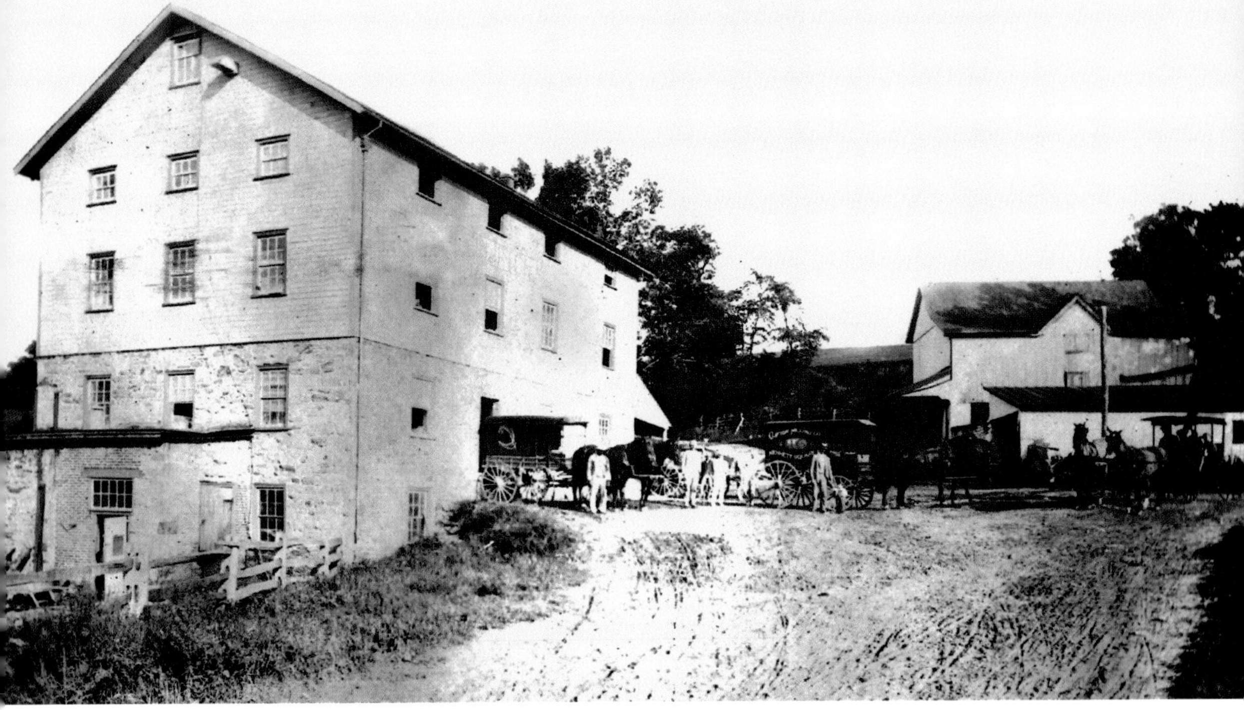

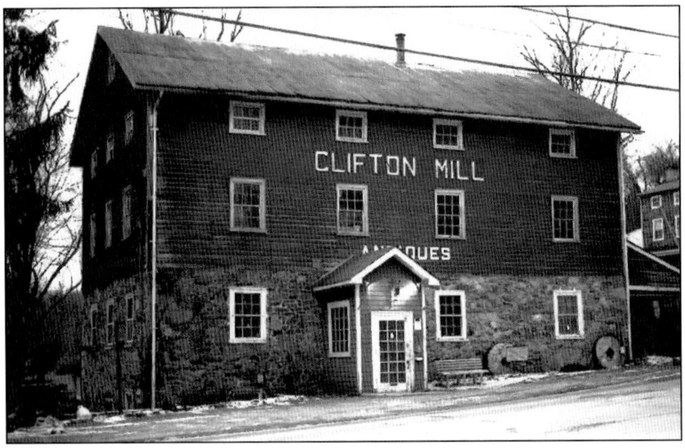

Clifton Mill on the Red Clay Creek was one of the oldest mills in continuous operation in eastern Pennsylvania. It was built between 1715 and 1741 and, under many different owners and operators, was in continuous operation until 1936. The mill burned in 1866 but was immediately rebuilt. The original overshot wooden waterwheel was 16 feet high and 7 1/2 feet across. It was replaced in 1911 with a metal wheel. The mill ground corn, wheat, and barley. The products were used locally, but most were shipped to Wilmington. In later years, the mill ground grain for nationally known product brands of Swan's Down and Cream of Wheat. Today, the mill is used as an antique shop and can be seen on Route 82 south of Kennett Square.

This building in West Sadsbury Township was the home of the Chalfant Motor Company, one of the pioneers in the manufacture of horseless carriages in the United States. Brothers Harry, Howard, and Fillmore Chalfant produced their first auto in 1906. The 22-horsepower vehicle was expensive, selling for approximately $1,200. Chalfant automobiles were produced for the next several years; engines increased in power to 40 horsepower, and the price increased to $1,300. Chalfant was but one of approximately 1,800 U.S. auto makers before 1930. In 1912, the brothers bought out the other stockholders and continued to produce automobiles until 1918. Approximately 200 Chalfants were built in all. This building through the years has housed the production of fireworks and toys and is now home to an automotive restoration company.

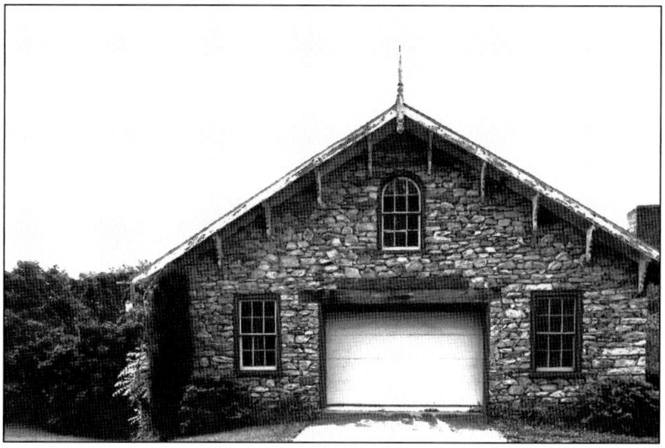

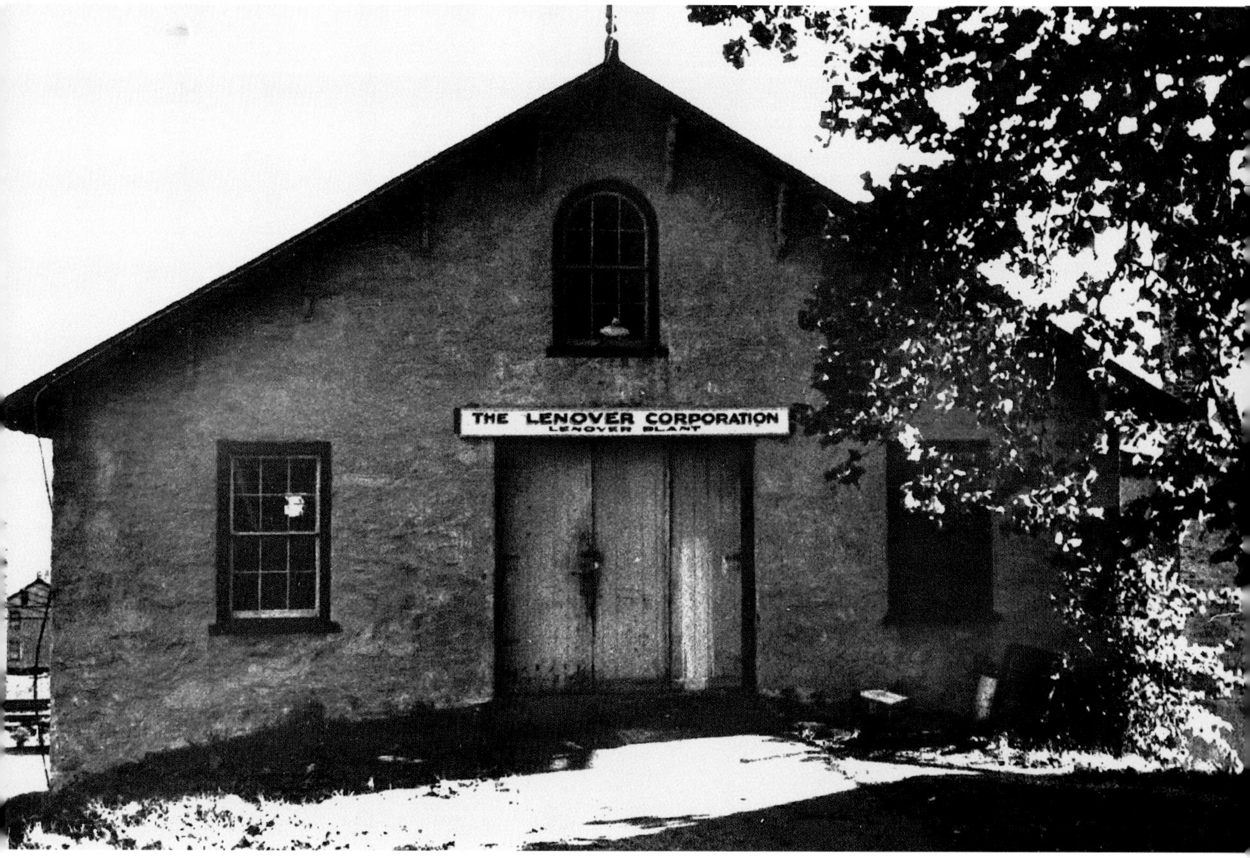

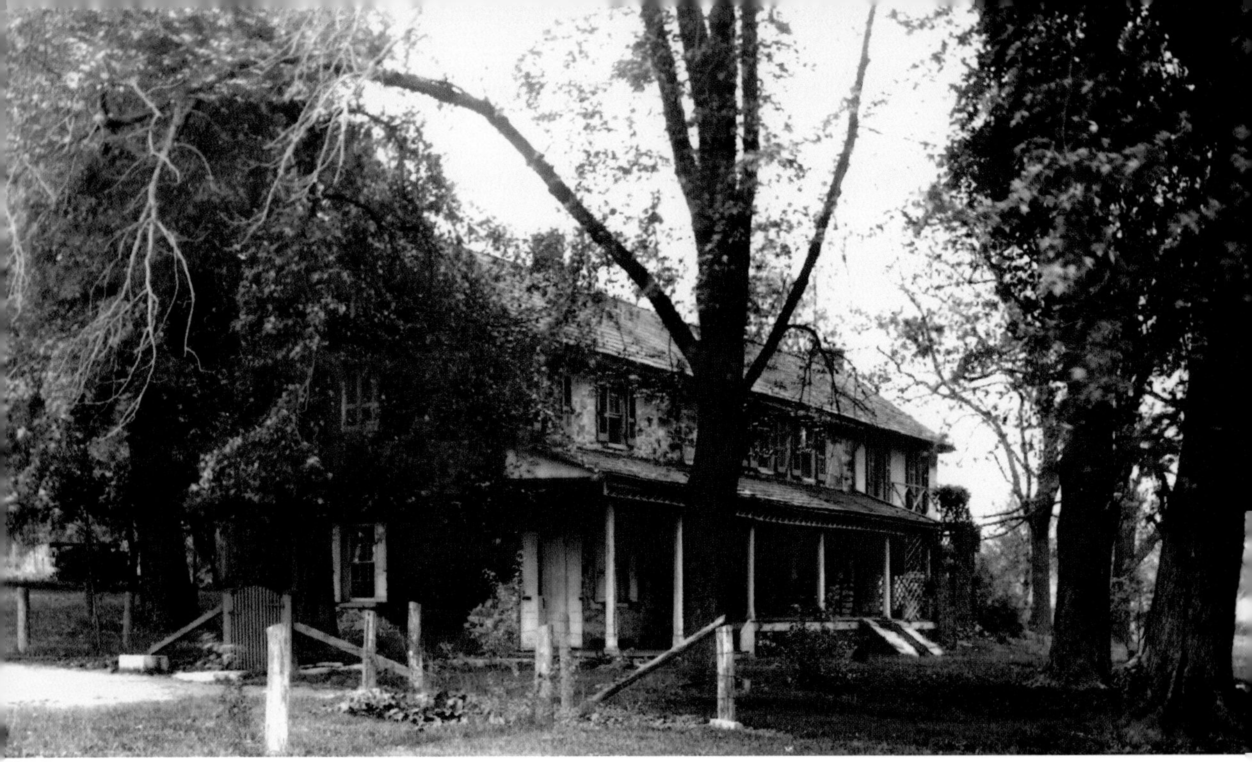

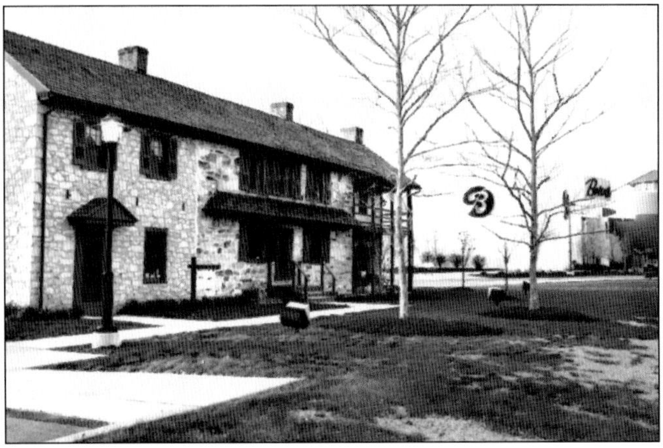

The Zook House in Exton, built by early settler William Owen in 1750, was home to eight generations of the Zook family. Moritz Zug (Zook), grandson of an Anabaptist preacher, moved from Berks County and purchased the home in 1770. It became a haven for Amish and Mennonite travelers who were migrating westward to Lancaster County and Ohio. The building was restored and preserved by the Rouse Company during the construction of Exton Square Mall (1971–1972) and became the headquarters of the West Whiteland Historical Commission. When Exton Mall expanded, the building was relocated to its present nearby site. Today, it houses the main offices of the Chester County Conference and Visitor's Bureau.

The Willistown Inn was the center of activity on West Chester Pike. It was first established as a hotel for passengers on the stage line from Philadelphia to West Chester. The earliest record of the inn is an 1808 application for a tavern license, submitted by owner Henry Bowman. Beginning in 1898, it became a stop for the West Chester and Philadelphia trolley, as seen in the historical photograph. The inn was used as the Willistown Post Office from 1854 until 1905. Today, the old inn has a new life as the Wachovia Securities investment office, and the old barn has become an antiques shop. The stucco was removed from the building in 2002.

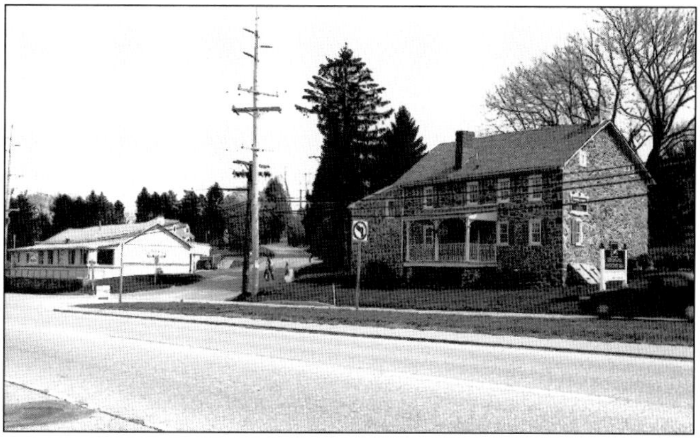

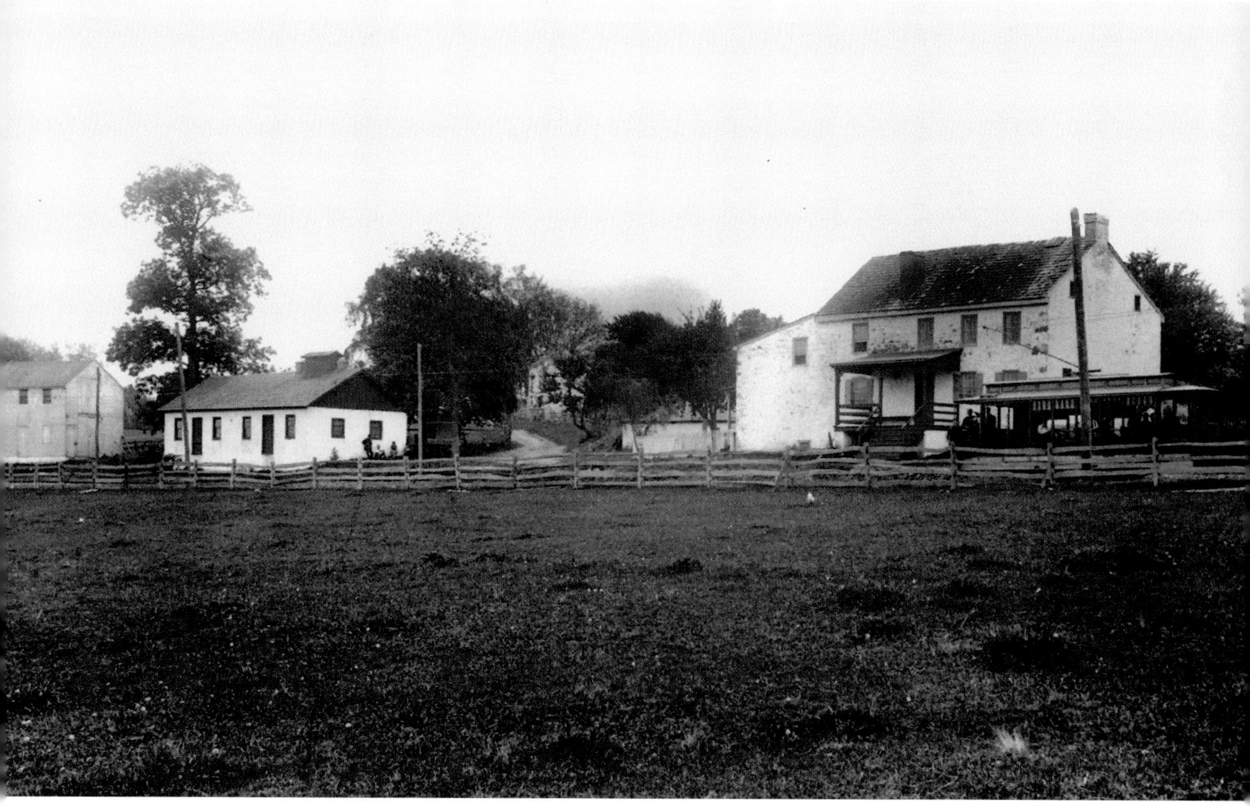

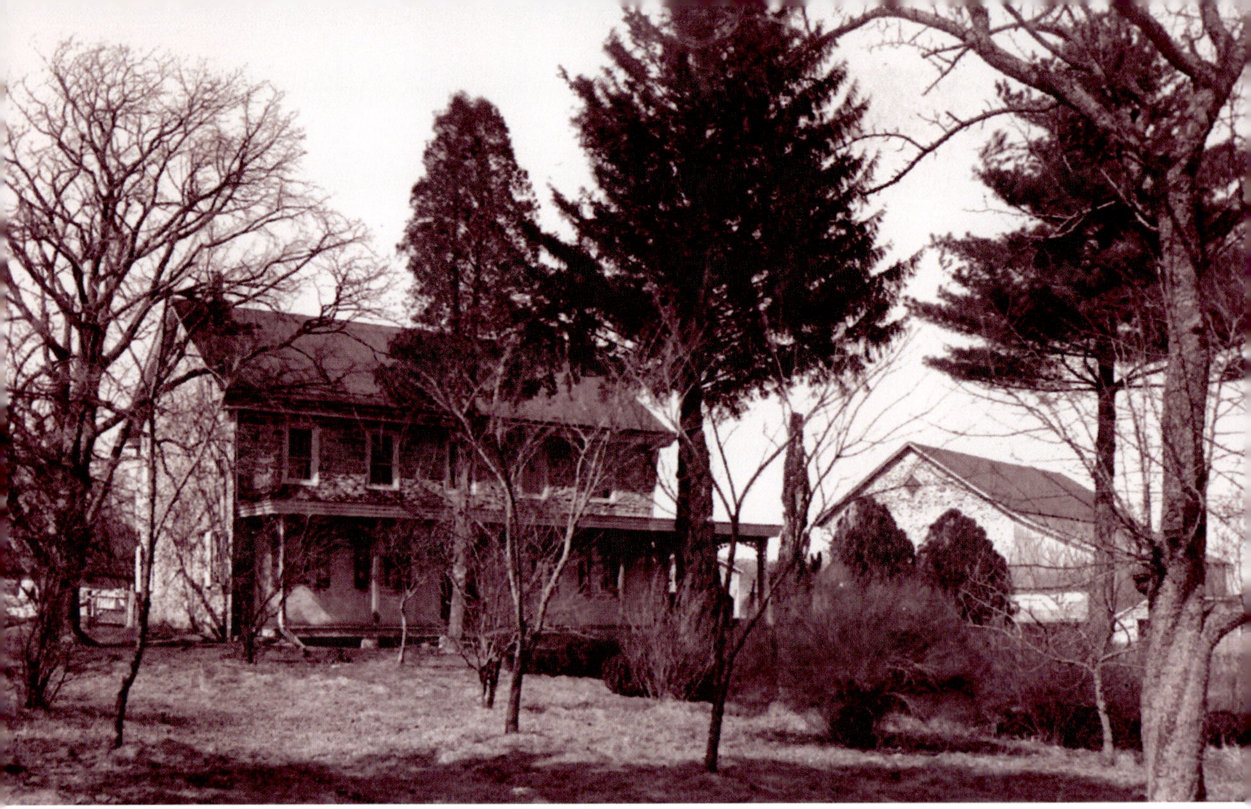

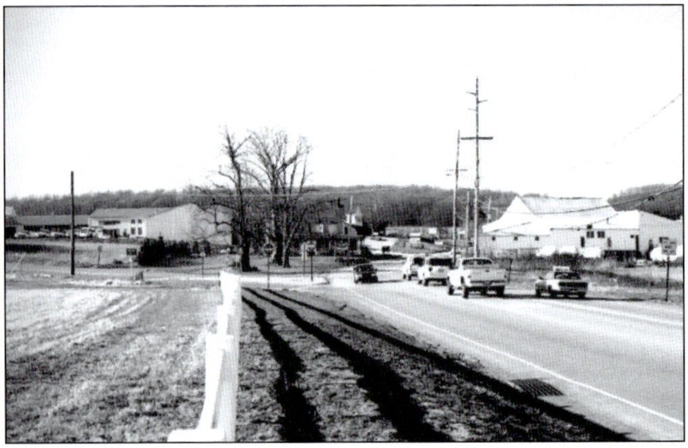

Daniel Keeley and his wife, Catherine Hartman Keeley, raised 10 children on their prosperous 150-acre farm in Upper Uwchlan Township. In 1870, their herd of 21 cows produced 13,500 gallons of milk. They raised corn, oats, wheat, and potatoes and had an orchard of 40 apple trees. Their son Marion took over the farm's operation when Daniel became too elderly to farm in 1893. Today, the homestead has been converted into the Clay Lady gift shop. The barn, which is across Pottstown Pike from the house, is now occupied by a trucking company.

This three-and-a-half-story barn in East Bradford Township housed the prize sheep of Joseph Cope during the mid-19th century. Subsequent owner Herman Hoopes transformed the working farm into a gentleman's country estate when he purchased it in 1896. He stabled his Arabian stallion and other fine horses in this barn. After a devastating fire in the 1930s, the barn was rebuilt to only three stories. It was used as dairy barn and riding stable. During the 1950s, it fell into disuse. The current owner purchased the property in 1979 and renovated it into a spacious three-story house.

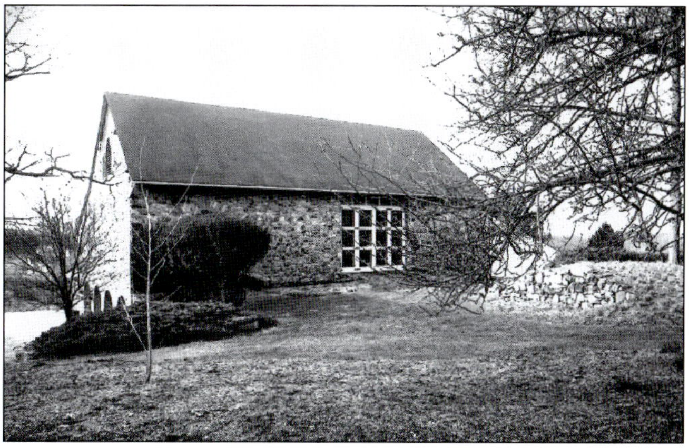

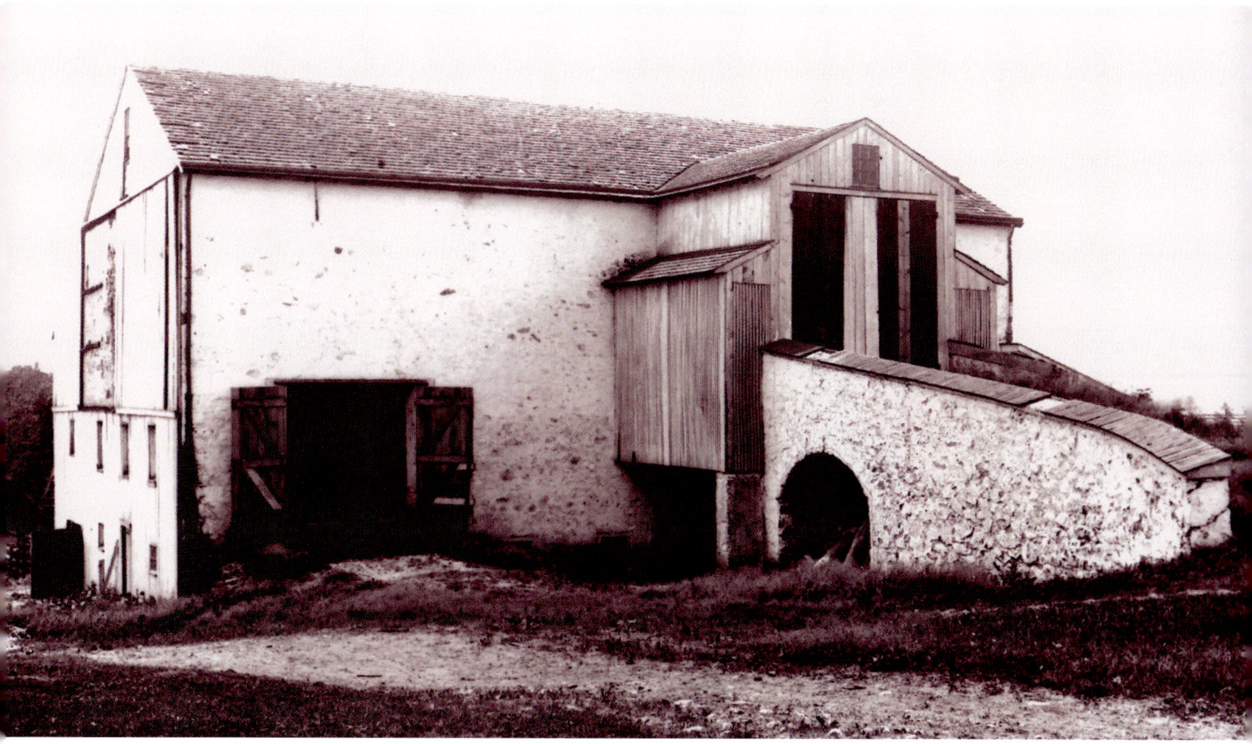

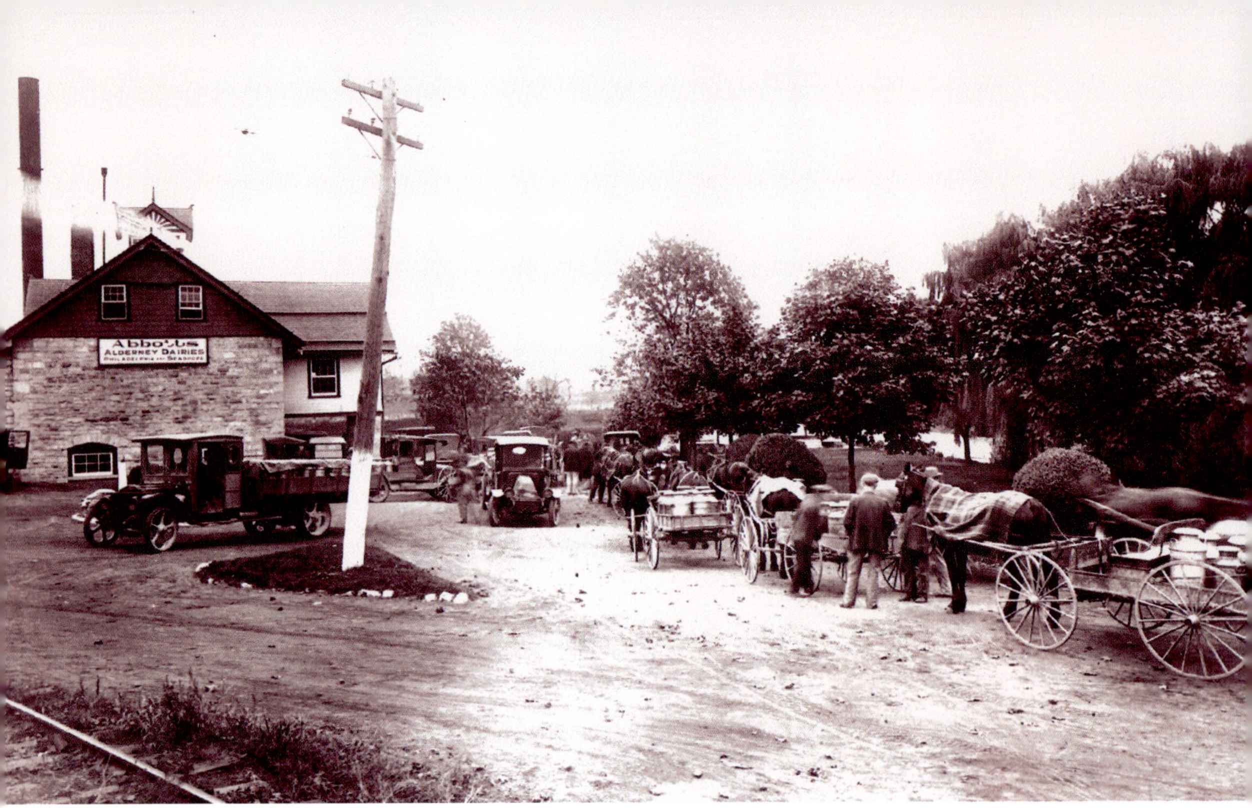

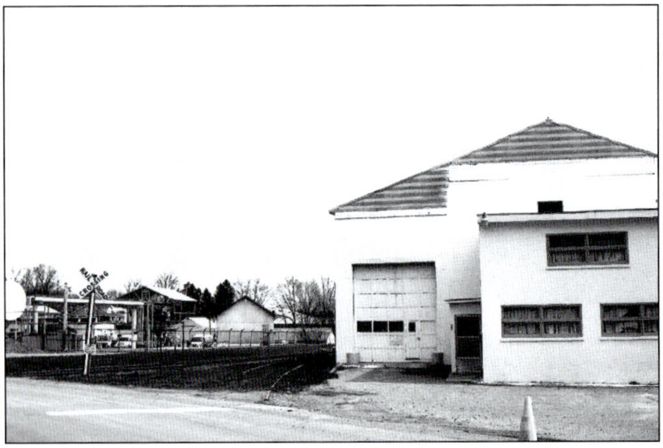

Abbott's Dairy in Oxford was founded in 1906 by George Abbott, a Philadelphia milk dealer. Abbott's Dairy introduced grade A milk in Pennsylvania. Milk produced under sanitary conditions had a lower bacterial count that qualified it to be sold as grade A. Farmers were paid a bonus for the clean milk. Communities that used the grade A milk saw a marked decline in infant mortality. Today, the Abbott's Dairy building has been converted for use as a mushroom-distribution house. Chester County was the leading producer of mushrooms in the nation until recent years.

In 1887, E. H. Herr began a creamery in the village of Glenroy, West Nottingham Township. The Glenroy Creamery flourished under the ownership of Turner and Wescott, who purchased it in 1898. They shipped milk from Chester and Lancaster Counties to Philadelphia and its environs. They also produced cream, butter, and condensed milk. A fire closed down the operation temporarily in 1953, but the plant reopened. Eventually, the plant was purchased by a frozen orange juice company that processed pulp shipped in from California. Currently, the site is occupied by Cowboy Way Limited, a western wear shop.

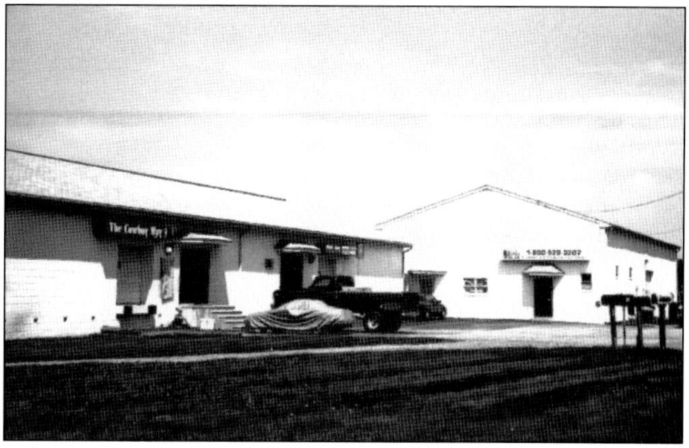

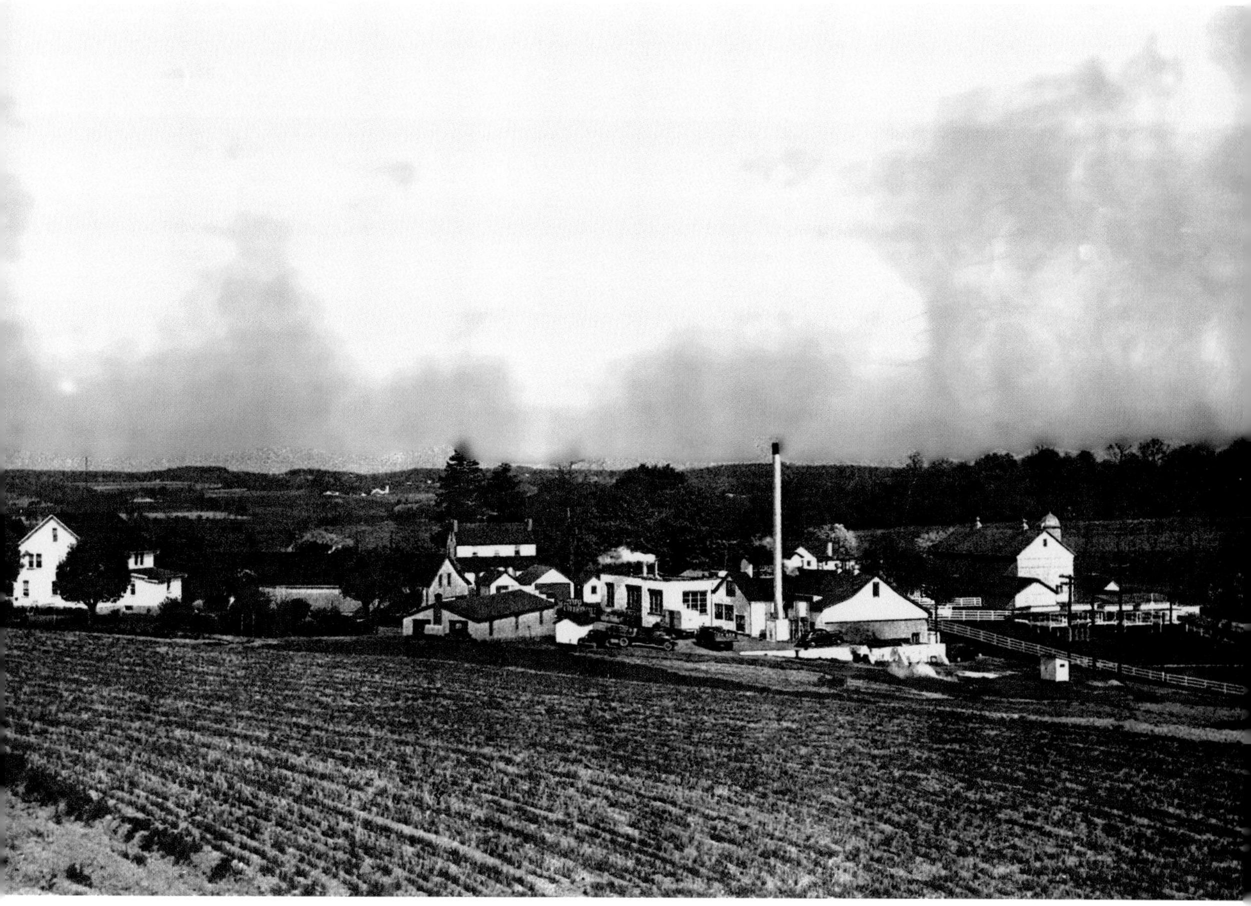

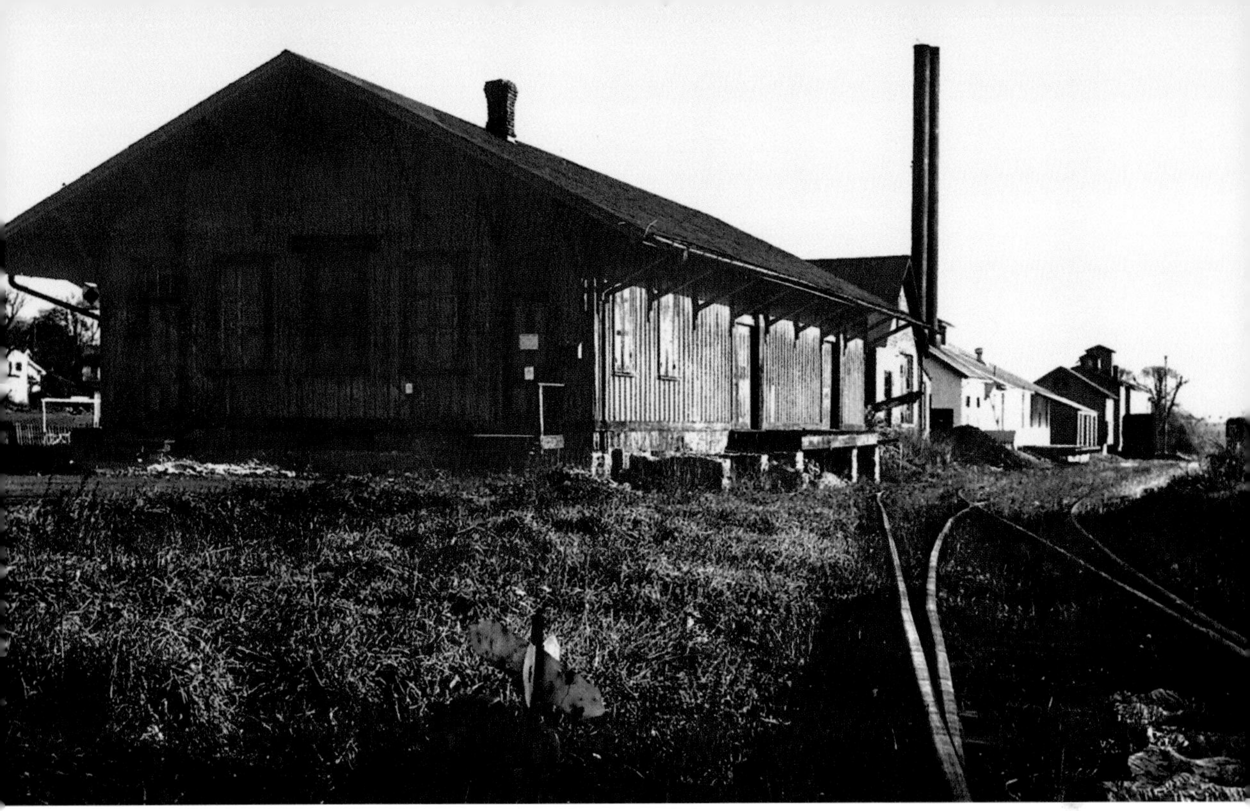

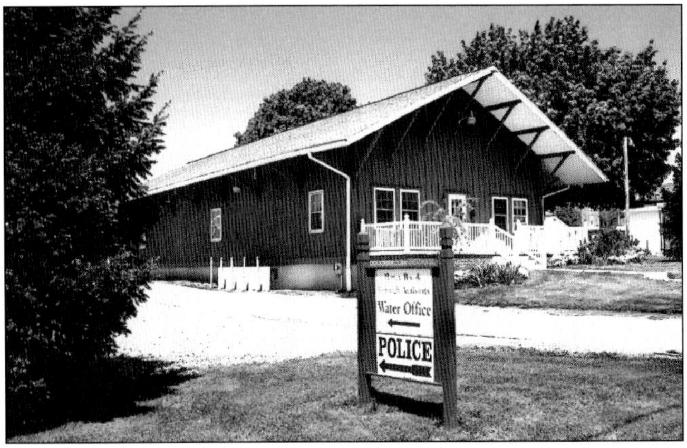

When the Pennsylvania Railroad ran a branch to Honey Brook from Downingtown in 1854, it had a dramatic effect on the local economy, especially after the line was extended to New Holland and then to Lancaster by 1890. Farmers could then send their products to market cheaply and efficiently. Milk was put on ice and shipped to Philadelphia every day. The development of the automobile and good roads in the early 20th century had an impact on the railroad. Passenger service was suspended in 1930. Today, the railroad station has been moved across the street from its original location and serves as the Honey Brook Borough offices.

Built about 1848, the Hickory Hill Store in Elk Township operated as a general store until 1987. The store also housed the post office from 1850 until it was discontinued in 1932. Charles McComsey and later his son, Millard McComsey, ran the store for 60 years. The store sold everything from candy and groceries to animal feed, horse collars, and tractors. More important than the everyday necessities that the store provided, it served as a communications center for the community. Some of the neighbors gathered there in the evening to play cards and talk. This group was known as the Hickory Hill Store Box Club because they sat on packing boxes. They had their own float in the neighborhood Victory Parade in September 1945. Today, the old store is a delicatessen.

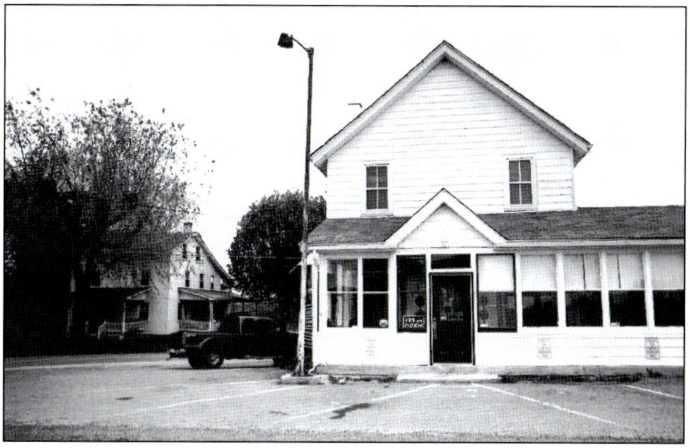

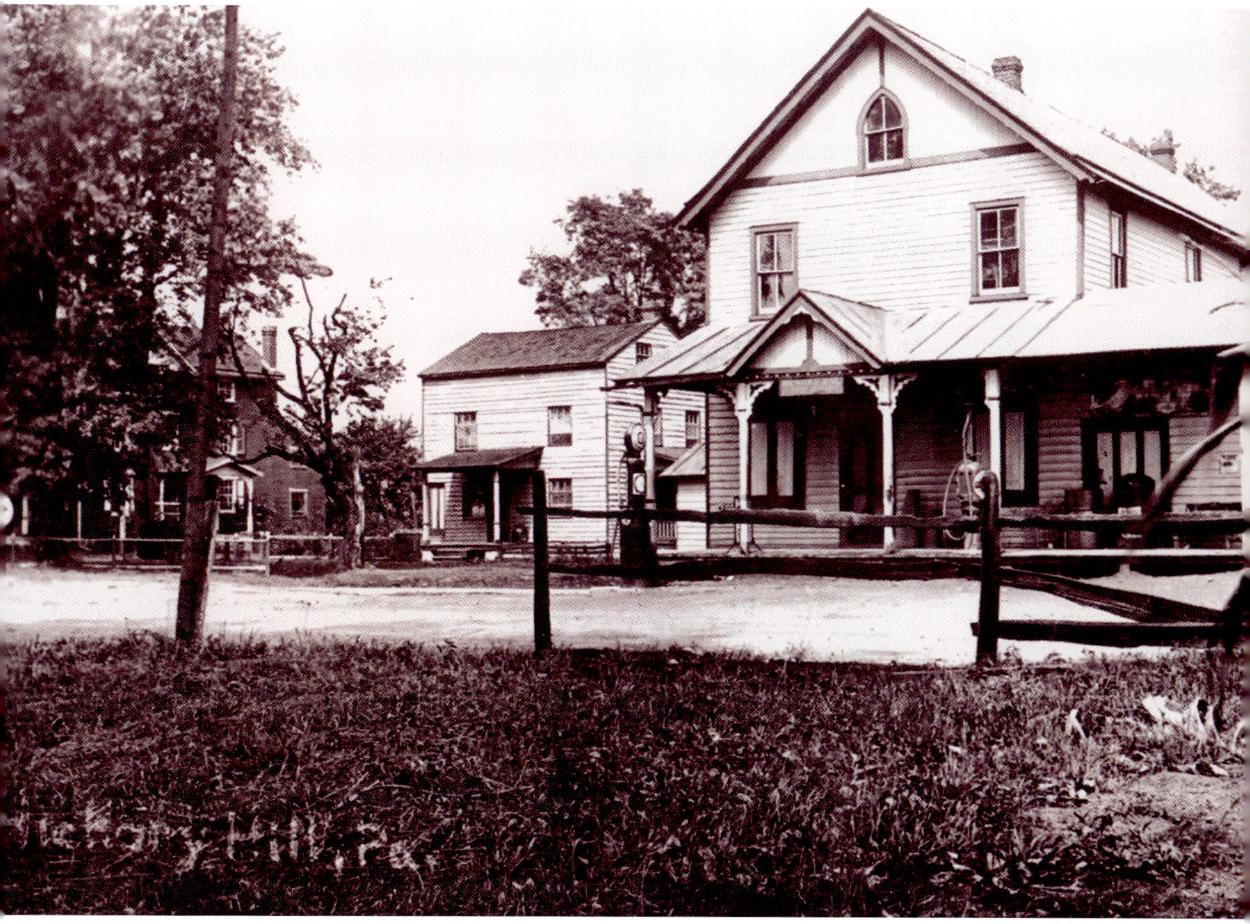

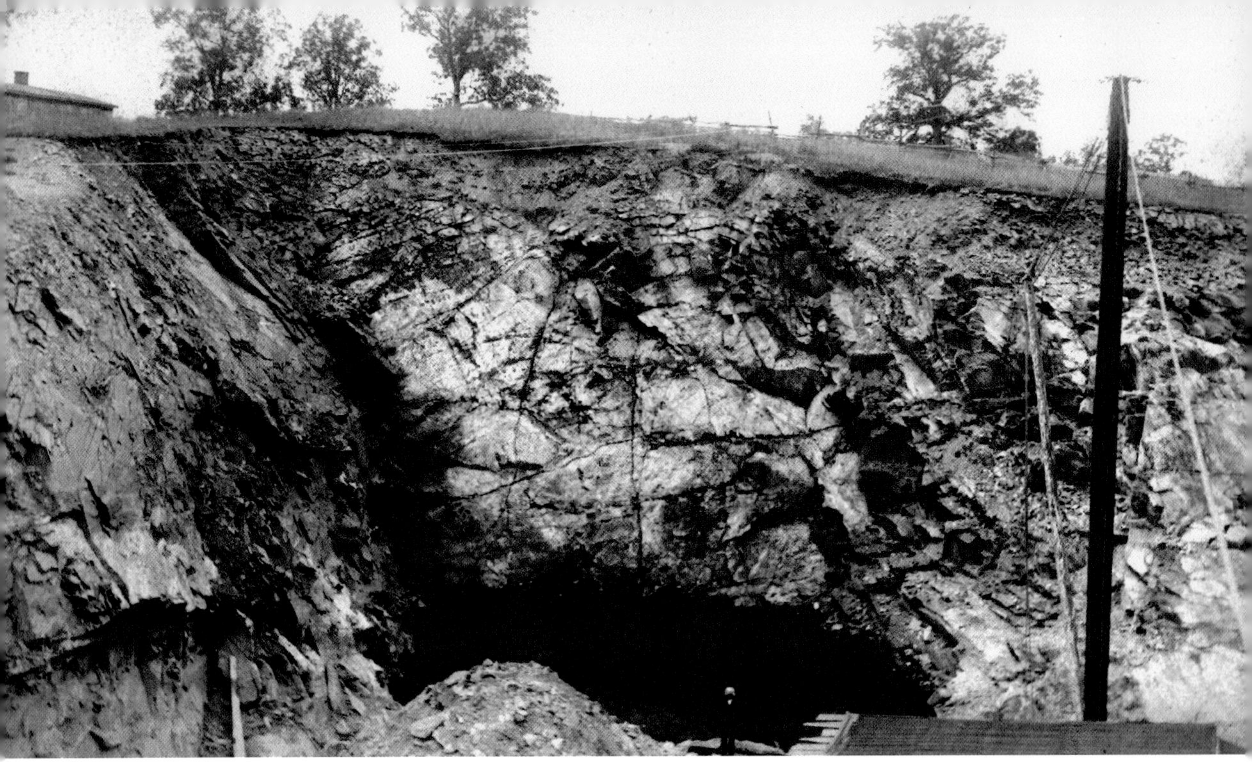

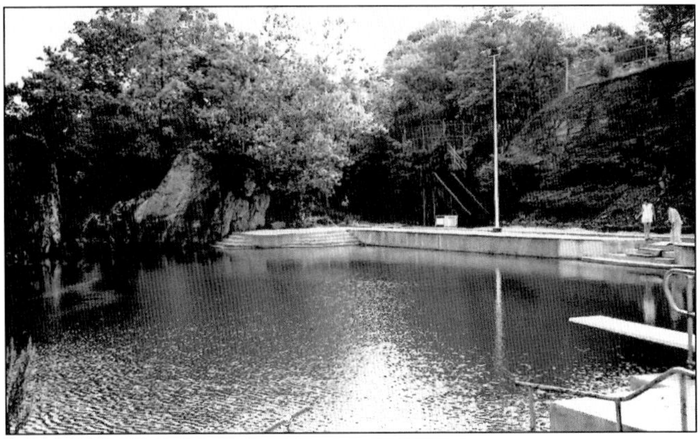

Joseph Hill Brinton operated the serpentine quarry on South New Street, Thornbury Township, from 1870 through 1899. During its heyday, 500,000 cubic yards of serpentine stone were cut and sold for building materials. The striking green stone is a familiar part of Chester County's architecture. Stone was shipped along the East Coast and as far west as Chicago. After a fire damaged the machinery, the quarry filled with 40 feet of spring water. In 1902, siblings Arthur and Lilly Brinton formed the Quarry Swimming Association as a private swimming club in which membership was by invitation only. Diving boards, bathhouses, and shady surrounding trees made it a popular swimming and picnicking spot. The Quarry Swimming Association purchased the quarry from Lilly Brinton in 1963. The association celebrated its 100th anniversary in 2002.

The Unionville Friends Meeting began in 1845 as an "Indulged Meeting." It was founded by Friends from neighboring meetings who wanted a meetinghouse in their own village. It was established as a preparative meeting in 1870, and the meetinghouse was used as a place of worship until 1939. After remaining deserted for several years, the building was purchased by the East Lynn Grange in 1949 to use as a Grange hall. The Grange members renovated the building themselves, constructing an addition that included a kitchen and restrooms. The East Lynn Grange celebrates its 100th anniversary in 2004. It is one of 11 active Granges in Chester County. East Lynn Grange holds an annual peach festival and chicken barbeque. It is one of the sponsors and organizers of the Unionville Fair.

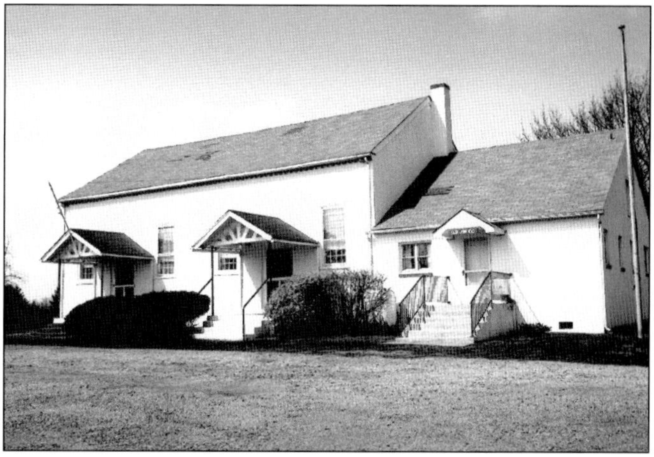

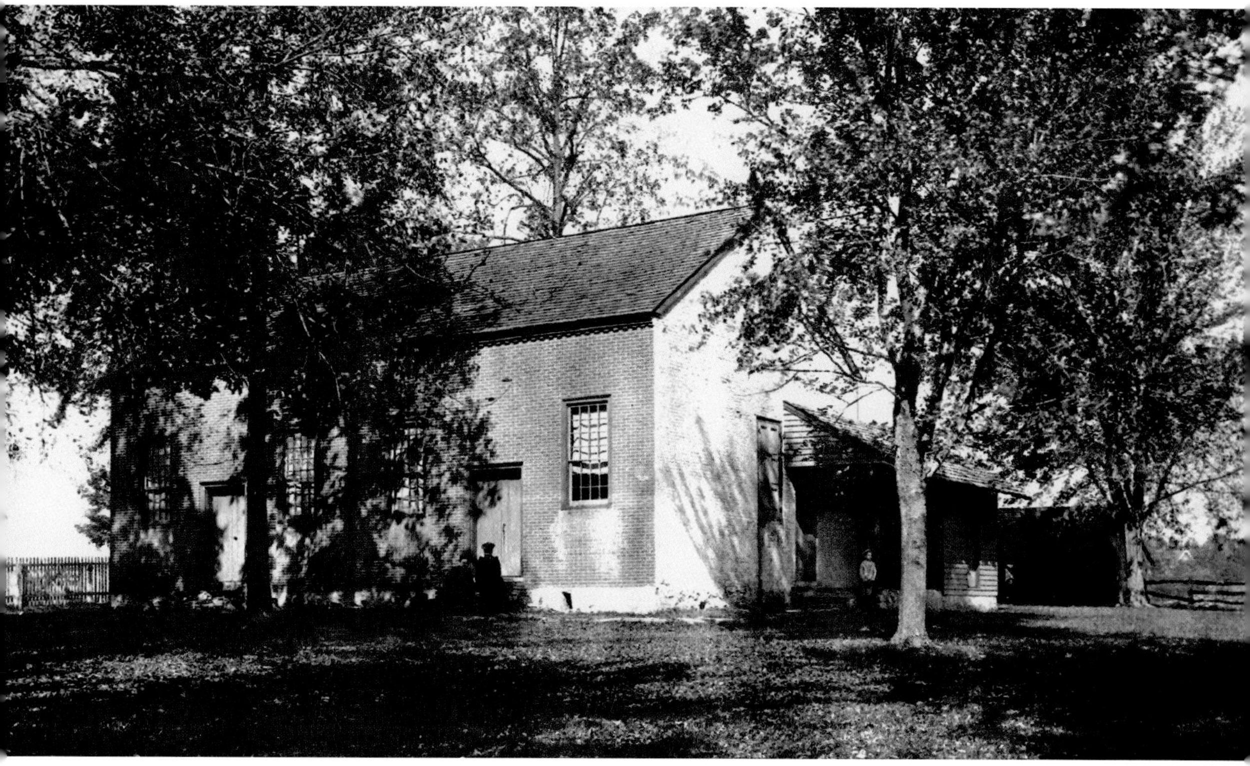

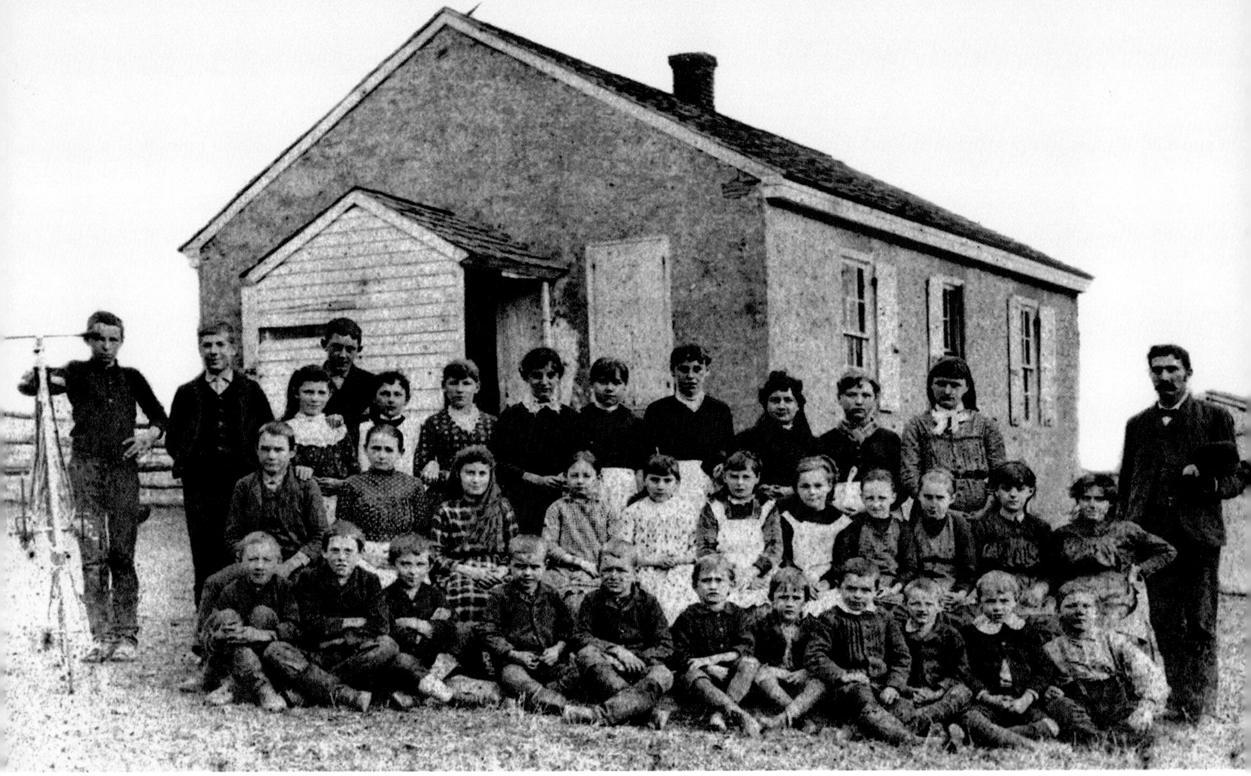

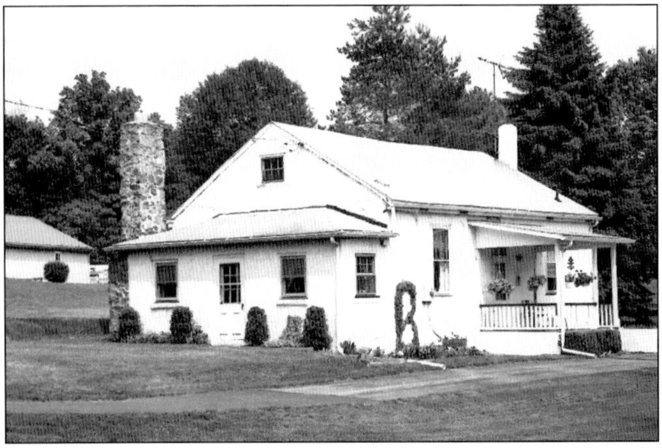

The Pughtown School in South Coventry Township was built sometime before 1832 and was in operation until 1924. The schoolchildren during the 1880s operated their own lyceum, modeled after popular adult lecture and entertainment programs. They recited poetry, sang songs, and staged debates. Some of the debate topics included "Did the Indian have a better right to America than the White Man?" and "Do men spend money more foolishly than women?" After the one-room schools were consolidated, this building was converted into a private home.

Built in 1908, the Pleasant View School in Upper Oxford Township served grades one through eight in the one-room schoolhouse. The school was finally closed in 1954, when the one-room schools were consolidated. Upper Oxford Township bought and converted the building into office space in 1977. In 2003, more than 300 people attended a reunion for the pupils of Pleasant View School. Now on permanent display in the township building is a quilt bearing the signatures of these pupils.

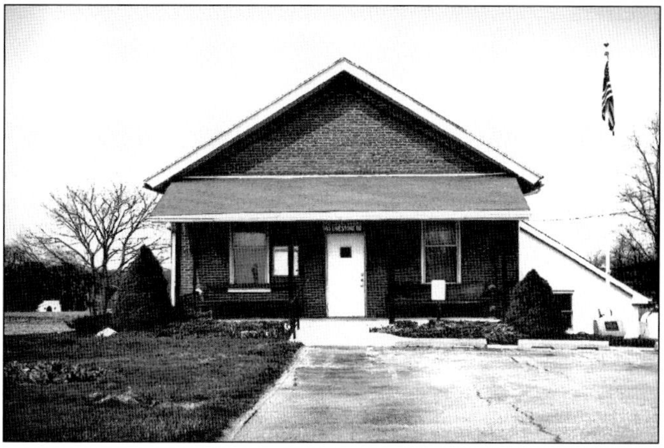

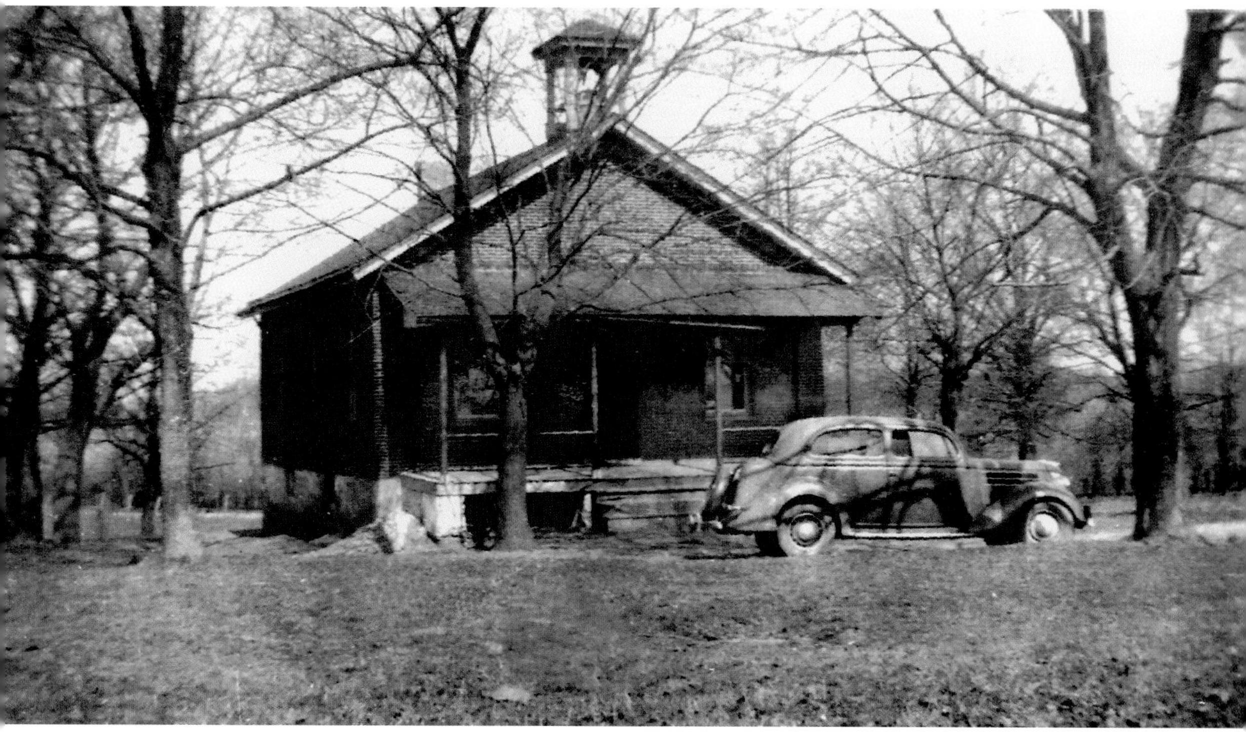

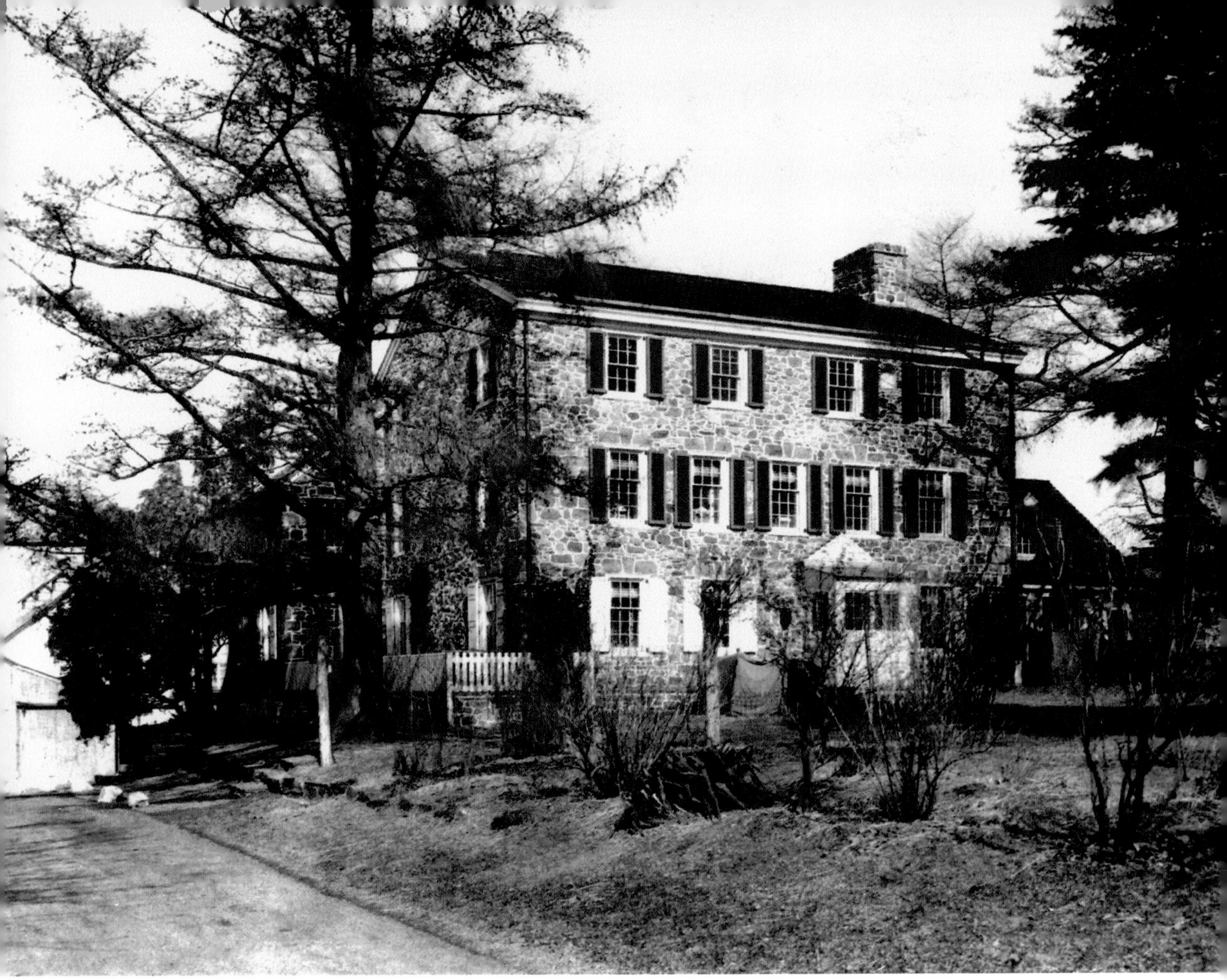

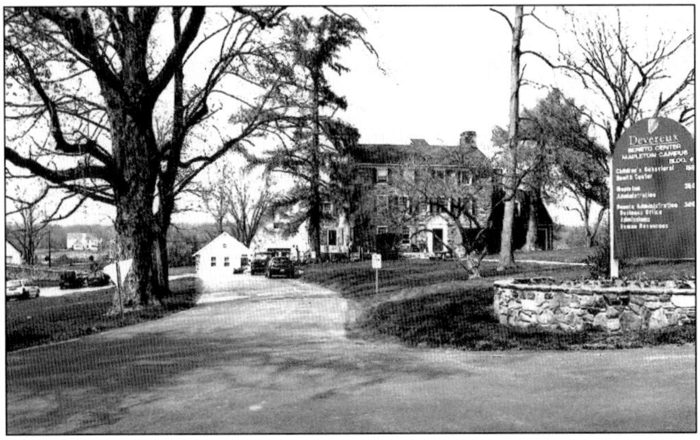

Mapleton Farm in Willistown Township had been in the Garrett-Cox family for 200 years when it was sold in 1926. The house was built in 1790, enlarged with the addition of a third story in 1858, and further remodeled in the early 20th century. After being used for general farming by the Garrett-Cox family, Mapleton Farm became a well-known name in thoroughbred racing under succeeding owners. The property changed hands again and became the Mapleton Campus of the Devereux Foundation in 1962. Devereux provides special education to children and adolescents with emotional and behavioral challenges.

Kimberton, in East Pikeland Township, was named for Emmor Kimber, who moved to that village in 1817. An activist Friend particularly interested in abolition and temperance, he established the French Creek Seminary for Females in a 1787 farmhouse that he enlarged. The school, which served between 30 and 50 students per term, flourished under Kimber for 30 years. The school closed upon Kimber's death in 1850 but was reopened as Kimberton Academy in 1858. It was run by Reverend Dim until 1873. Fire destroyed much of the building in 1940, and only about one-third remains today. An antiques shop is now located at the site.

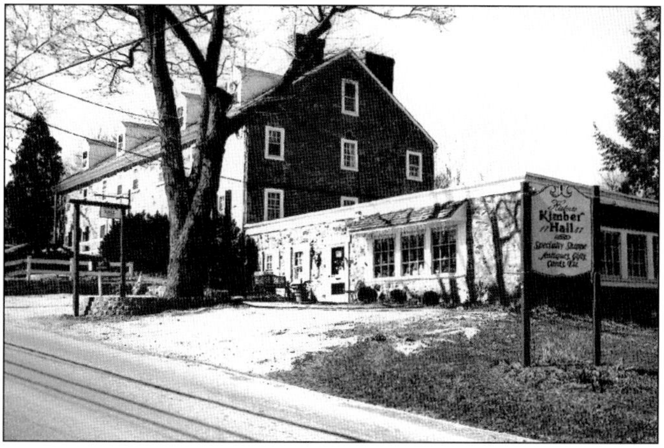

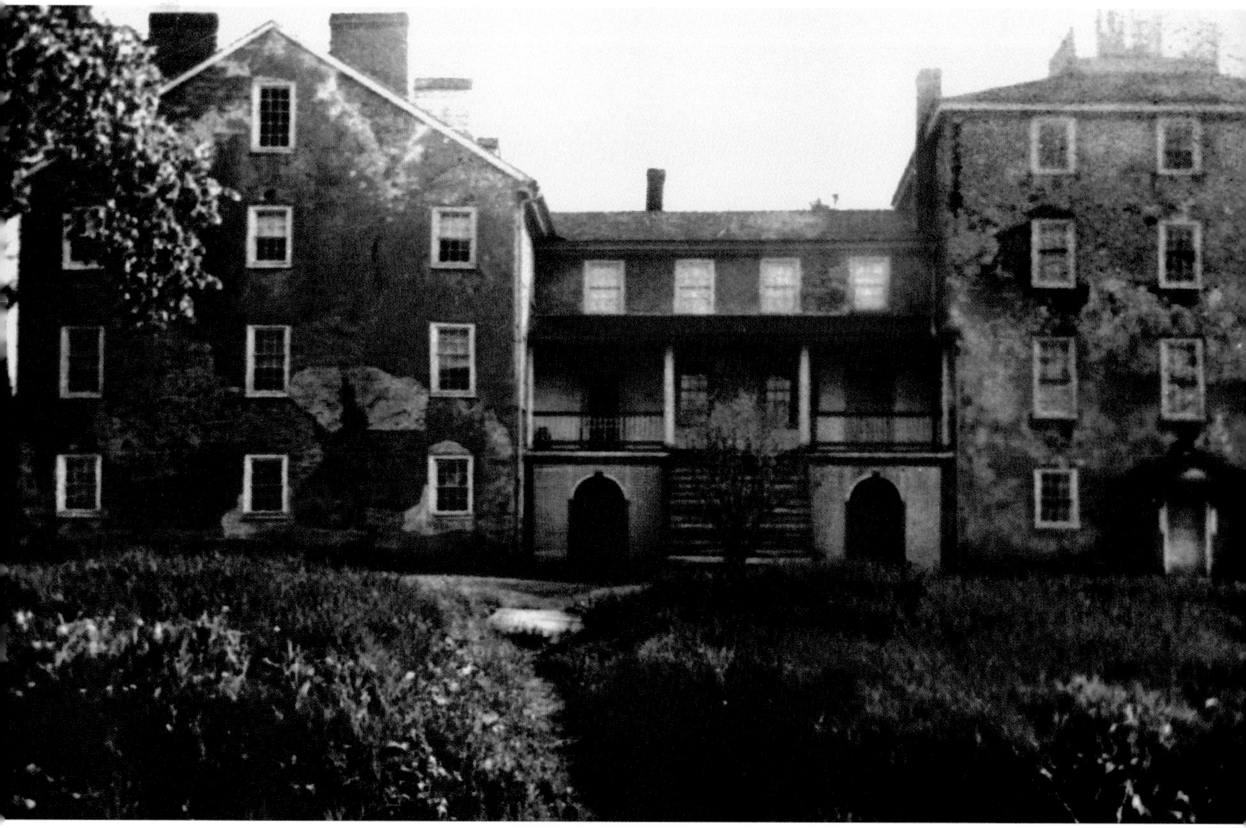

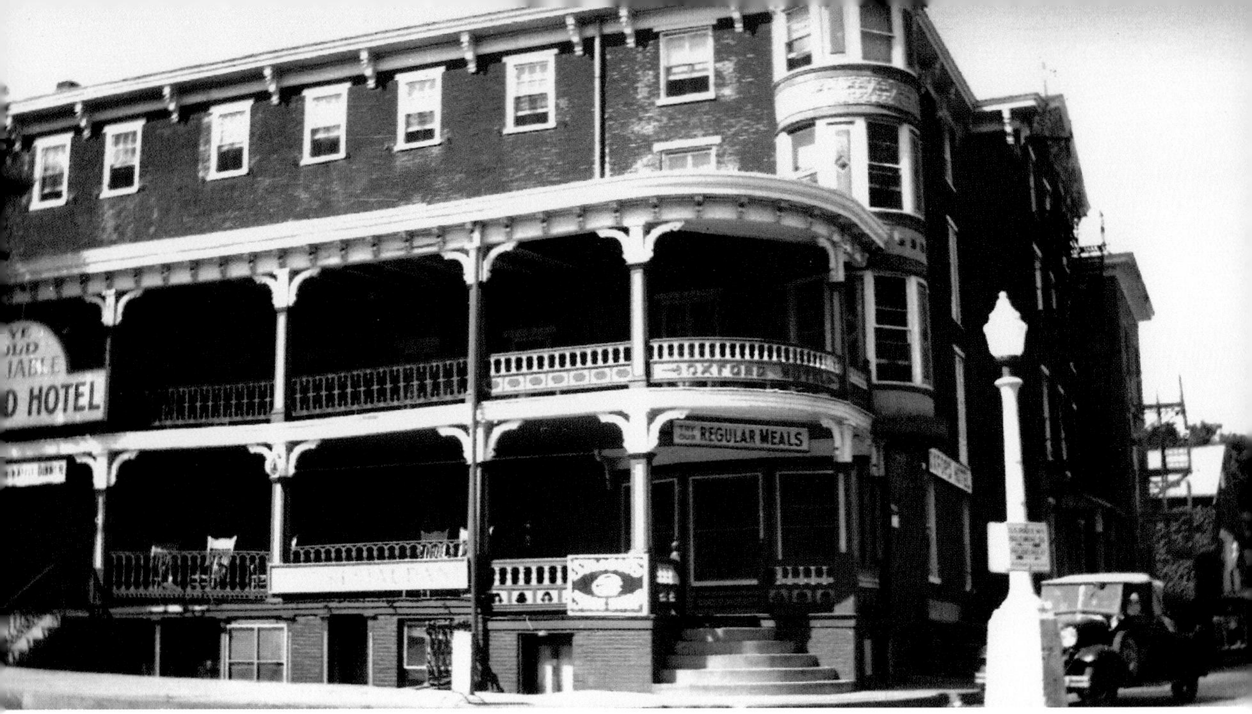

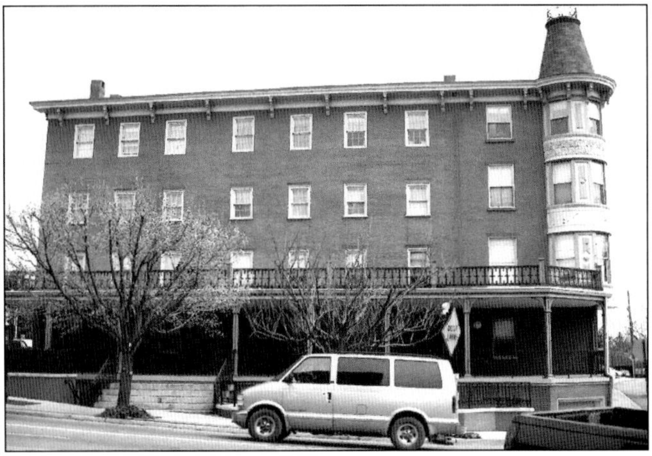

The original part of the Oxford Hotel is known to have been standing since 1759. By 1875, two stories had been added. The hotel was famous for its porches, shown in this photograph taken before 1935. Senators and state governors, including Andrew G. Curtin and Samuel W. Pennypacker, used the porches as platforms for speeches. In 1940, during an appearance by Henry A. Wallace, vice president of the United States, cracking noises were noted. A collapse was averted, but it was obvious the porch was unsound. The porches were removed during remodeling done in 1949. Today, the building houses senior apartments.

Col. Joseph D. Potts commenced building Langoma, a 68-room, cut-stone mansion, in 1890. The mansion is adjacent to the Isabella Furnace in West Nantmeal Township. The mansion's cost was approximately $175,000. Theophilus P. Chandler was the architect. Colonel Potts died in 1894 before completion of the mansion. His son, William M. Potts, gained possession and completed the structure in 1897, living there until his death in 1943. Today, the building is owned by the Religious Congregation of the Daughters of St. Mary of Providence, who provide assisted living for seniors and also use the facility as a conference and retreat center.

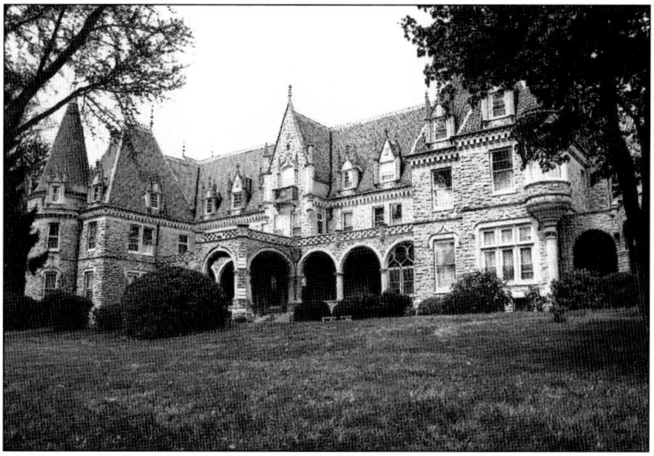

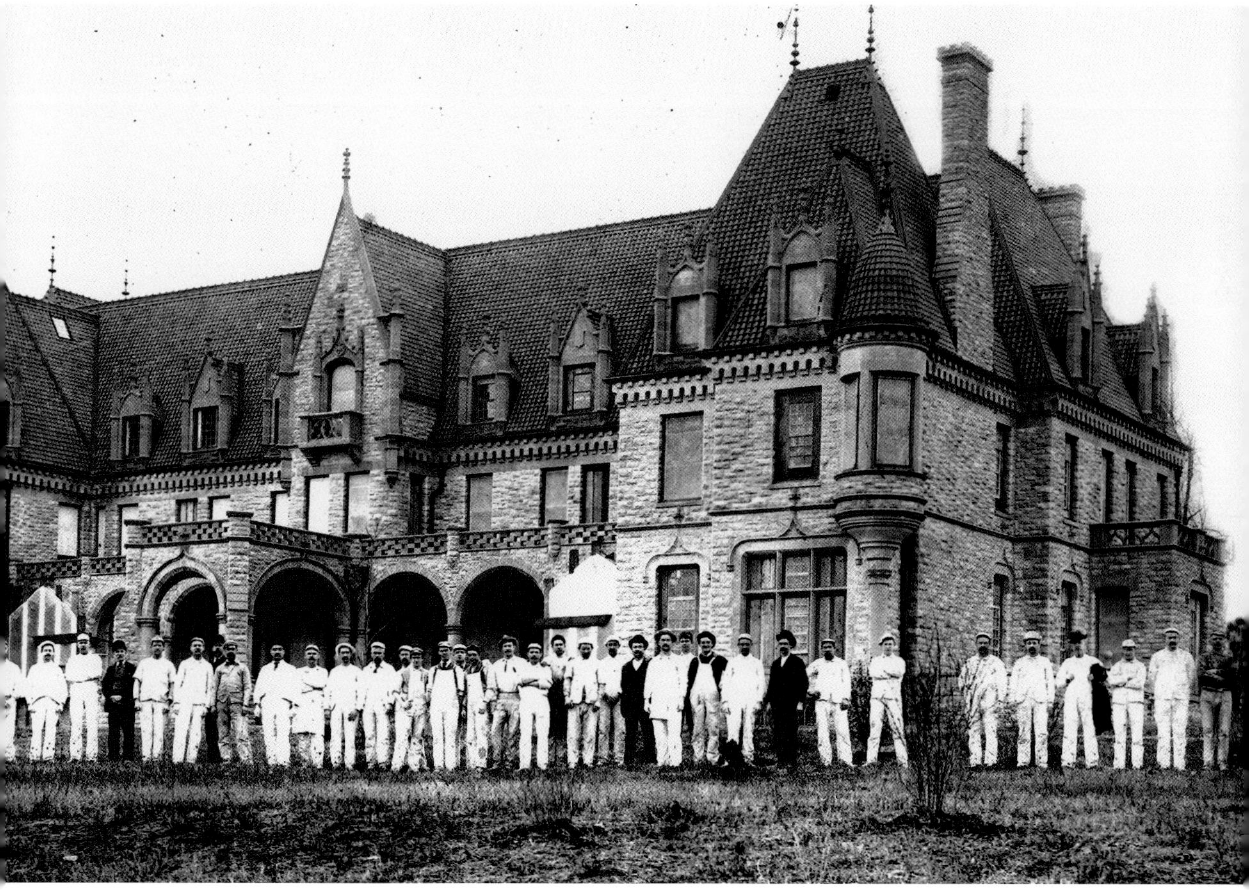

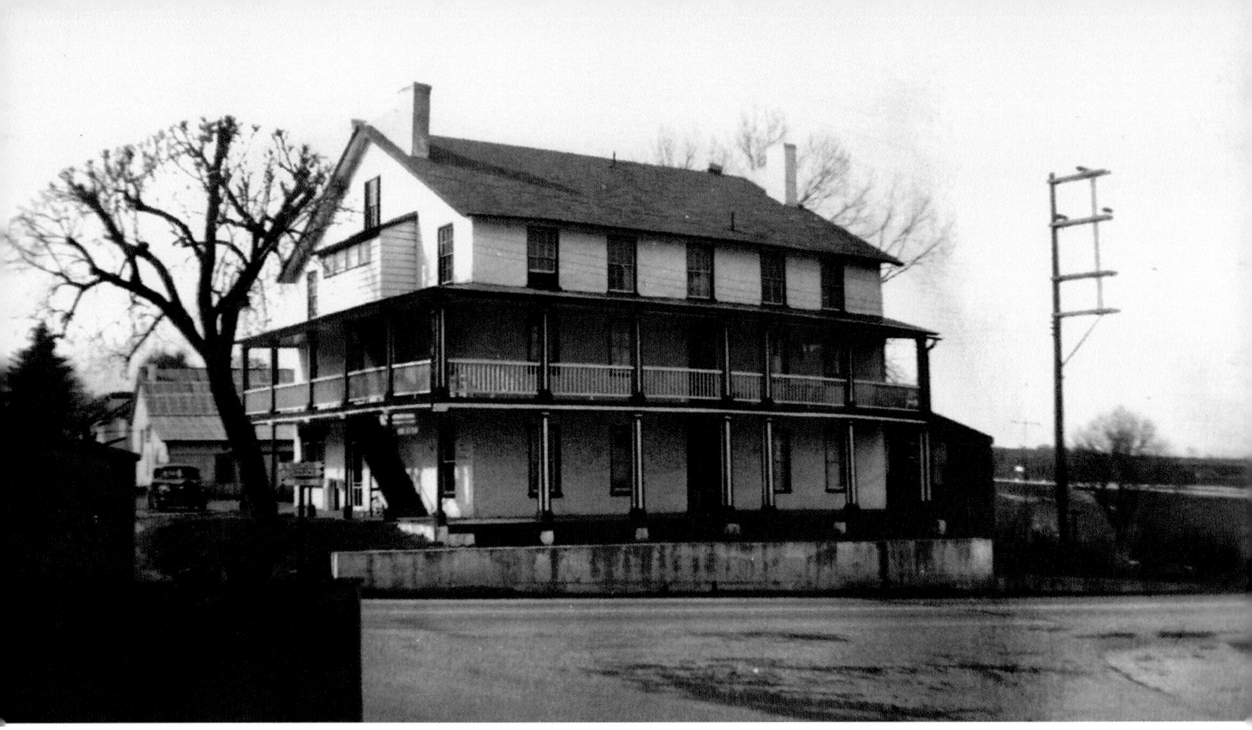

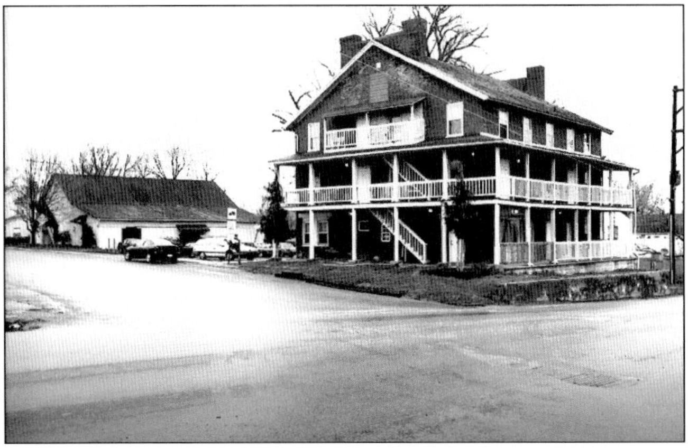

The Cochranville Hotel was built in 1809 by Samuel Cochran, a prominent figure for whom the town was named. A gentleman named Hollis ran the establishment for Cochran, who pursued political interests and spent most of his time in Harrisburg. Cochran served as a state legislator from 1816 to 1822. He was surveyor-general of Pennsylvania from 1800 to 1809 and 1821 to 1824. The hotel changed hands many times through the years. In 1948, the voters of West Fallowfield Township designated the area dry in a local option election, hurting the hotel business and spelling the eventual doom of the enterprise. Today, the structure is an apartment building.

The Avon Grove Consolidated School opened in 1929 through the efforts of the Avondale, London Grove, and West Grove School Boards to consolidate Avondale Vocational School and West Grove High School. Later, students from surrounding districts were included as well. By 1950, the Avon Grove School District needed larger facilities. They built a new high school and renovated this building for use as an elementary school in 1957. Today, the building houses the Avon Grove Charter School, for elementary school students.

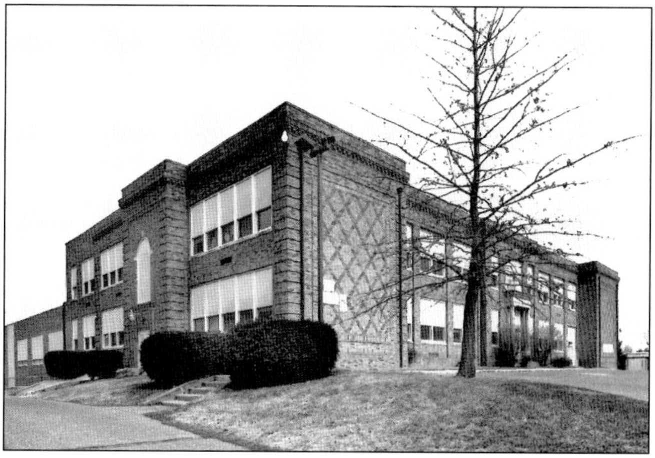

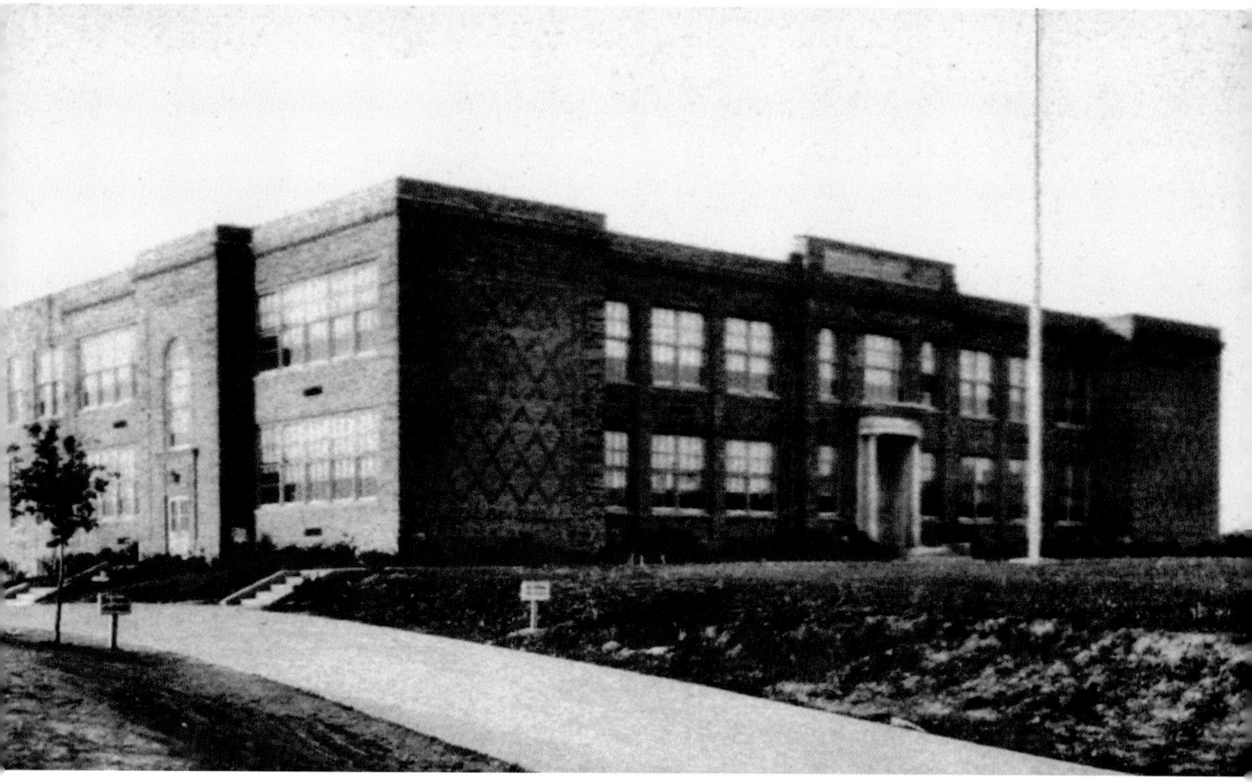

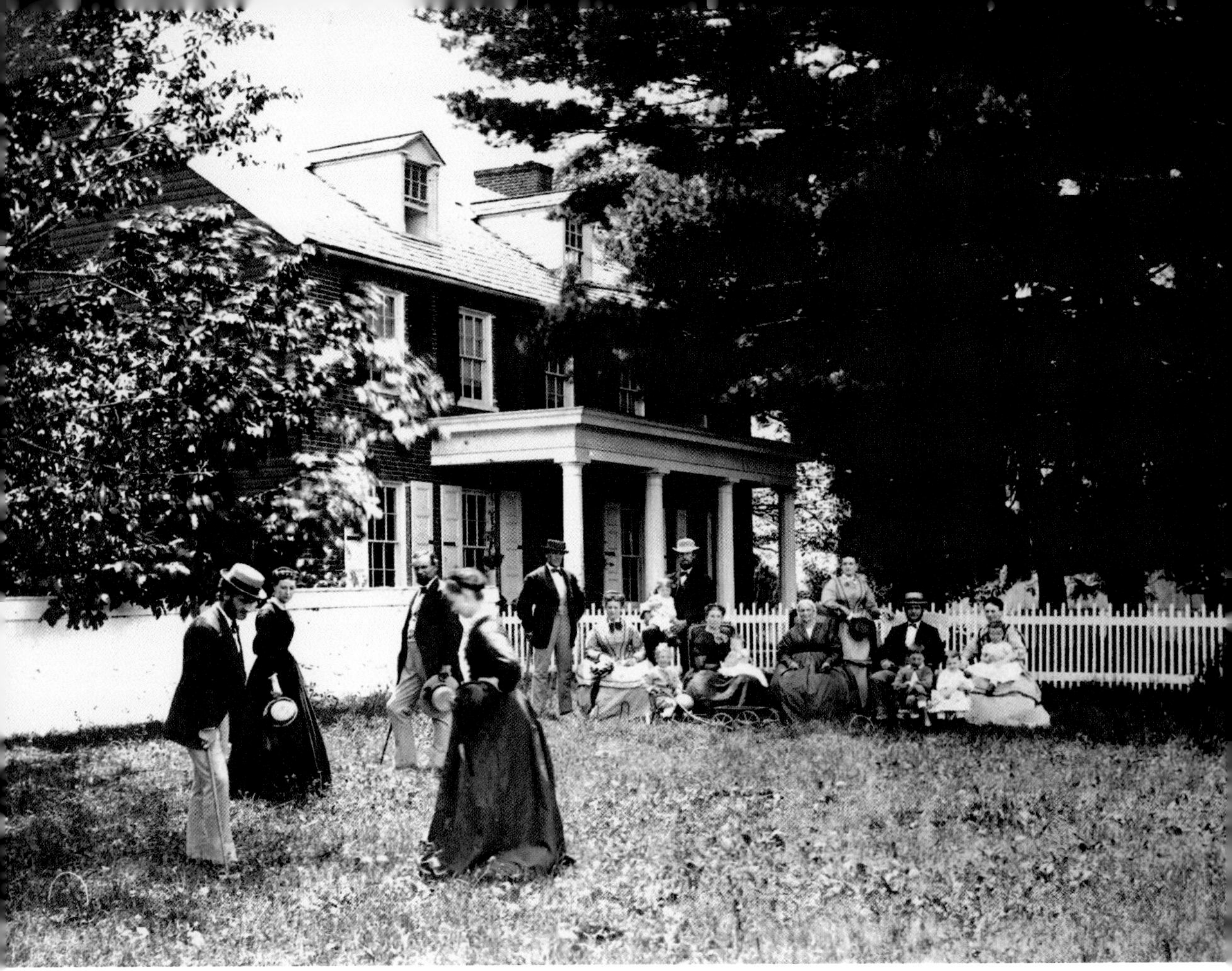

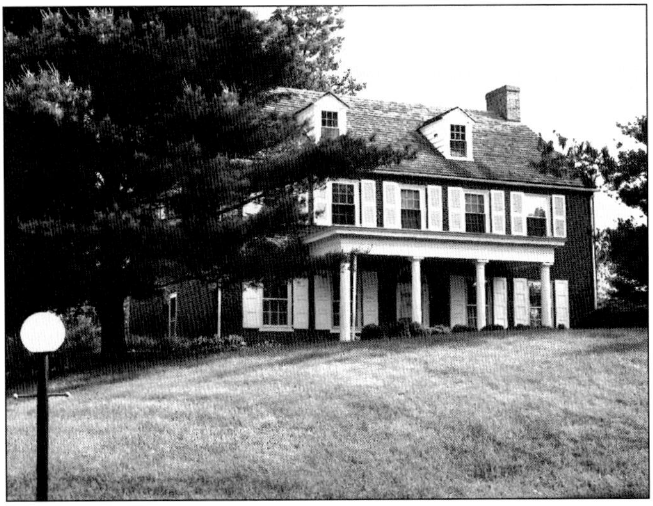

Ellerslie, in Pennsbury Township, was the summer home of Thomas H. and Sara P. Savery and family of Wilmington. The house, built *c.* 1827, is seen here in an 1873 photograph. The Savery family actively farmed the land. The property included a mill and a creamery that were torn down in the early 20th century. In 1975, the property was sold and Crosslands, a Friends life-care retirement community, was built. Today, Ellerslie serves as a guesthouse and meeting center for Crosslands.

The Schuylkill Canal was opened in 1824 by the Schuylkill Navigation Company, providing an avenue for transporting goods from Pottstown to Philadelphia. Industrial towns such as Spring City, seen in this 1905 photograph, grew up along the canal. It was eclipsed by the railroad as a primary mode of transportation in the 1870s. For many years, the canal was used for pleasure boating until it was filled in.

Chapter 2
Things That Aren't There Anymore

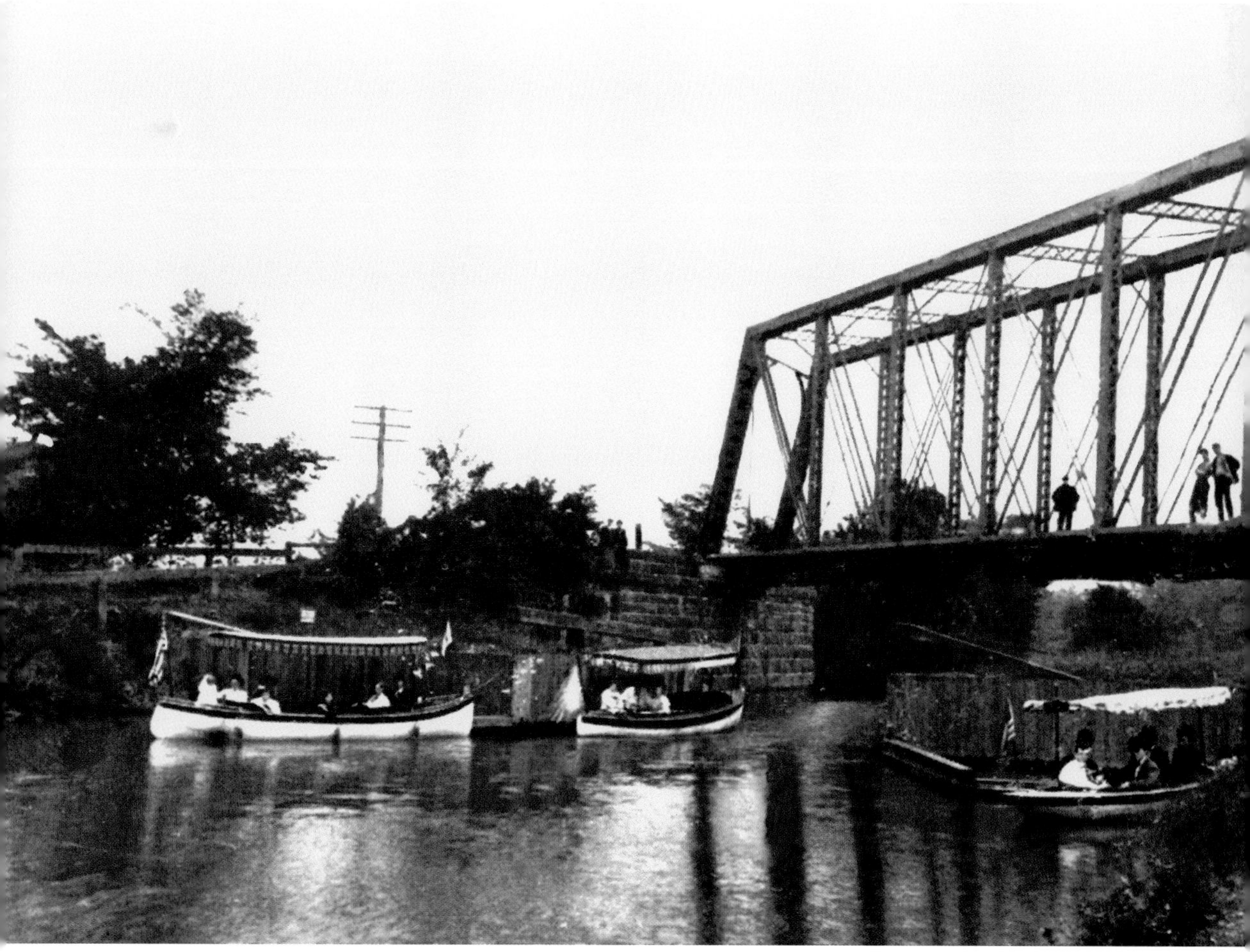

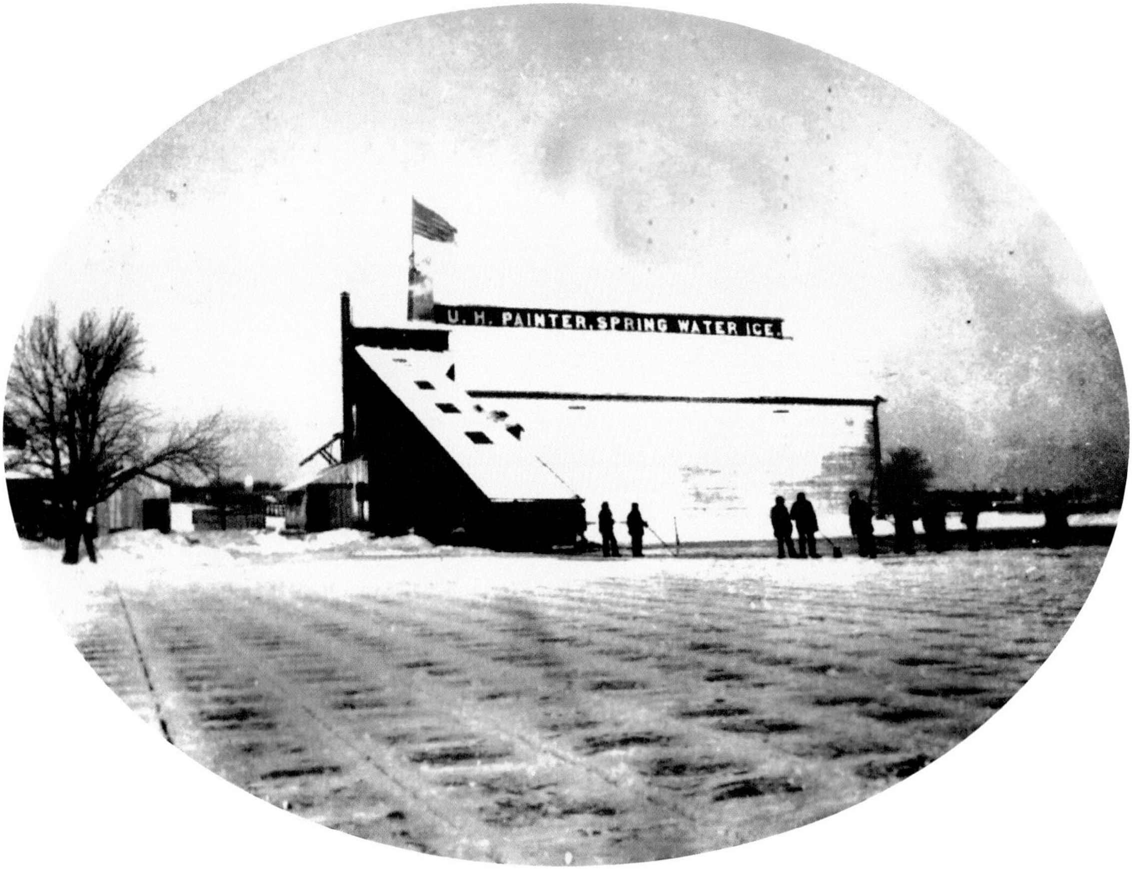

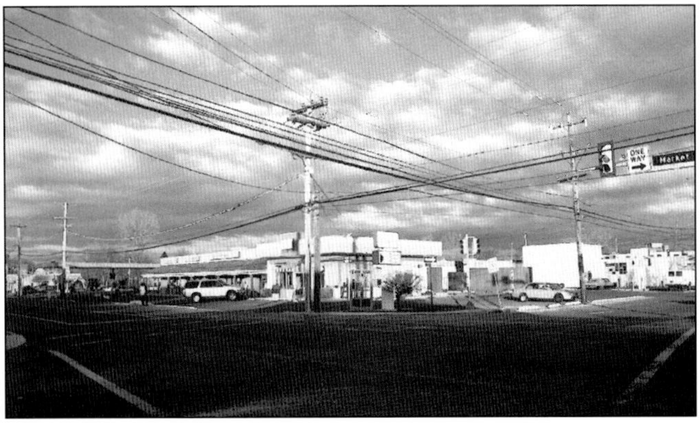

Uriah H. Painter began his ice and lumber business in West Chester in 1857. The Gay Street Ice House, pictured above, was erected in 1873 and enlarged in 1880. It occupied the block between North Penn Street and Worthington Street. Extending to Market Street was a two-acre artificial pond that produced 2,500 tons of ice per freezing. Once the ice was harvested, in blocks weighing 225 to 250 pounds, Painter permitted skating on the pond. His workers were able to harvest approximately 93 tons of ice per hour. The photograph shows the blocks measured out on the pond. About 5,000 tons of ice could be stored in the icehouse. Today, the pond has been filled in and is the site of a fast-food restaurant and a shopping area.

The Chester County Prison was located on the north side of West Market Street at the intersection of New Street. It was designed by the architect Thomas U. Walter, who designed the House and Senate wings and the dome of the U.S. Capitol in Washington, D.C. The prison, based on the latest in penal reform, was erected in 1838 and included 46 individual cells. It was enlarged in 1871. In 1955, it failed to meet Department of Welfare standards and was torn down in 1959. A new county building opened in 1962 on the site to house county offices and the Chester County Library. It was dedicated to honor Congressman Paul Dague in 1971. A new county justice center is now planned for this site.

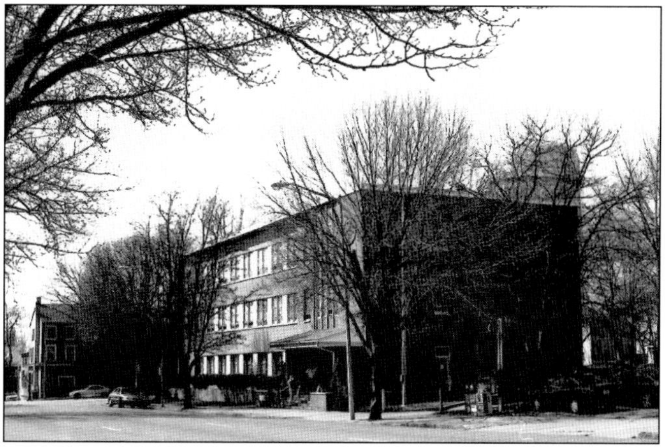

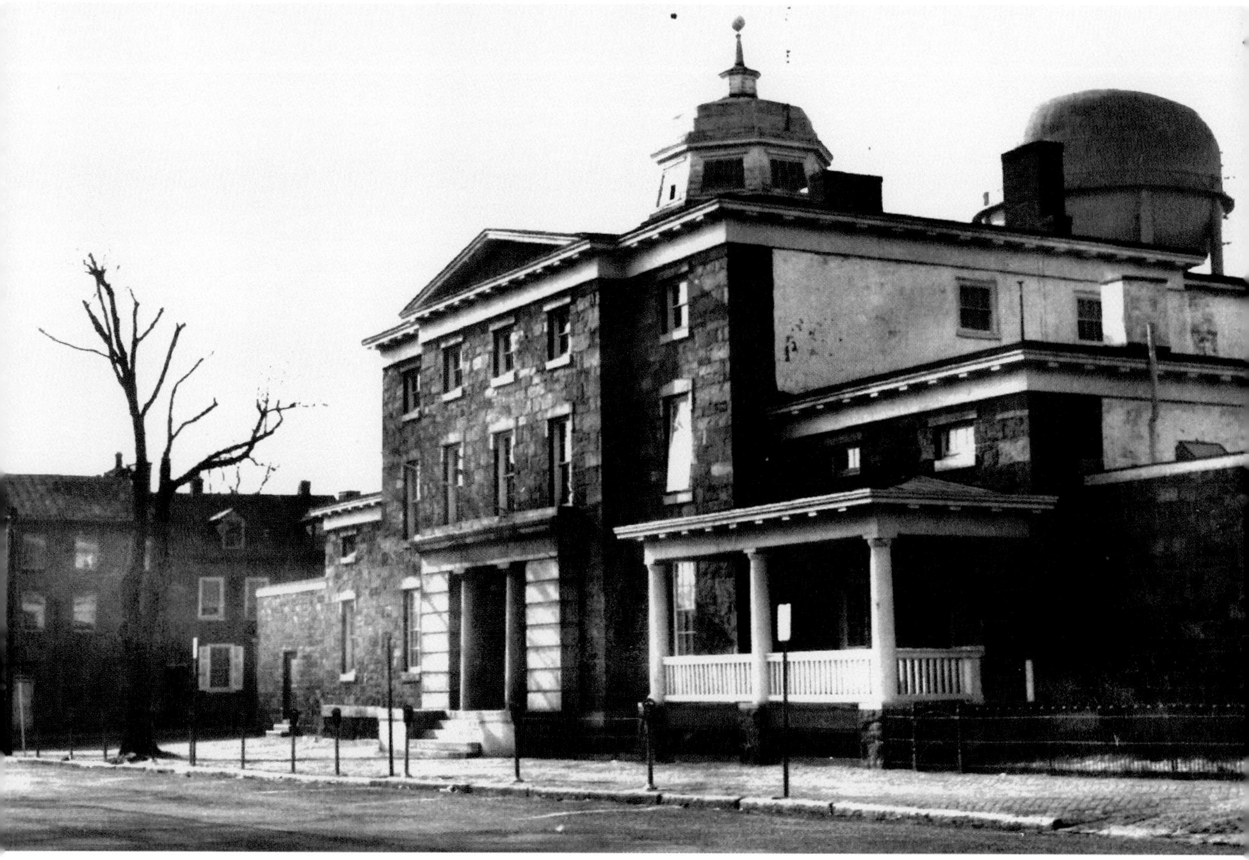

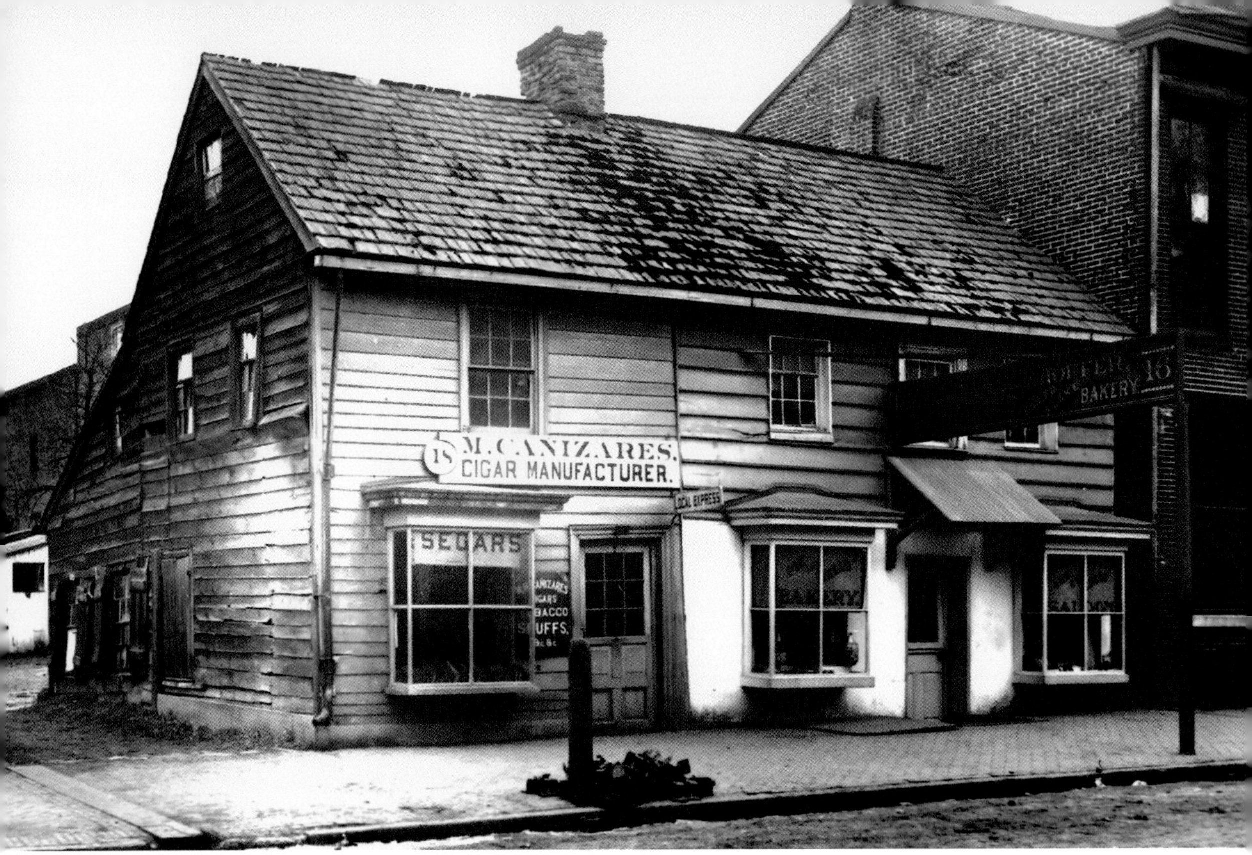

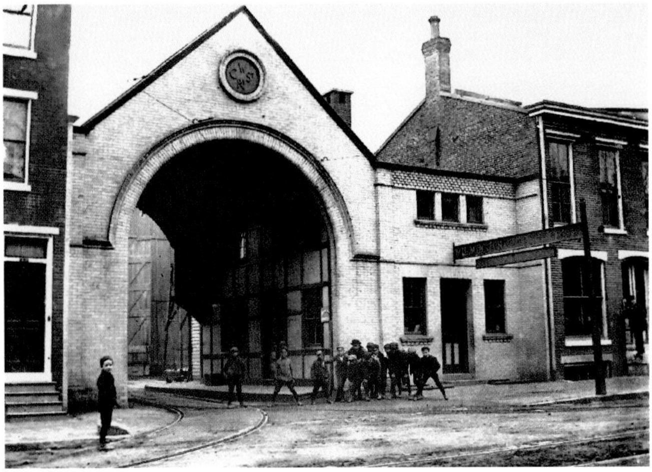

This site on South High Street, West Chester, has seen a dramatic evolution. The photograph above shows the log and frame structure on the site built before 1812. It was known as the Olof Stromberg house, for the Swedish shoemaker who lived there from 1818 until 1871. This was probably the oldest log structure in the borough when it was demolished in 1890 and replaced by a trolley barn. The West Chester Street Railway brought trolley service to West Chester in 1891. For a 5¢ fare, passengers traveled north and south on High Street or east and west on Market Street. The trolley expanded its service to include Lenape Park in 1892. It connected with lines in Downingtown in 1901 and Kennett Square in 1904. The trolley ceased operation in 1929 because it could not compete with bus transportation services or privately owned automobiles.

The *Daily Local News* was first published on November 19, 1872, by founder William Hodgson as West Chester's first daily paper. This building on South High Street was the paper's headquarters until it needed larger quarters. The office was demolished in 1973. The trolley barn and *Daily Local News* office on South High Street were replaced with a parking lot, and today there is a parking garage. Specially designed to blend in with the streetscape, the Bicentennial Garage was opened in 1999, when the borough of West Chester celebrated its 200th anniversary.

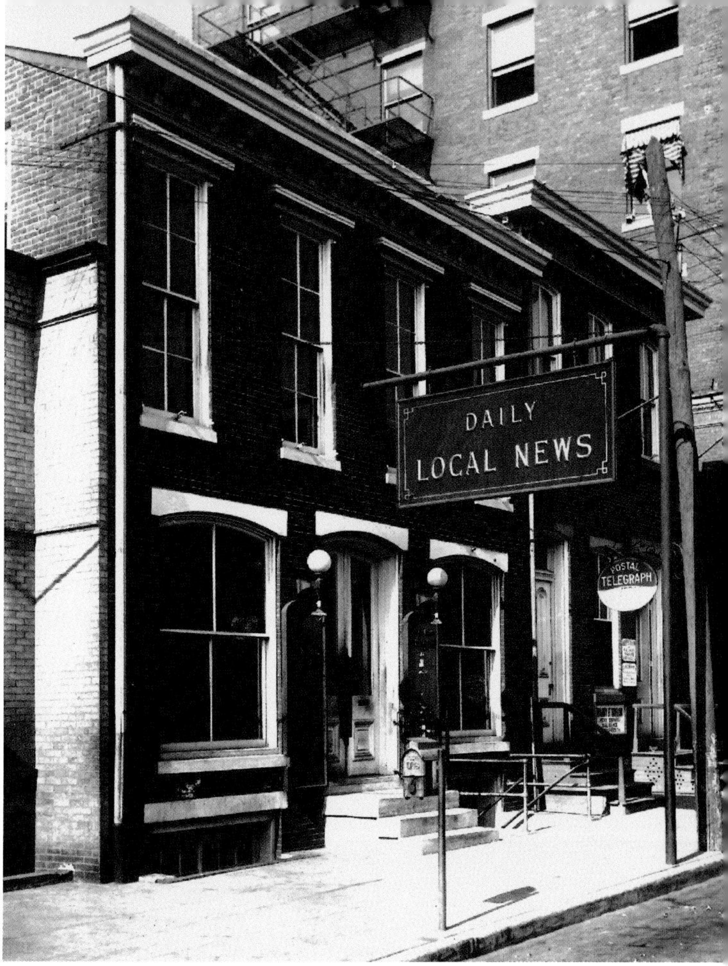

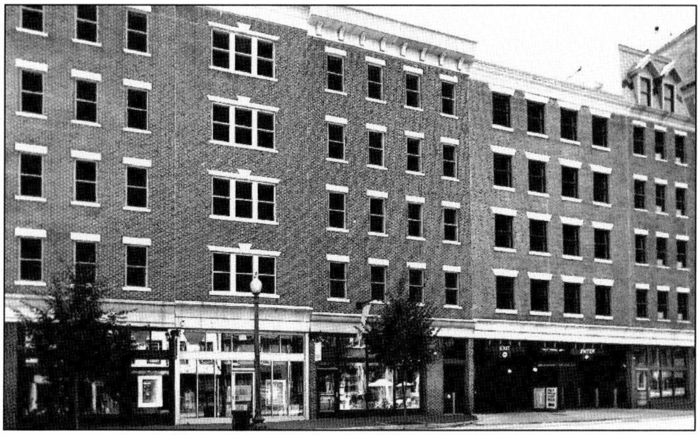

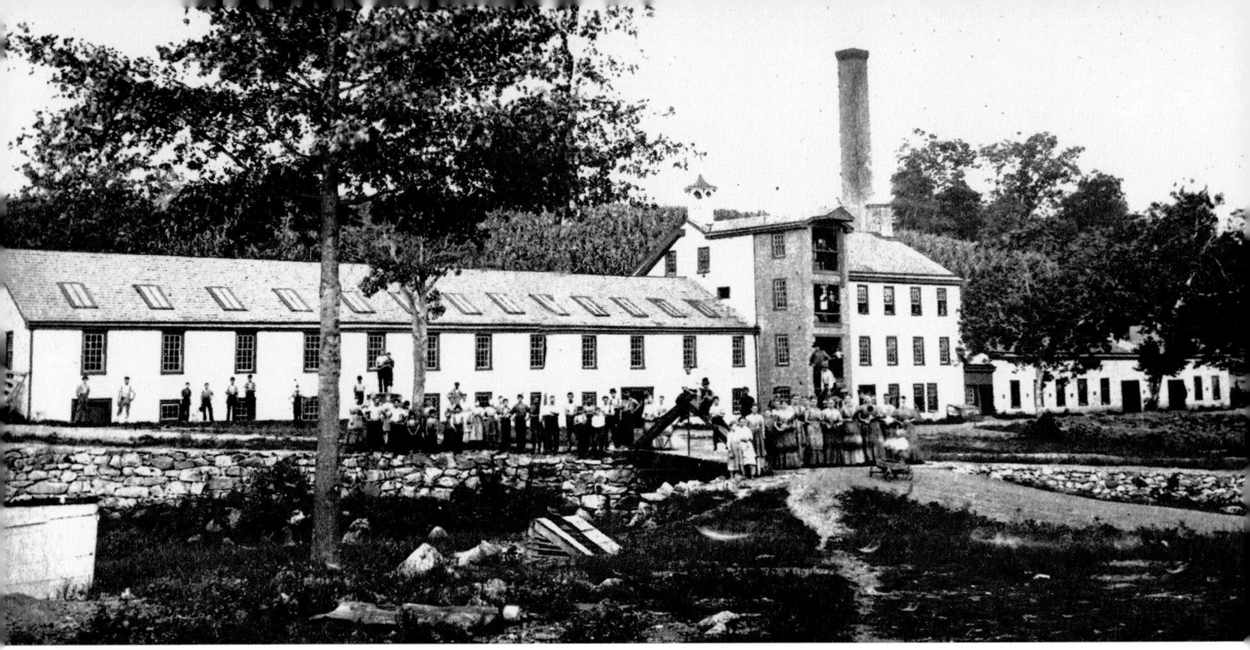

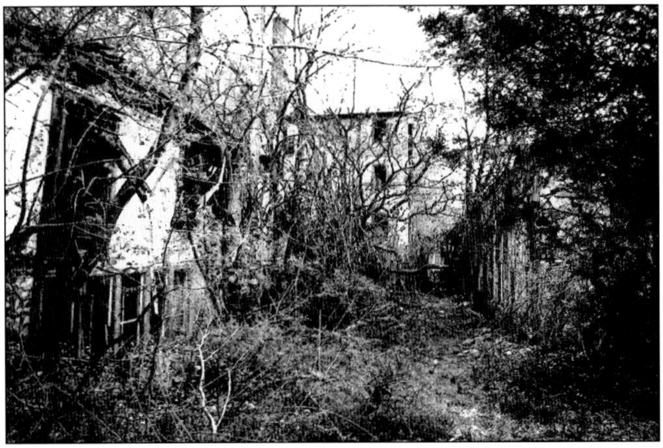

Bonds' Woolen Mill on Beaver Creek in East Brandywine Township was established early in the 1840s. The surrounding area became known as Bondsville. This textile-manufacturing mill changed hands many times and produced a variety of products during its long history. When the Roberts family ran it during the 1870s, it manufactured Kentucky jeans cloth. At that time, 100 employees worked 12-hour days, 6 days a week. Early in the 20th century, owner Fred Pearson used the mill to dye plush, silk, and chenille. In 1932, Collins and Aikmen bought the mill and greatly enlarged it. They manufactured cloth for automobile upholstery and, during World War II, made lining fabric for U.S. Air Force jackets. During its heyday in the 1940s, the mill employed 300 to 400 people. It closed in 1954.

These row houses along Bondsville Road were originally constructed by the Roberts family, owners of Bondsville Mill, as housing for their workers in the mid-19th century. This was the only settlement in Chester County that was constructed as a company town. One row of mill workers' dwellings still remains on Bondsville Road in East Brandywine Township. The other row of houses was torn down during World War II to create a parking lot and a memorial marker for fallen soldiers.

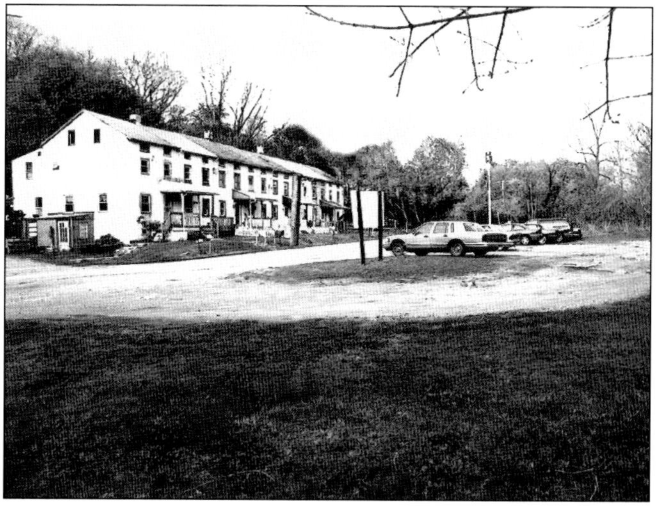

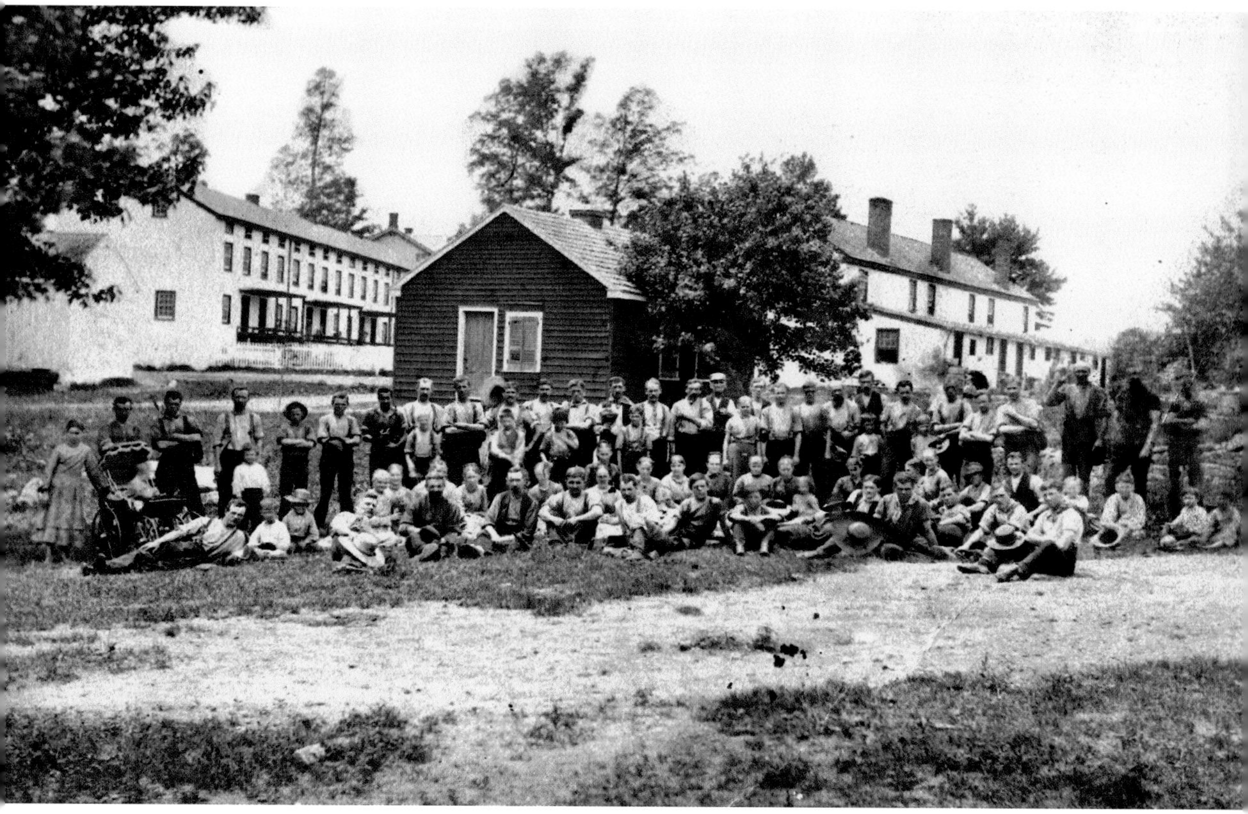

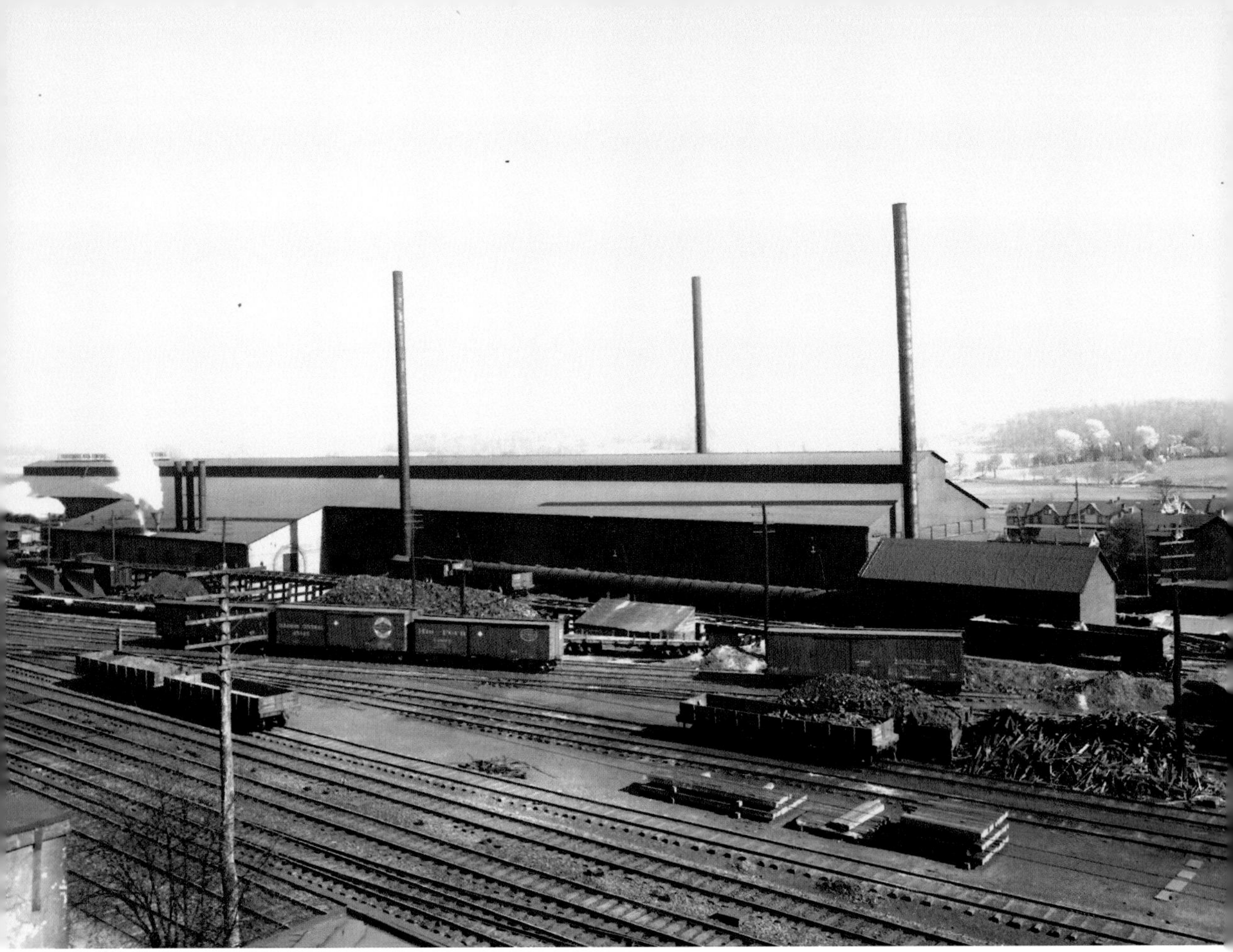

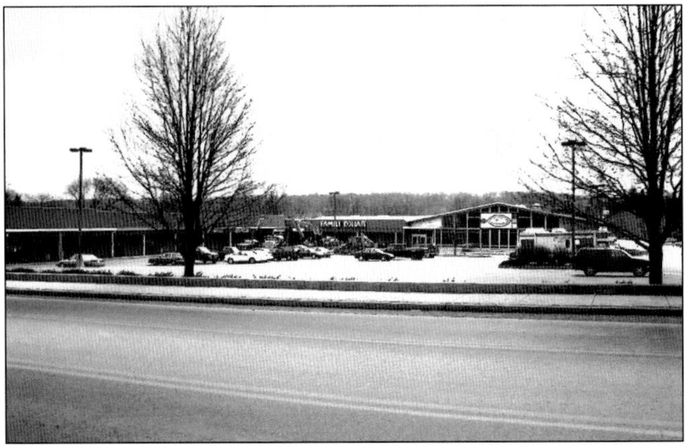

The Parkesburg Iron Company was founded by Horace Beale. In 1872, he moved Thorndale Iron Works to Parkesburg into buildings that were used by the Pennsylvania Railroad as car shops. The company was the main industry of Parkesburg for 55 years until the mill failed and was shut down in 1927. Peak employment came in 1917, when some 900 worked in the mill. During the first decade of the 20th century, virtually every railroad in the country used boiler tubes made of Parkesburg iron, the best available. Illness forced Beale to retire in 1924. The demand for boiler tubes slackened after 1925, causing the business to decline. Today, there is a shopping center on the site.

David and Henry Potts established the Isabella Furnace in the early 1830s for the purpose of making iron from the iron ore that was found in the surrounding area. The furnace, located in West Nantmeal Township, was named after Henry Potts' wife and produced cannon balls during the Civil War. In 1880, millionaire civil engineer Col. Joseph D. Potts purchased the furnace and later began building a palatial mansion adjacent to it. In 1890, an explosion blew the top off the furnace. Potts died in 1894, and a year later the furnace closed down. Today, part of the furnace has been restored as a private home and part remains unchanged.

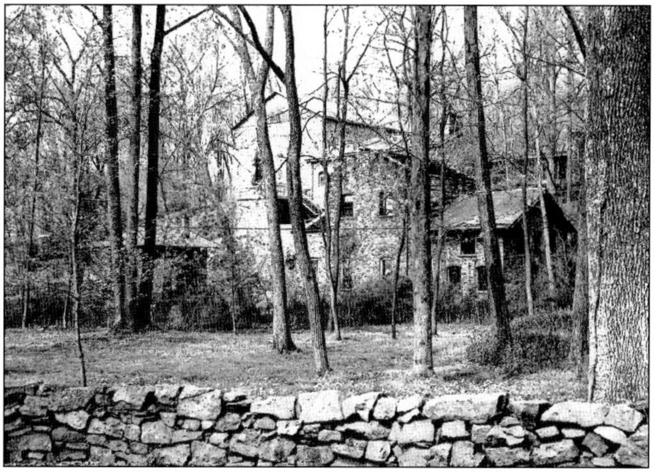

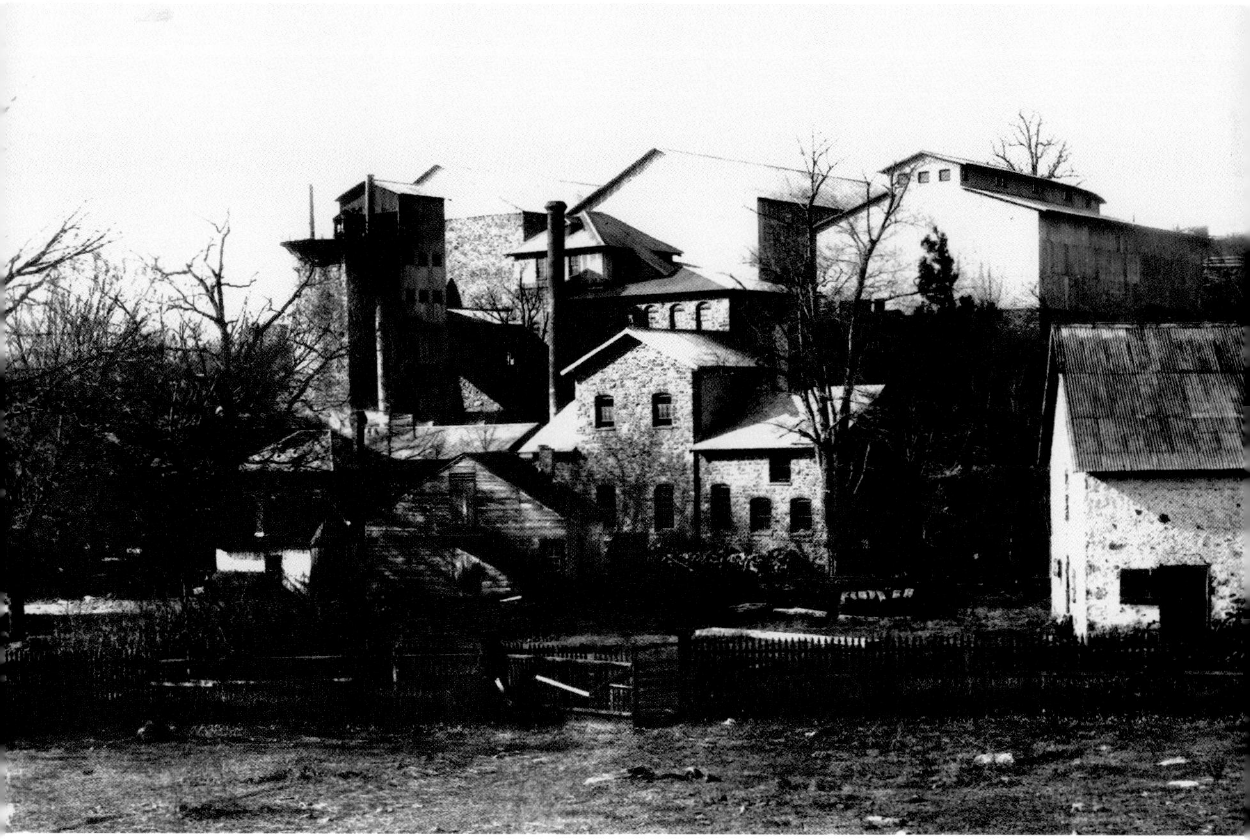

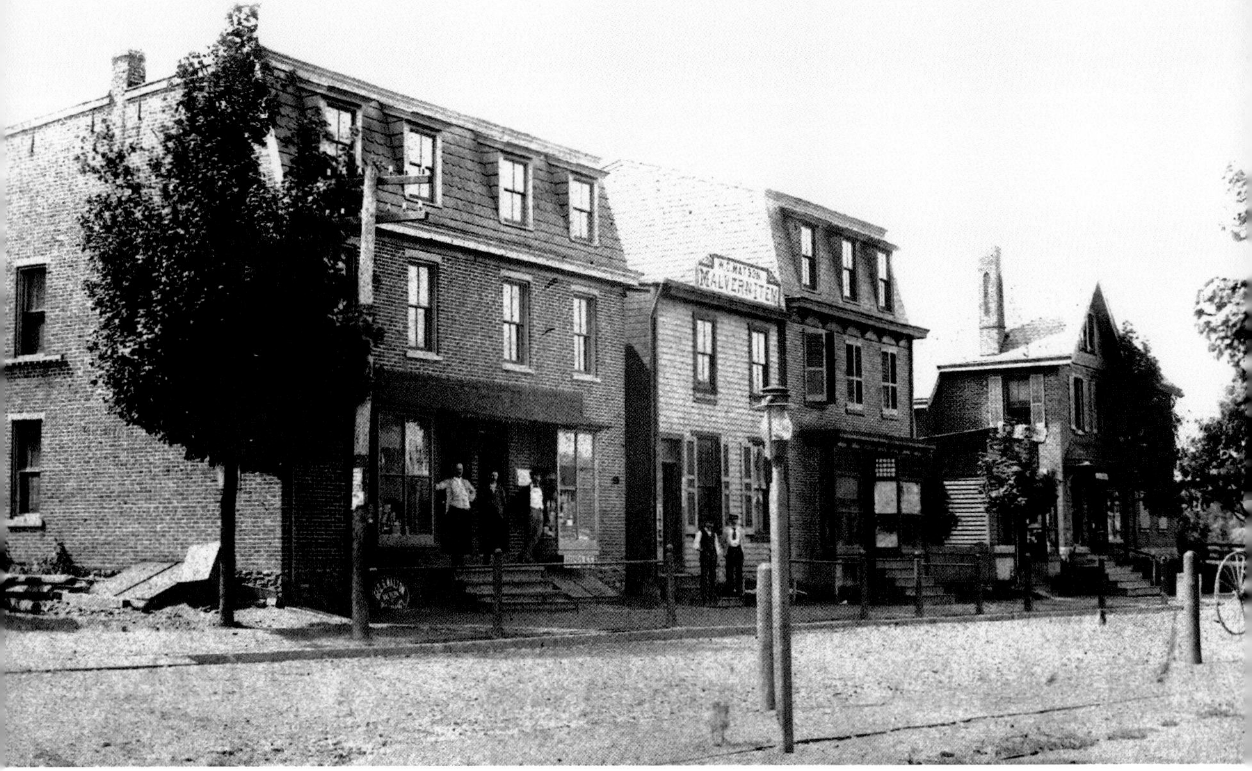

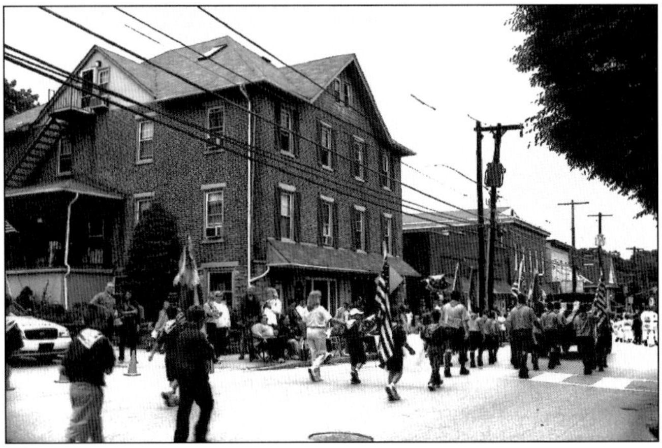

This 1888 view of the south side of King Street in Malvern shows the office of the *Green Tree and Malvern Item,* the borough's first newspaper. First published in 1878, it was founded by Herbert Gill, the son of Malvern's sheriff. The office did job printing and published the newspaper on a weekly basis every Saturday. After 1882, the paper changed its name to simply the *Item*. The paper changed hands a number of times and was published into the early 20th century. Today, many small town newspapers are a thing of the past. The frame building where the *Item* was published has since been replaced by a new structure. A Memorial Day parade passes down King Street in the present-day image.

John N. Chalfant began his business in 1873 with a modest hardware store known as the Kennett Hardware House. In 1884, he joined with J. N. Marshall and expanded the business into the Kennett Agricultural Warehouse. They sold agricultural machinery and building, blacksmith, and wheelwright supplies. They supplied everything from mowing machines and seeds to horseshoe nails, just what every farmer needed in the agriculturally rich area. In 1993, Genesis Health Ventures purchased the properties in the Chalfant block on East State Street, Kennett Square, to build their new national headquarters. Genesis HealthCare is one of the nation's largest providers of long-term care and rehabilitation therapy in the eastern United States. They operate Genesis ElderCare skilled nursing centers in 12 states and offer Genesis Rehabilitation Services in 21 states.

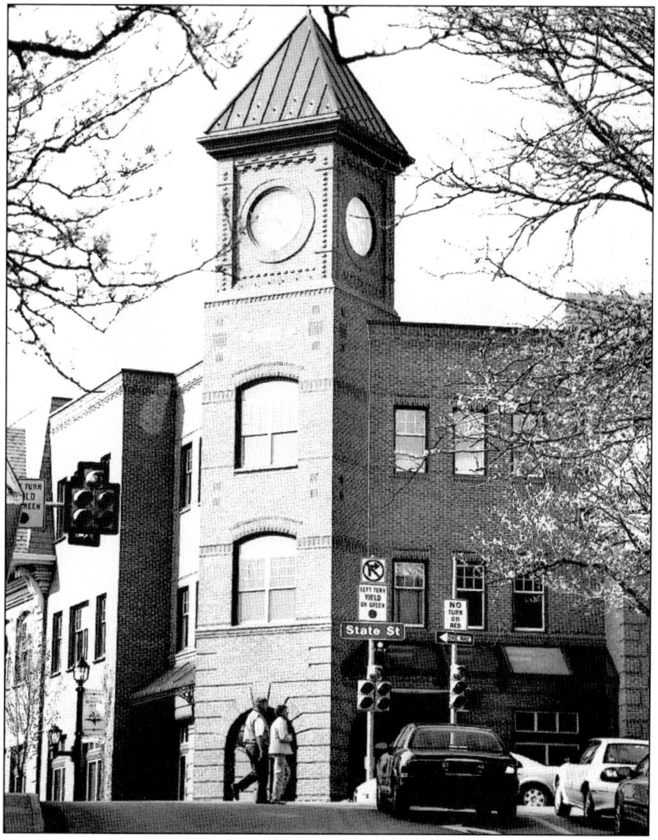

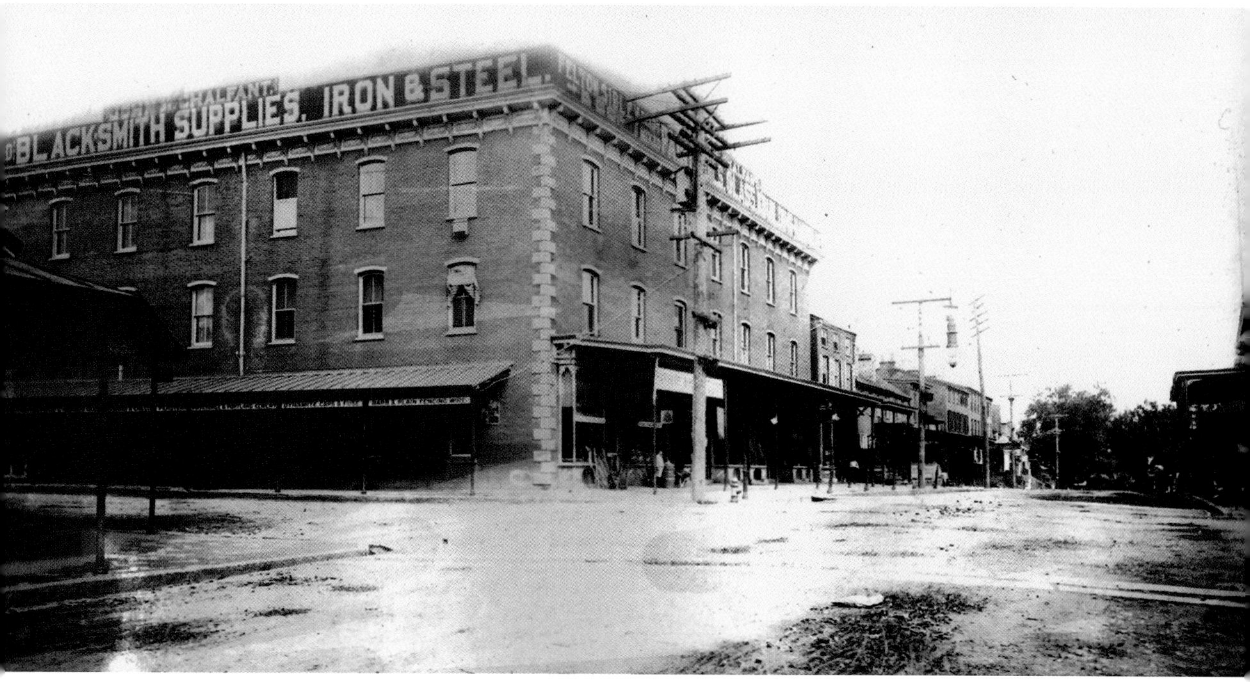

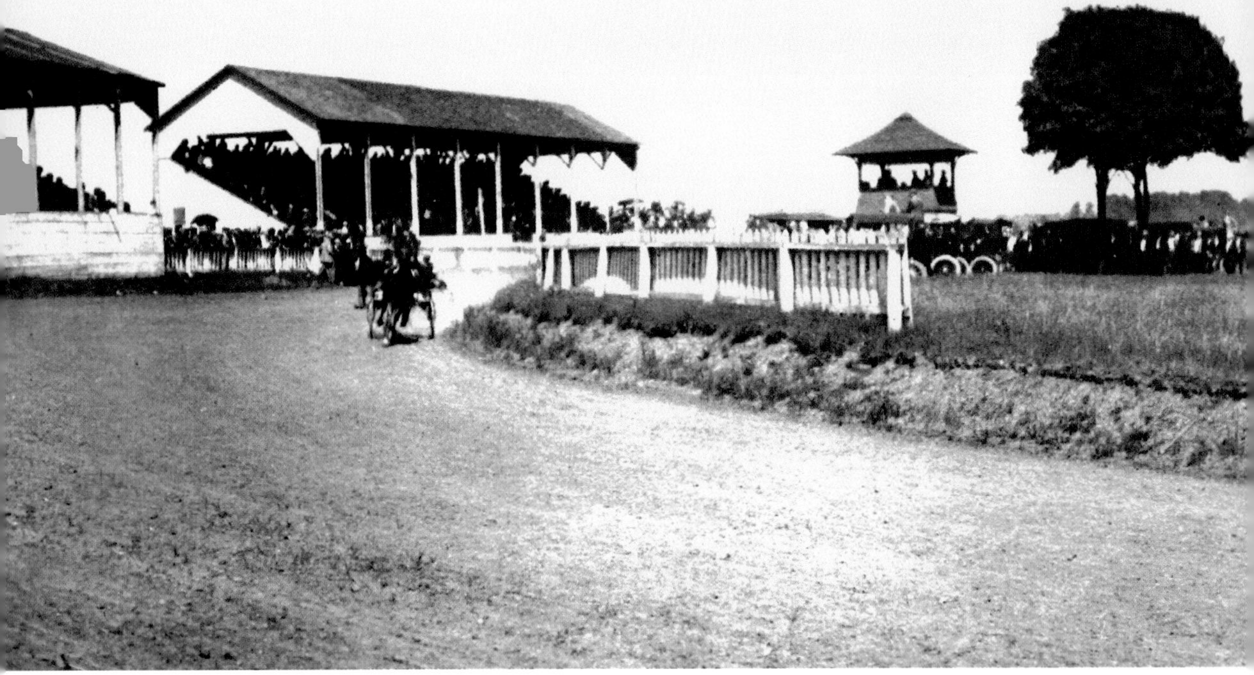

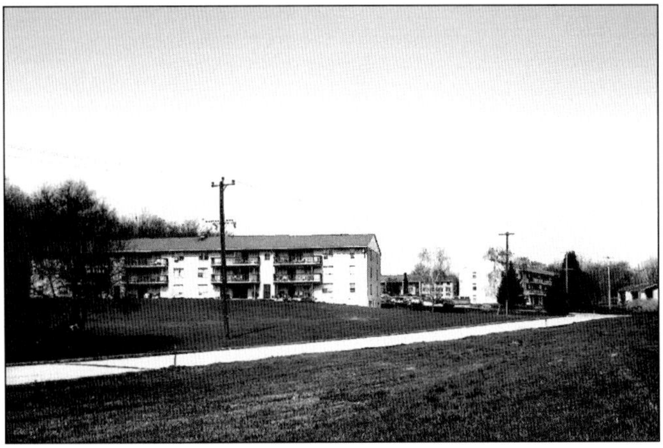

In 1870, the Oxford Agricultural Society purchased land in Oxford convenient to the railroad for a fairground. That year, the first annual fall agricultural fair featured exhibitions of farm animals, products, implements, trotting races, a corn-husking competition, and a parade featuring 116 yoke of oxen. The event drew 12,000 visitors from the surrounding area. Exhibits of hard cider and wines were stricken from the program, and gambling on the races was discouraged. The fair was held continuously until 1915. Thereafter, the fireman's carnival was held at the fairgrounds. Today, an apartment complex and a housing development are at that location.

In 1915, the YMCA building in Coatesville was completed at a cost of $155,000. It replaced the original YMCA, which had been destroyed by fire in 1913. A new dormitory wing was added in 1923. Relief in the form of free meals and shelter was provided during the Great Depression. The auditorium was used as a movie theater; proceeds from the theater went to help further the many activities sponsored by the YMCA. Spirited athletic activities, particularly amateur basketball, flourished there over the years. The building was later demolished, and in 1978 construction commenced on Coatesville Towers, today a senior retirement community. Local YMCA programs and activities are now run by the Brandywine YMCA, located on Hurley Road.

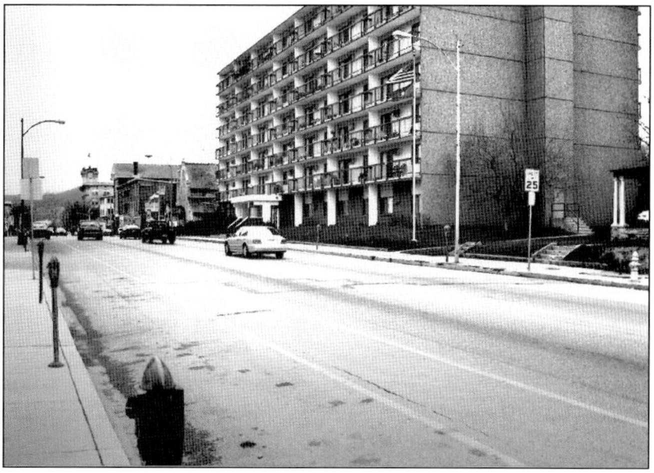

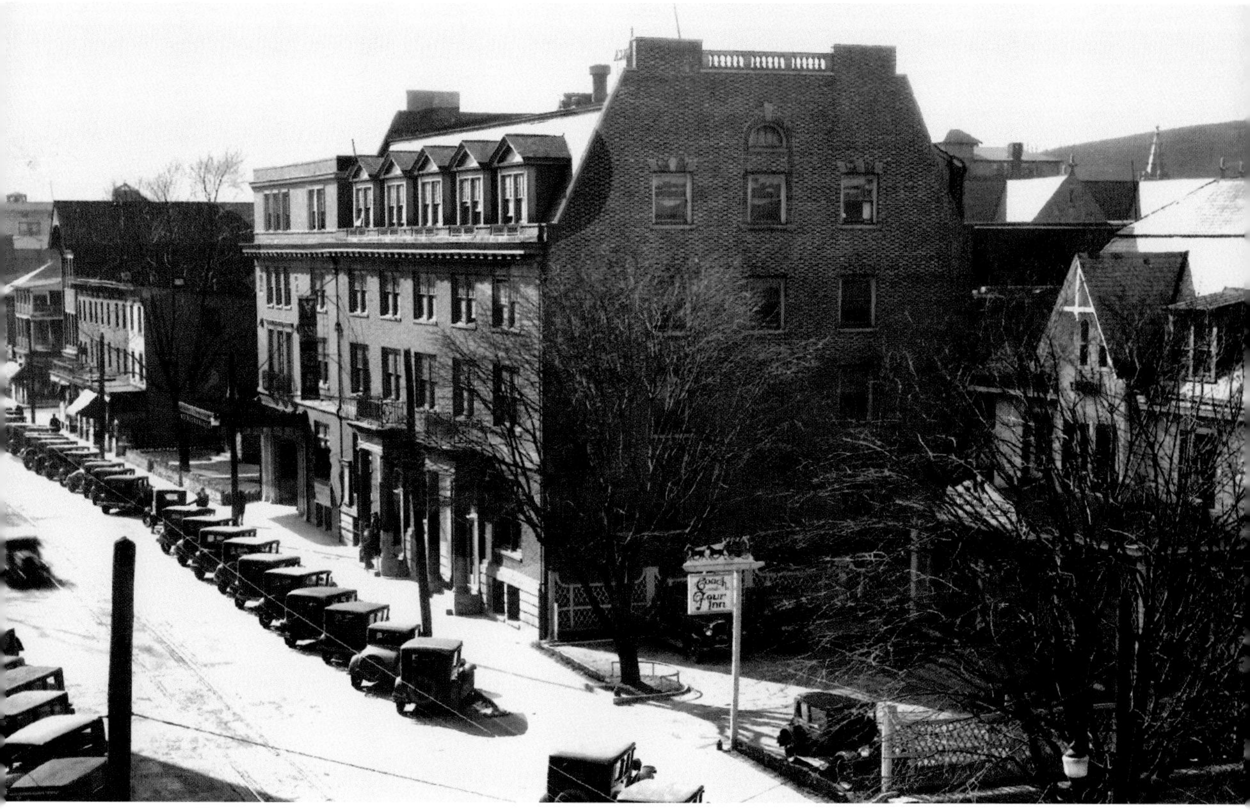

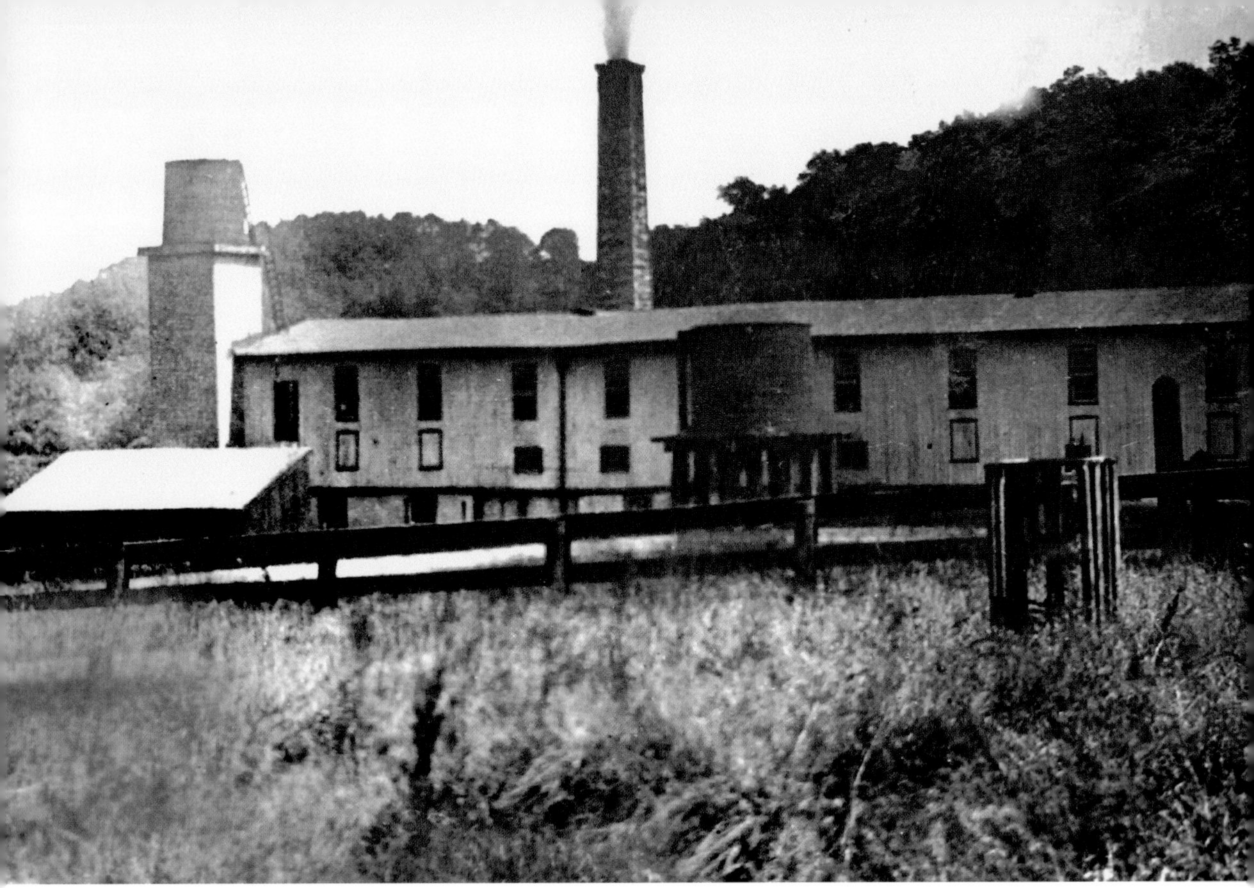

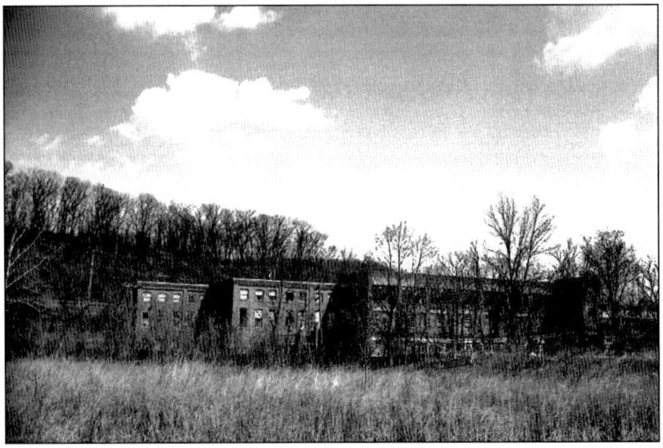

Known as Mode's Mill, Dove Mill or Megargee Mill, this mill in Modena has a long history. In 1776, William Mode established a gristmill and in 1812 converted it to a paper-making mill. His son Alexander, due to the low volume of water in the creek, installed a steam engine to drive the mill. In 1881, the Megargee brothers bought the mill shown in this 1895 historical photograph. In 1907, a two-story addition was built, which included an electric generator to operate the mill. The mill changed hands many times in the succeeding years. In 1946, owner Beach and Arthur installed a treatment plant for the wastewater discharged into the Brandywine. They made paper tablecloths, napkins, plates, and cups. Today, the buildings are abandoned, idle for more than 20 years.

Thomas Parke established the Swan Hotel and Tavern in Downingtown in 1806. Beginning in 1814, a stage line from Downingtown to Philadelphia stopped daily at the hotel. Many livestock sales were held in the hotel yard and barns. Cows, mules, and pigs were unloaded from the adjacent railroad. The hotel was extensively enlarged and remodeled by owner Theodore Hallman in 1895. In 1902, the West Chester and Downingtown trolley stopped conveniently in front of the hotel. During the 1950s, the hotel restaurant and ballroom hosted elegant coming-out parties for debutantes. The hotel was purchased by Downingtown Savings and Loan in 1965 and was demolished to make way for a modern bank building and parking lot. Today, that building houses the First Financial Bank.

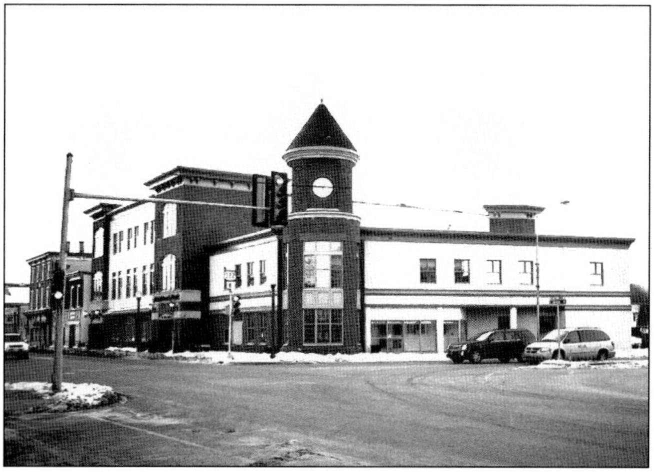

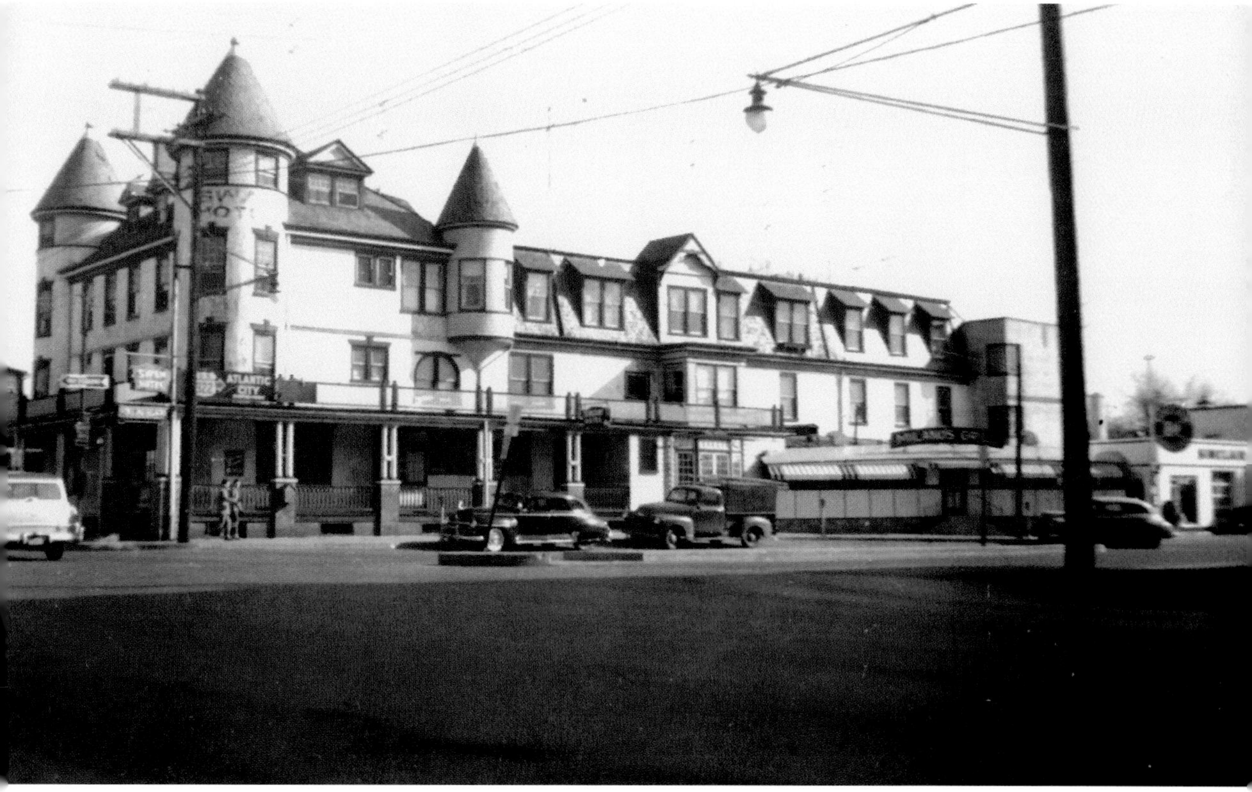

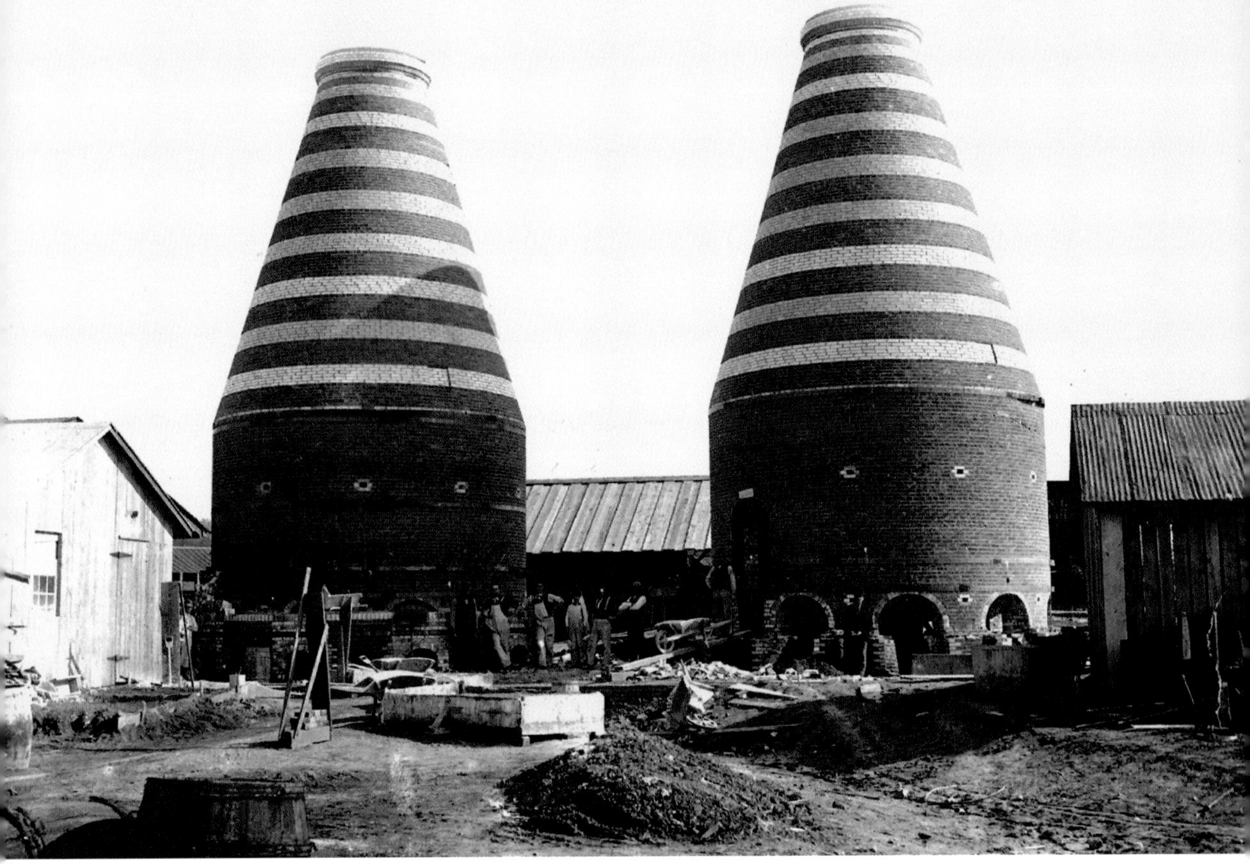

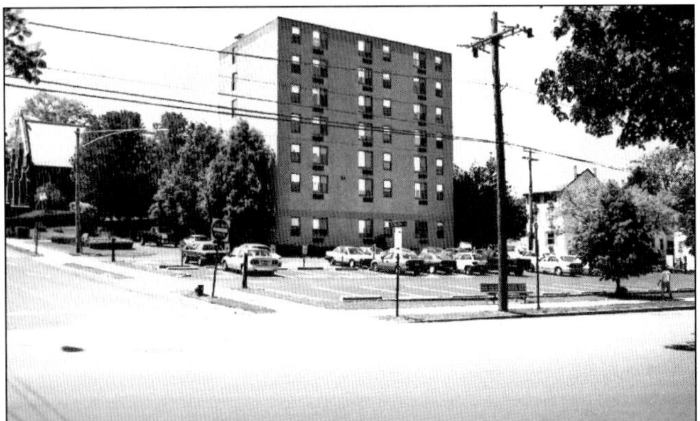

W. Schrieber established the Phoenix Pottery, Kaolin, and Fire Brick Company in 1867 and made firebricks for the Phoenix Iron Company. Changing hands in 1877, it became known as Griffin, Smith and Hill. The company was best known for its Etruscan majolica ware. Majolica pottery is made in fanciful naturalistic forms that are brightly hand-painted. After a devastating fire in 1890, majolica was no longer manufactured in Phoenixville. The pottery buildings located at Church and Starr Streets in Phoenixville were torn down shortly after the beginning of the 20th century. Currently, the site is occupied by a high-rise apartment for seniors.

Later known affectionately as "Old Main," the structure was built in 1871 as a classroom building and dormitory for the West Chester State Normal School, a state-chartered teacher-training institution. Designed by architect Addison Hutton, the building was a fine example of the type of educational architecture in vogue following the Civil War. Large wings were later added, making it the largest serpentine building in the United States at the time it was demolished in 1971. Today, the original arch that was over the front doorway has been preserved and can be seen standing next to "New Main" at West Chester University.

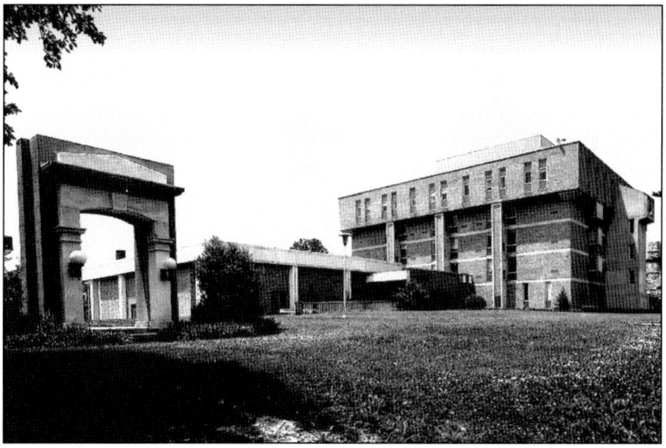

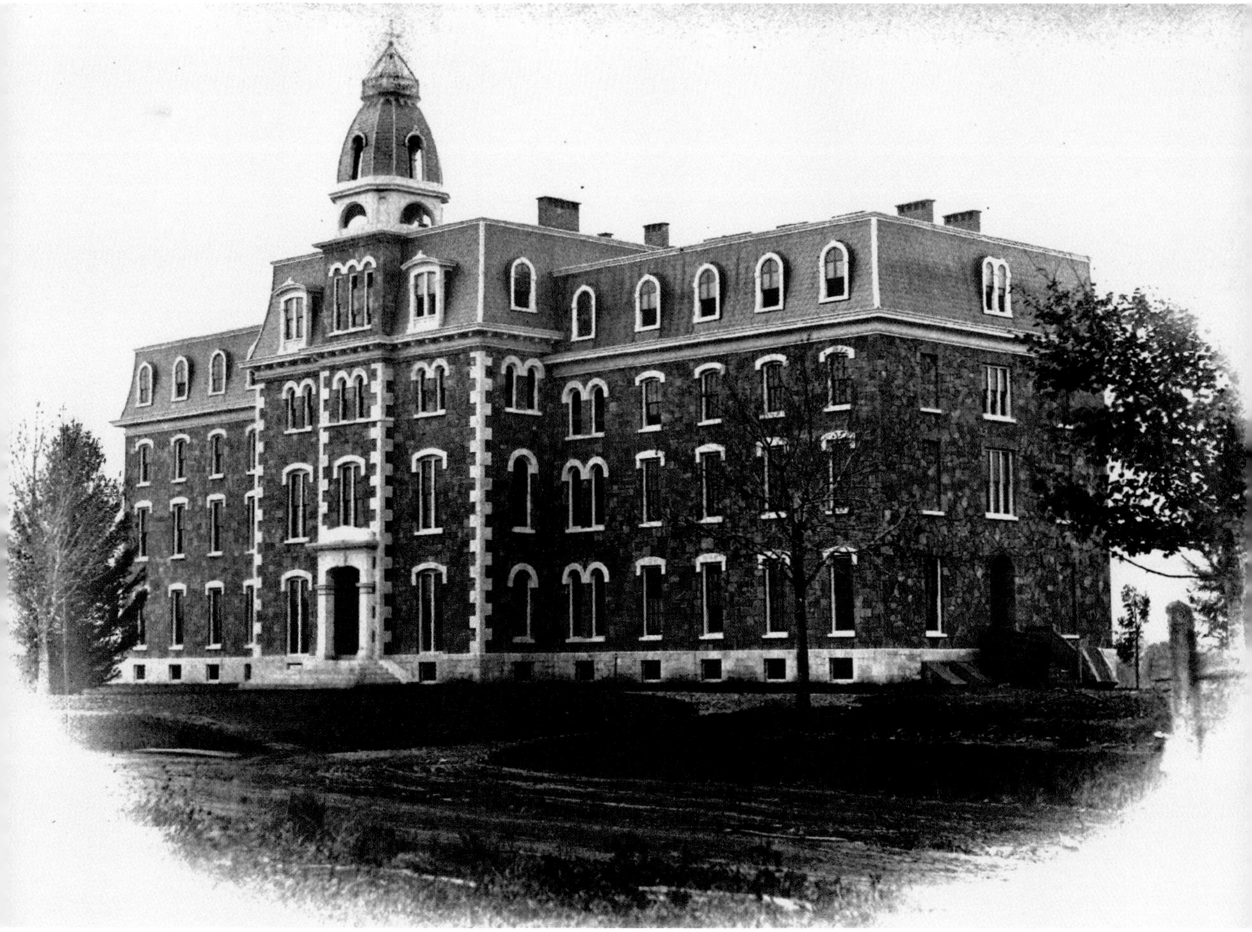

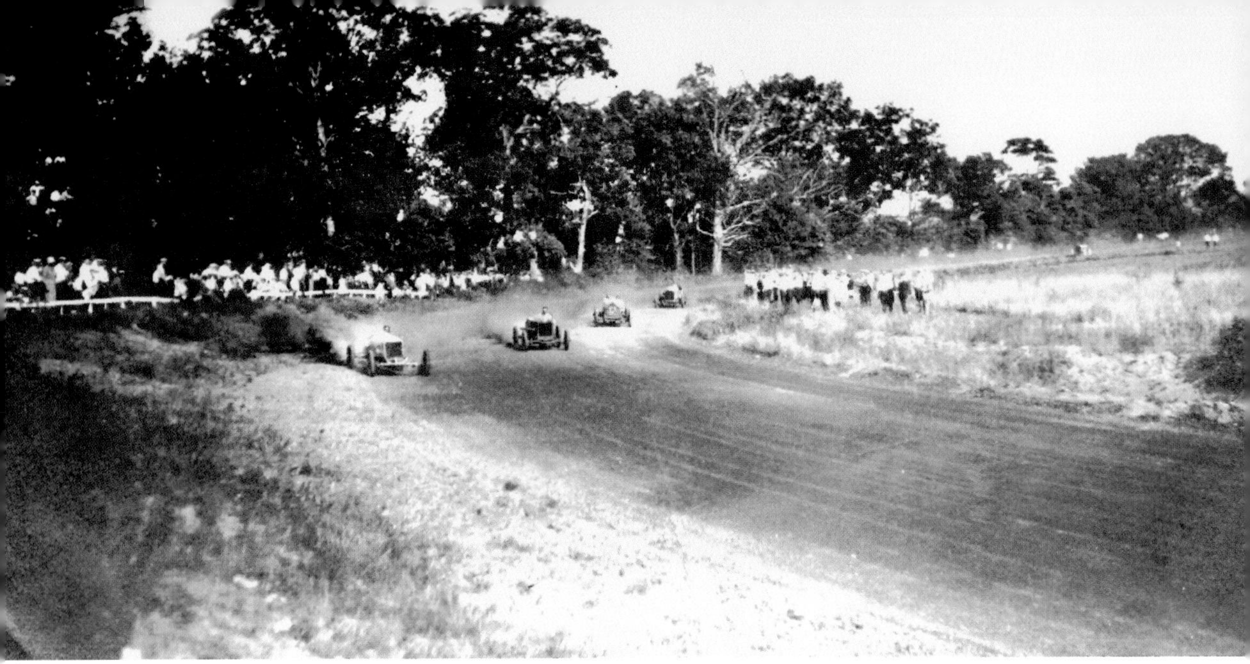

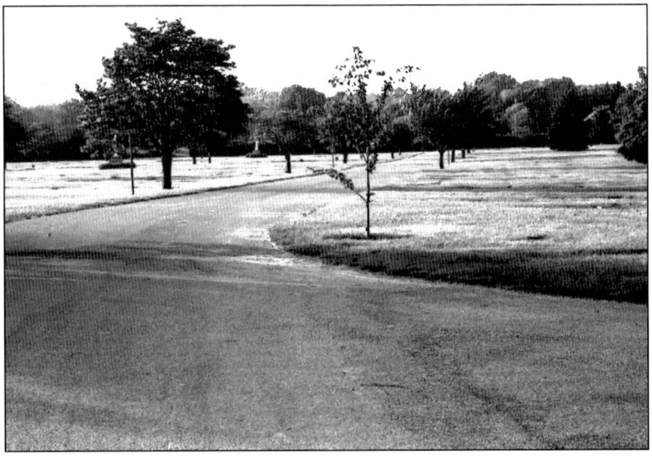

Located on West Chester Pike about a mile east of West Chester, the old Chester County Fair Grounds were the scene of many types of events, including foot, horse, and auto races. It was also known as Sheller's Track, named for owner Charles Sheller. The photograph above shows racing cars circling the narrow half-mile oval *c.* 1920. The infield was used for football and baseball contests. Beginning in 1898, it was the site of an annual West Chester Stallion Show, which featured speed trials and jumping contests. The West Chester and Philadelphia trolley cars frequently passed the fairground gates affording easy access to the events. In 1938, the grounds were sold to Rolling Green Memorial Park, and today they are a cemetery.

London Grove Friends Meeting, as seen below *c.* 1910, looks much the same today. The large stone meetinghouse was constructed in 1818 for the London Grove Friends, who had been meeting for over 100 years in smaller quarters. Treasured by the active Friends of today's meeting is a historic great white oak tree, present when the meeting was originally established.

Chapter 3
Places That Have Been Preserved

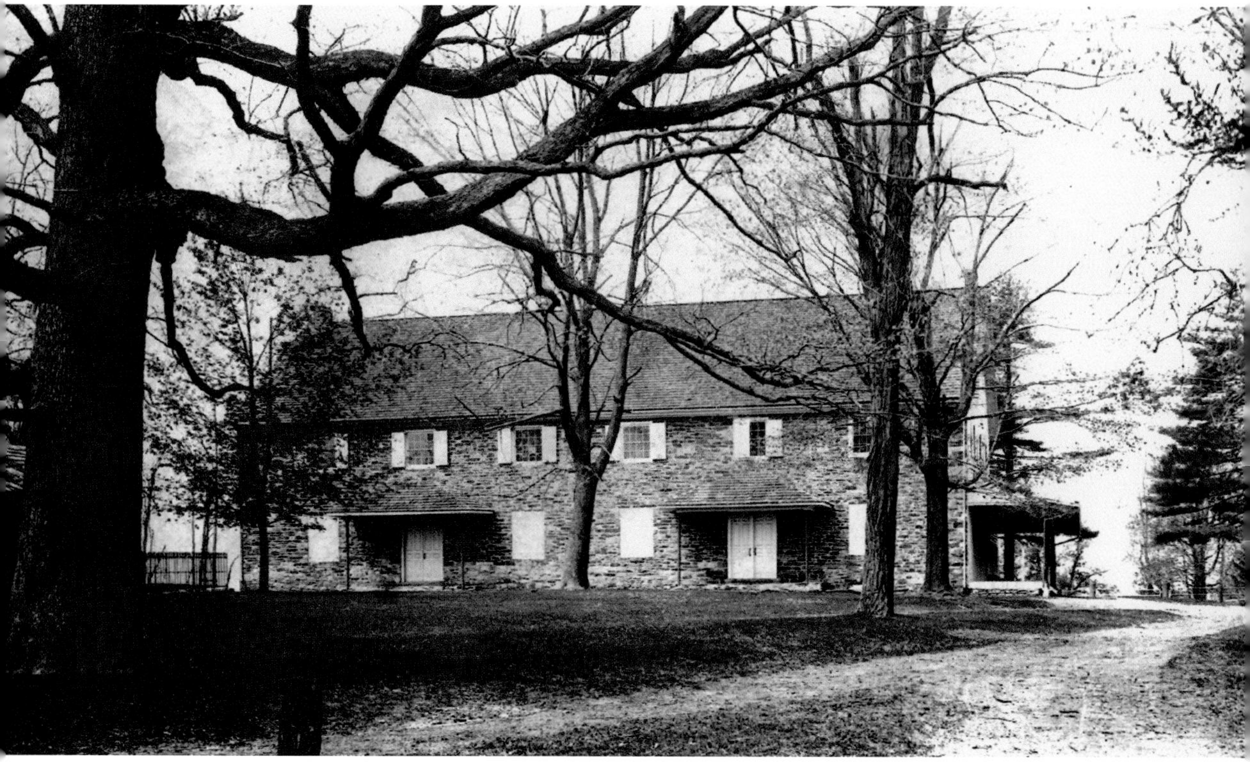

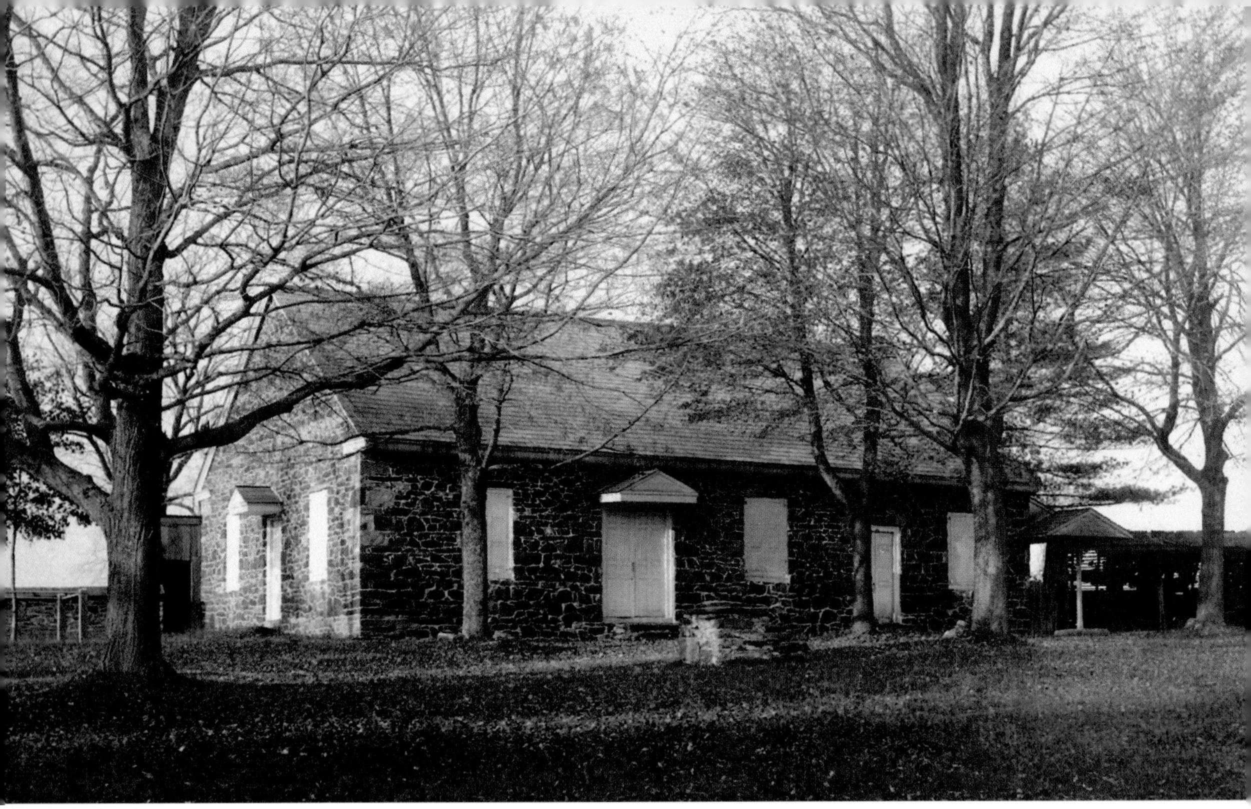

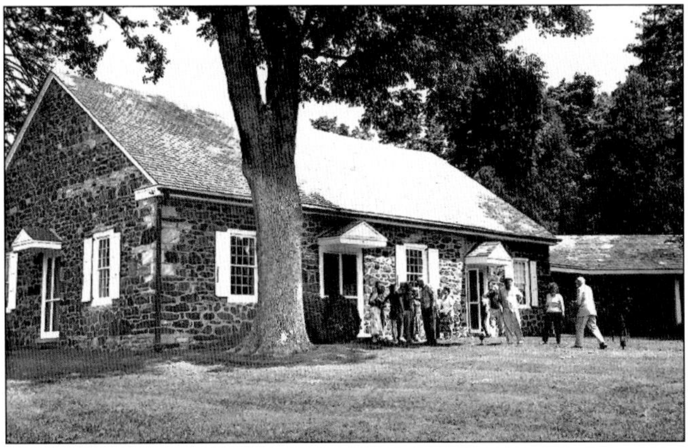

Originally formed as Birmingham Preparative Meeting in 1690, Friends met in private homes to worship and in a log meetinghouse. Friends have been meeting for silent worship in the Birmingham Meetinghouse since it was built in 1763. The building briefly served as a field hospital at the time of the Battle of Brandywine in 1777. Both British and American soldiers are buried in a mass grave located in the cemetery adjacent to the meetinghouse. In general, Friends opposed war and took a neutral position during the American Revolution. The original building included sheds for sheltering horses during worship. These sheds were removed in 1940 and replaced with a small frame addition. This, in turn, was replaced in 1968 with a gray-stone activities building, including a kitchen, classroom areas, and restrooms.

The Barns-Brinton House was built in 1714 by blacksmith William Barns on the road that became Baltimore Pike. He applied for a license to operate a tavern here in 1720. In 1753, James Brinton purchased the house, and it remained in the Brinton family for over 100 years. After falling into disuse, the Chadds Ford Historical Society purchased the Barns-Brinton House in 1969 and restored it. The house is now open on a seasonal basis for tours. Today, over 36,000 vehicles pass by this landmark daily. Note that the path of Route 1 has changed from when the historical photograph was taken *c.* 1890.

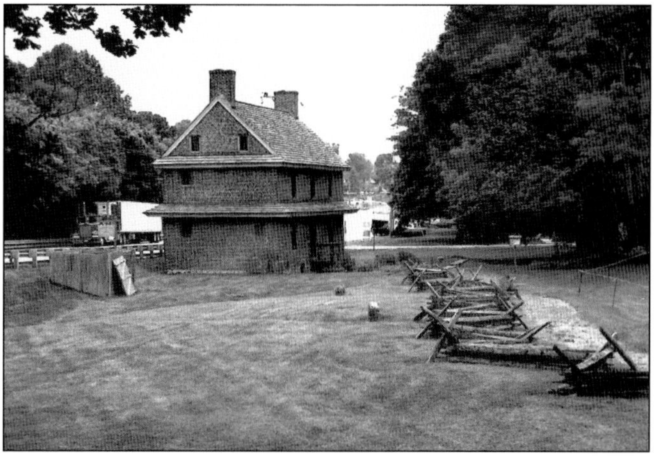

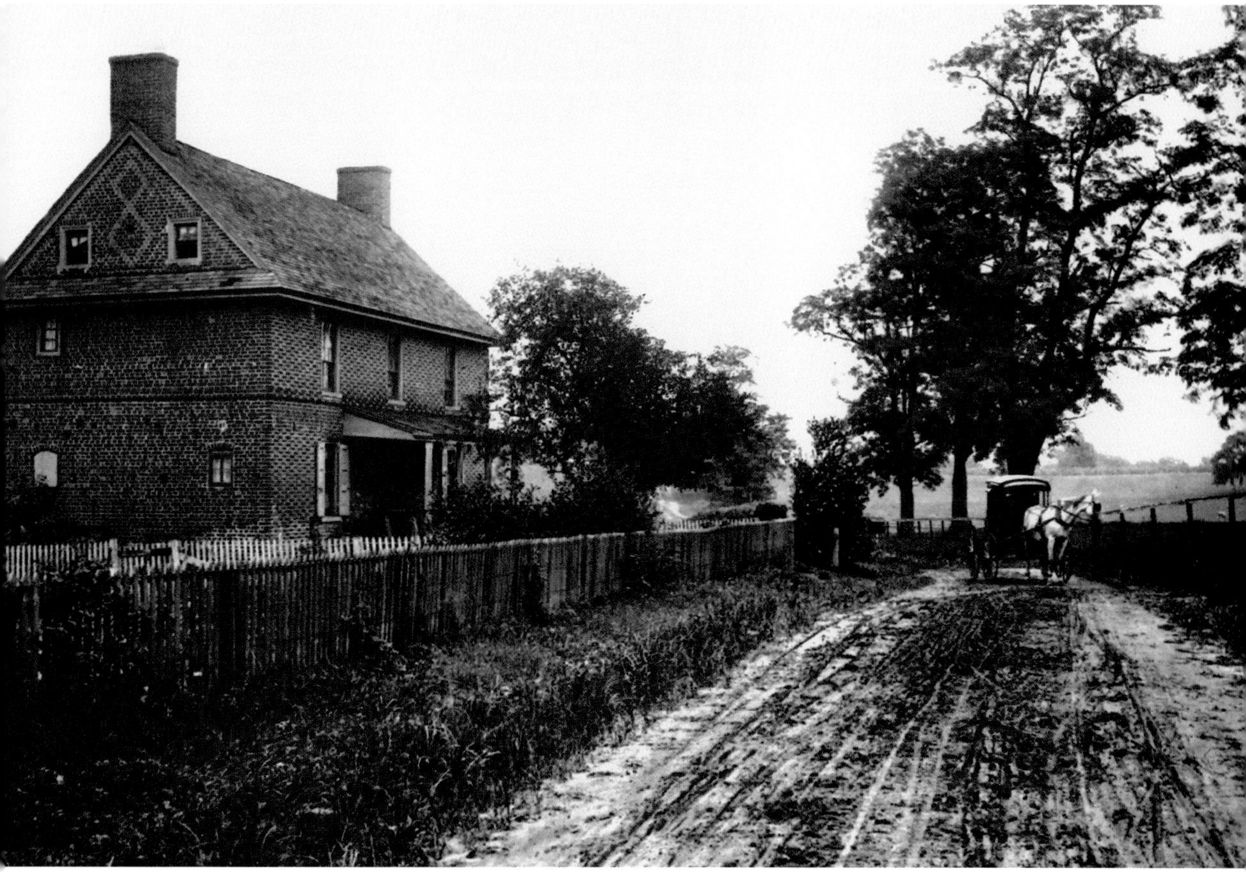

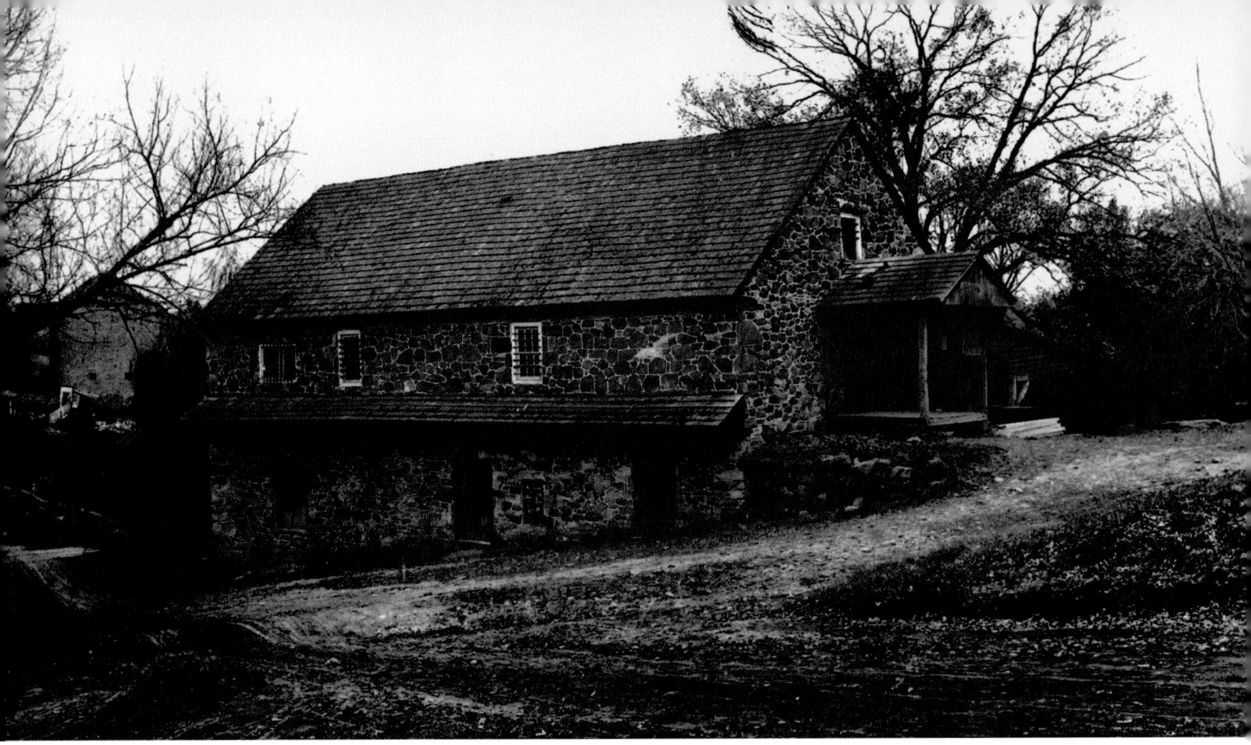

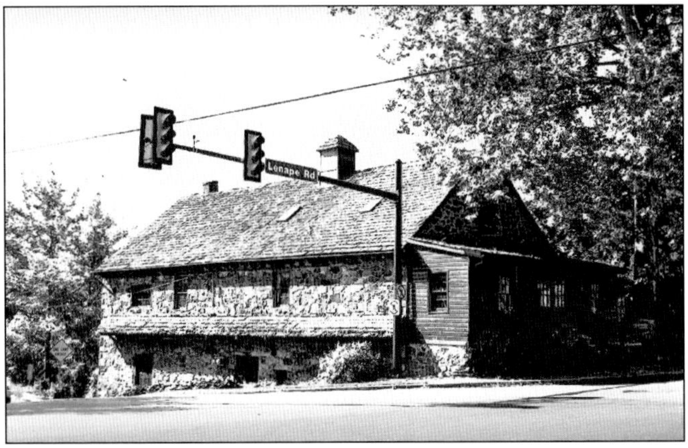

Strode's Mill was built in 1721 to grind wheat grown in the fertile Brandywine Valley. During the Battle of Brandywine in the American Revolution, British soldiers stole flour from the mill. The mill became known as Strode's Mill when John Strode purchased it in 1737. The Strode family operated the mill for nearly 150 years until it was sold in 1878. After being used by a variety of businesses, the mill was again used to grind grain for Pepperidge Farm Bakery in Downingtown in the 1950s. In 1968, PennDOT proposed razing the structure to eliminate a dangerous curve in the road. Concerned citizens petitioned to save the mill. PennDOT drafted an alternative plan that was acceptable to all. Currently, the mill is a private residence and art gallery.

The first Yellow Springs Inn on this site dates from 1750. Parts of this building date from the 1760s, with subsequent additions ongoing until 1876. It was once the hub of a fashionable spa retreat. Many wealthy Philadelphians came to "take the waters" in the mineral springs. In September 1777, George Washington stayed at the inn. Other famous visitors over the years included Daniel Webster, Henry Clay, DeWitt Clinton, and singer Jenny Lind, the Swedish Nightingale. The spa reached its peak around the time of the Civil War. After the war, it became a boarding school, the summer campus of the Pennsylvania Academy of Fine Arts, and housing for employees of a movie production company. Today, it is once again a fashionable restaurant, the Inn at Yellow Springs.

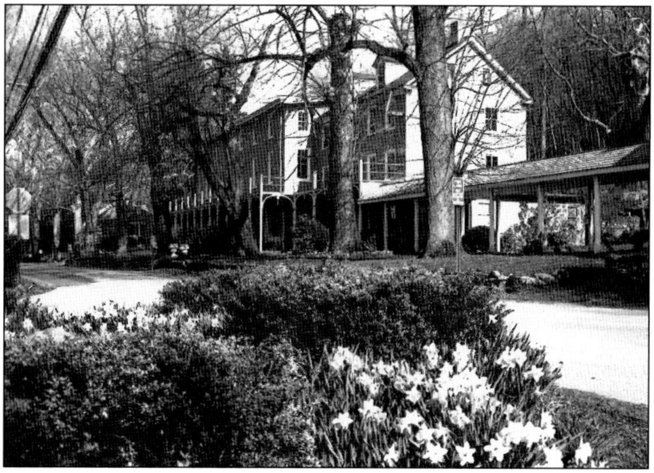

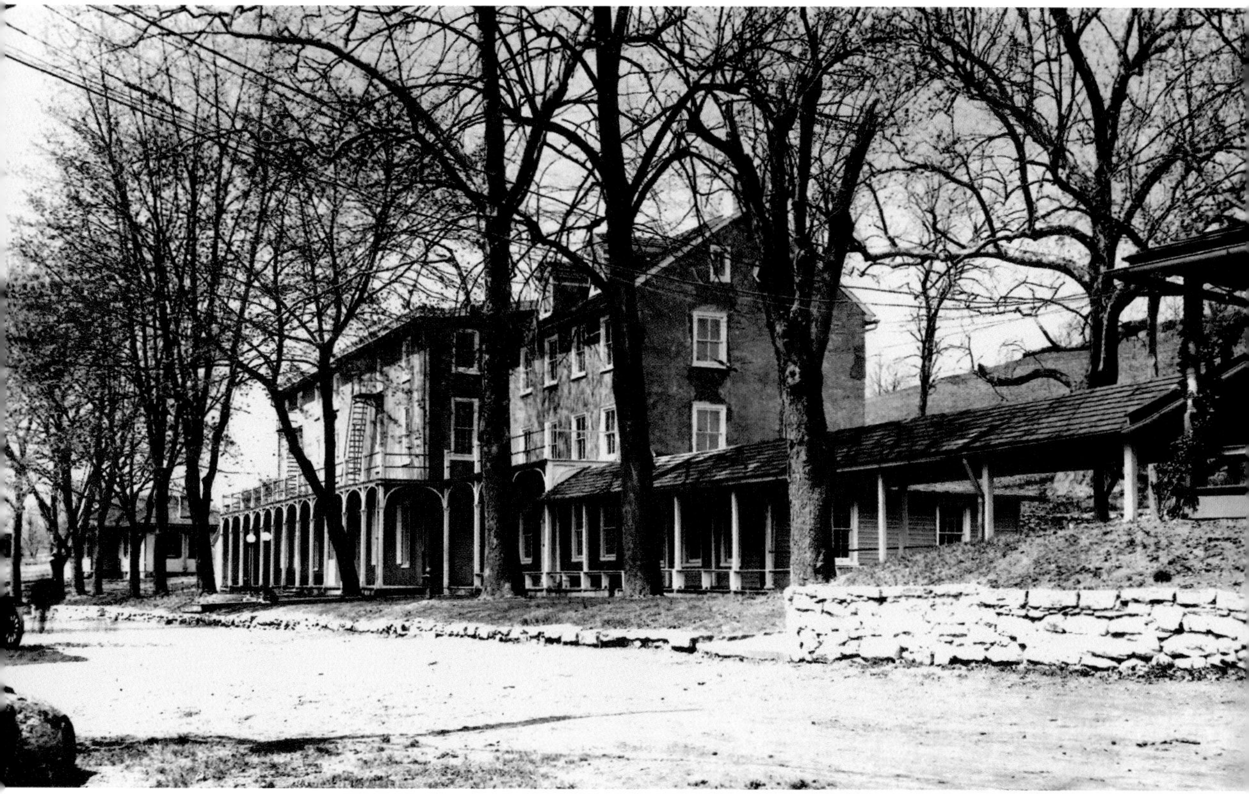

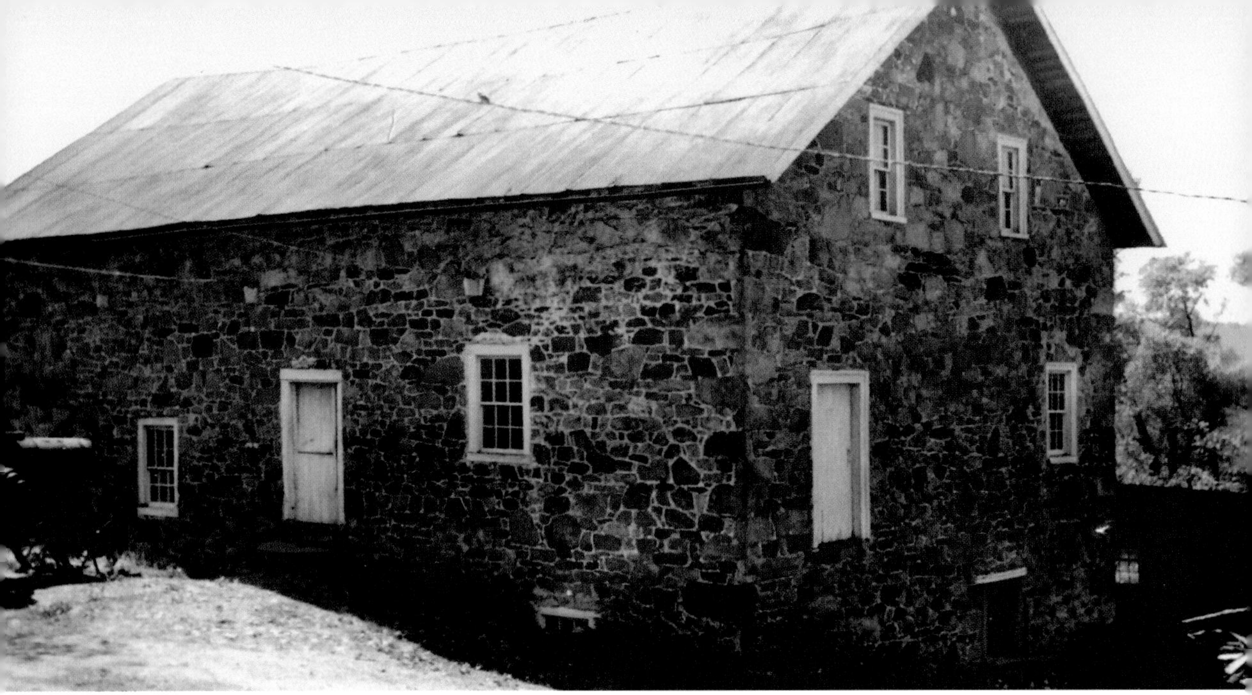

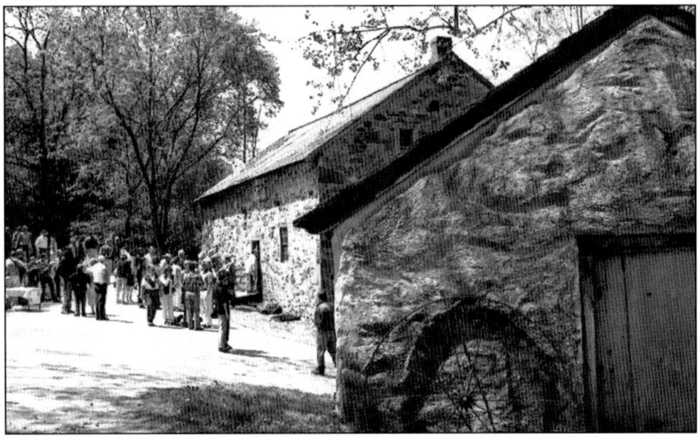

Samuel Lightfoot, a surveyor and one of Pikeland's earliest settlers, constructed Anselma Grist Mill on Pickering Creek in 1747. Subsequent owners adapted the ideas of the inventor Oliver Evans, and by the 1820s the mill was automated by use of conveyors and elevators. The mill's wooden waterwheel was replaced by a steel wheel in 1906. Through the efforts of the Mill at Anselma Preservation and Educational Trust, the structure has been restored as an operational museum. It is the most complete example of a custom grain mill that reflects changing technology over a period of three centuries. The photograph below shows the opening celebration of the site in 2004, billed as the "first turn of the wheel."

Primitive Hall in West Marlborough Township was built in 1738 by Joseph Pennock. A judge, Pennock may have held court in his house. The large manor house consists of a center hall and four rooms downstairs, a large hall and four rooms upstairs, a full attic, and two separate cellars. It measures 52 feet wide and 40 feet deep. Architecturally and historically, it is considered one of the more important houses in Pennsylvania. Owner Stewart Huston began the restoration efforts in 1920 to remove the gabled roof and porches added in the 19th century shown in the historical photograph. Currently, it is maintained by the Primitive Hall Foundation and is open to the public by appointment only.

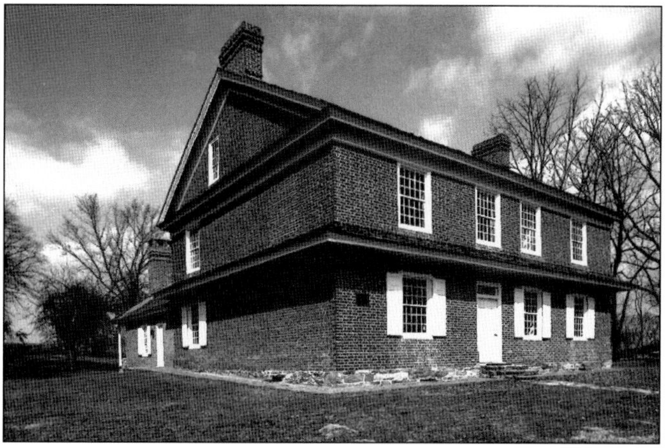

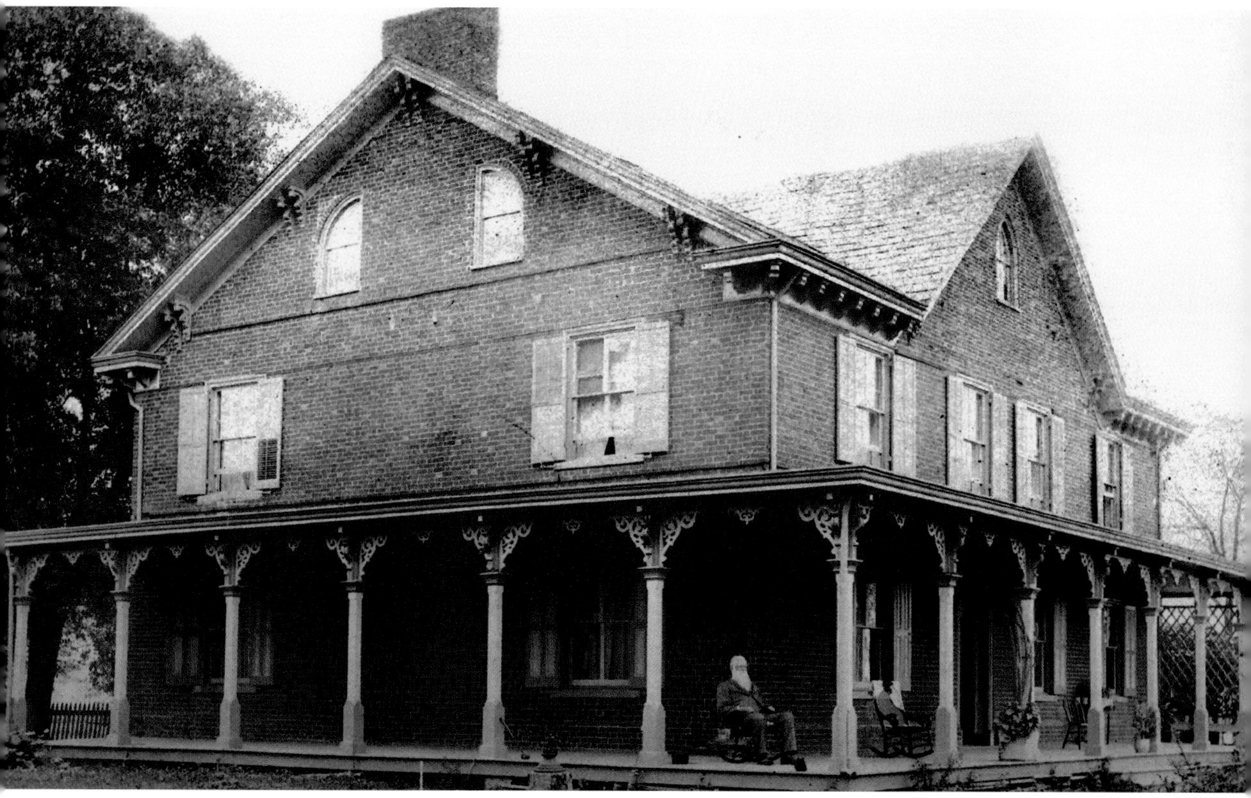

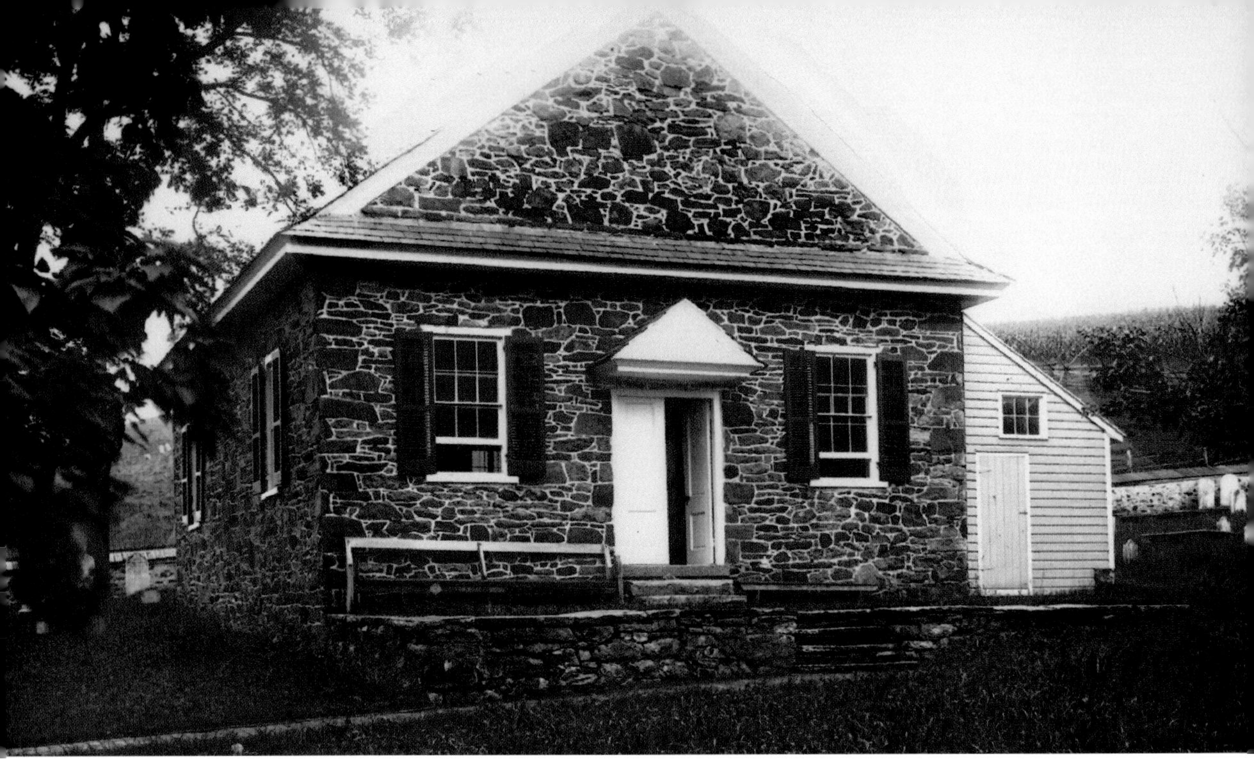

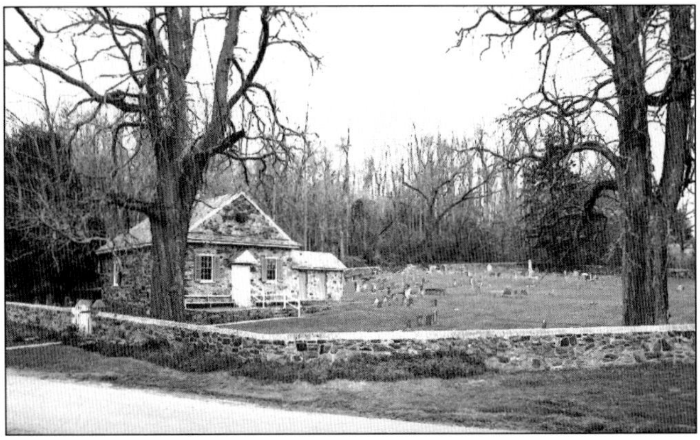

The London Tract Baptist Church held services in this building, constructed *c.* 1729, for more than 230 years. In the 1960s, a project calling for the building of a dam across White Clay Creek threatened to flood the area, potentially putting the building under 20 feet of water. This would have necessitated the removal of the structure. The project never came to fruition, and the building was spared. In 1984, the DuPont Company donated the land to Pennsylvania and Delaware, and the White Clay Creek Preserve was created. The church serves as the visitor center for the 1,225 acres located in Chester County and is administered by the Pennsylvania Bureau of State Parks.

Westtown School was founded in 1799 by Philadelphia Yearly Meeting as a boarding school for Quaker boys and girls. The early curriculum for students included mathematics, grammar, penmanship, geography, surveying, bookkeeping, and science. Practical studies for girls included sewing and embroidery. A classical education, including Greek and Latin, was added in 1830. The school was greatly enlarged in 1888, when a new main building was constructed. The Quakers were progressive in their outlook, providing physical education for boys and girls beginning in the late 1880s. Today, Westtown School offers a college preparatory education for pre-kindergarten through 12th grade. The 600-acre campus features 17 buildings, athletic fields, an arboretum, and a lake. The student body totaling 781 represents students from 20 different countries and from all faiths and ethnic backgrounds.

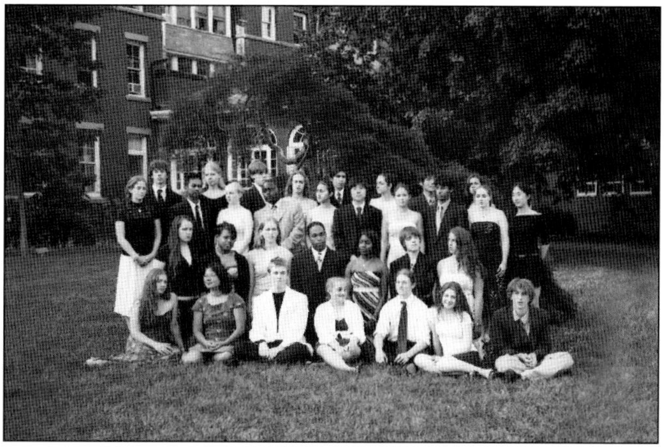

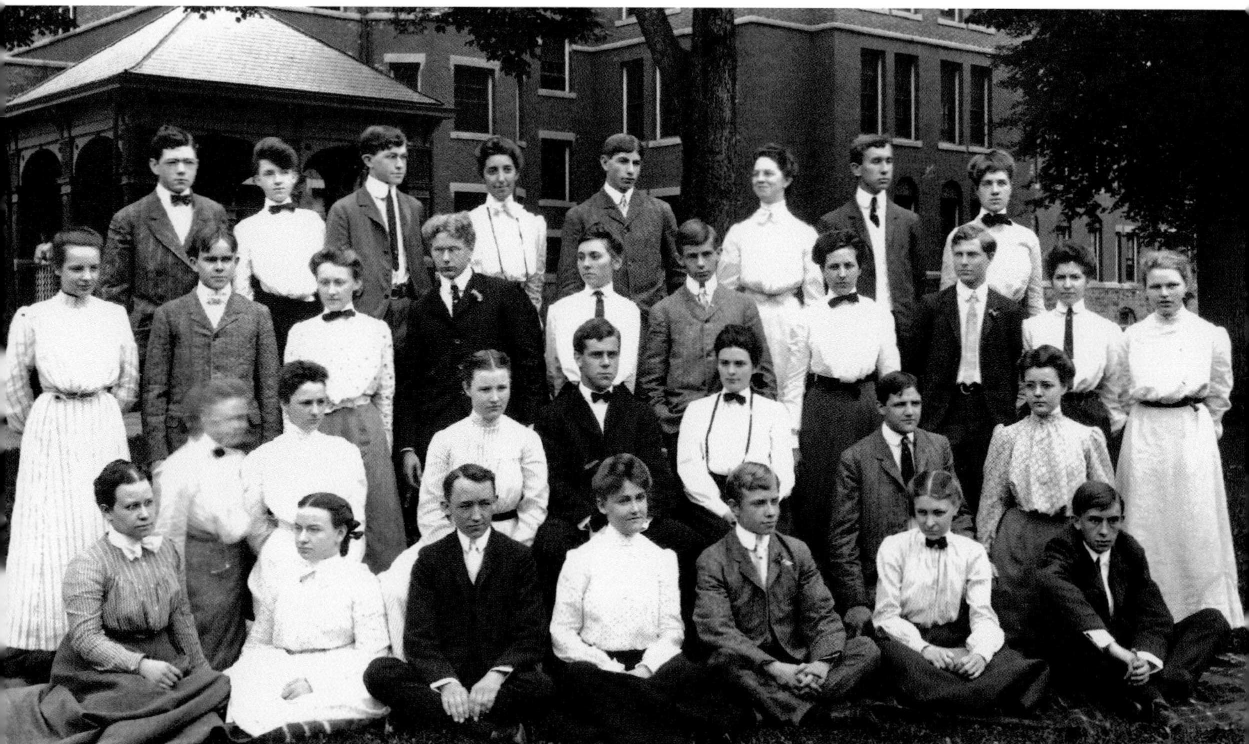

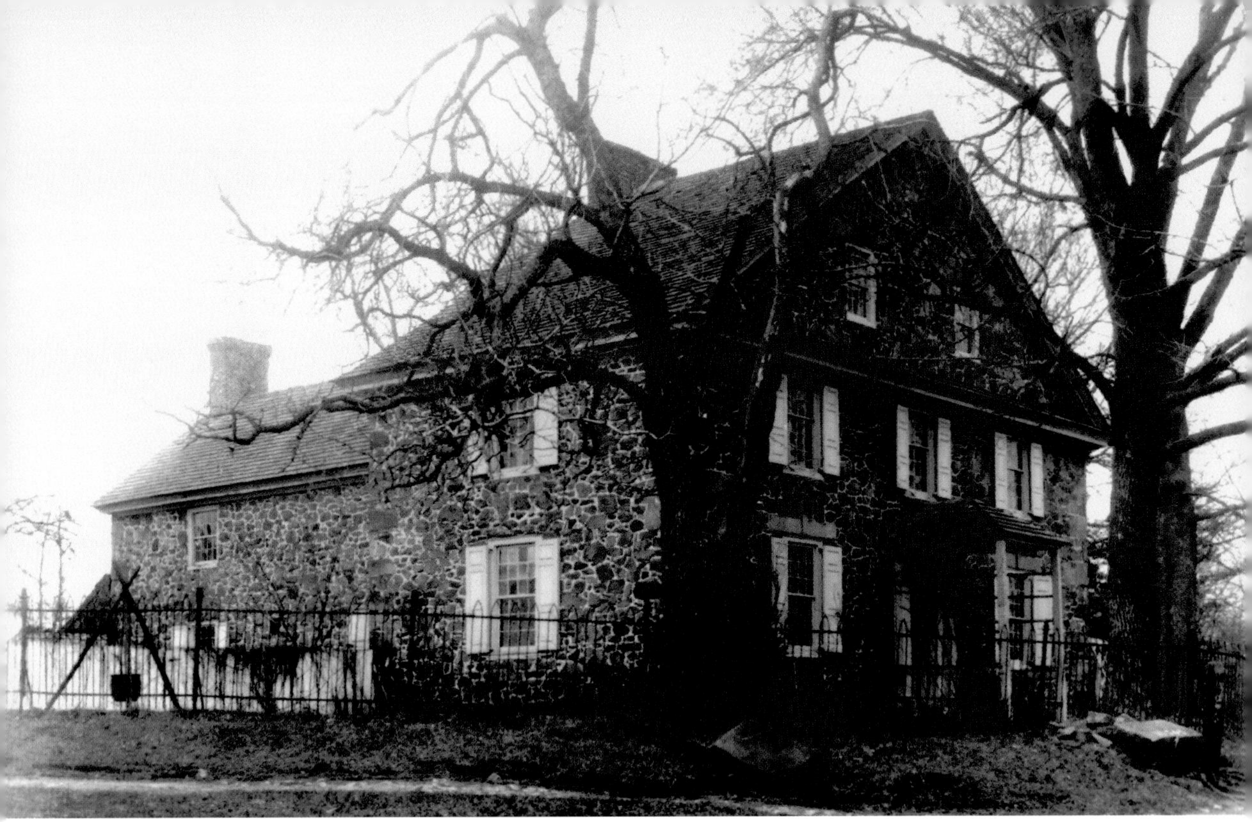

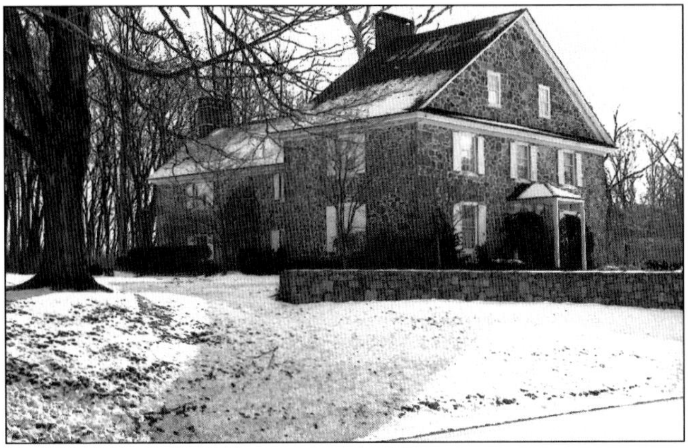

Bull Mansion was named for Thomas Bull (1744–1837), a lieutenant colonel in the Revolutionary War, a stonemason, and the manager of the Warwick Furnace. On his land in East Nantmeal Township, he built a mansion, blacksmith shop, barns, tenant houses, gristmill, and sawmill. His son Rev. Levi Bull (1780–1859), a well-known clergyman, also made Bull Mansion his home. The property was purchased by Levi's son Thomas Kempis Bull (1810–1893), a gentleman farmer who served in the Pennsylvania state legislature from 1846 to 1848. Bull's daughter Caroline J. Bull (1863–1942) inherited the mansion and shared the home with her cousin Octavius Bull, who took the 1905 photograph shown here. Currently, the mansion is no longer in the Bull family. It is still surrounded by the quiet countryside enjoyed by its builders so long ago.

In 1771, Mark Bird, a key figure in Colonial iron making, established Hopewell Furnace near present-day Elverson. The site today represents the iron plantation as it was in the 1820–1840 period. Hopewell, famous for its cast-iron stoves, stayed in operation until 1883. The photograph below was taken in 1887 as the facility was falling into disrepair. The federal government purchased the property in 1935 and designated it a national historic site in 1938. Restoration has continued through the years. The cast house shown here was where molders cast iron into stove plates and other items. Live demonstrations of the various aspects of iron making are held periodically at the site, which is administered by the National Park Service.

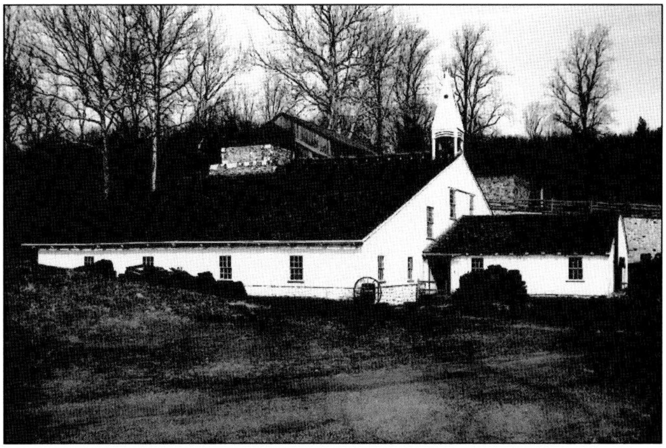

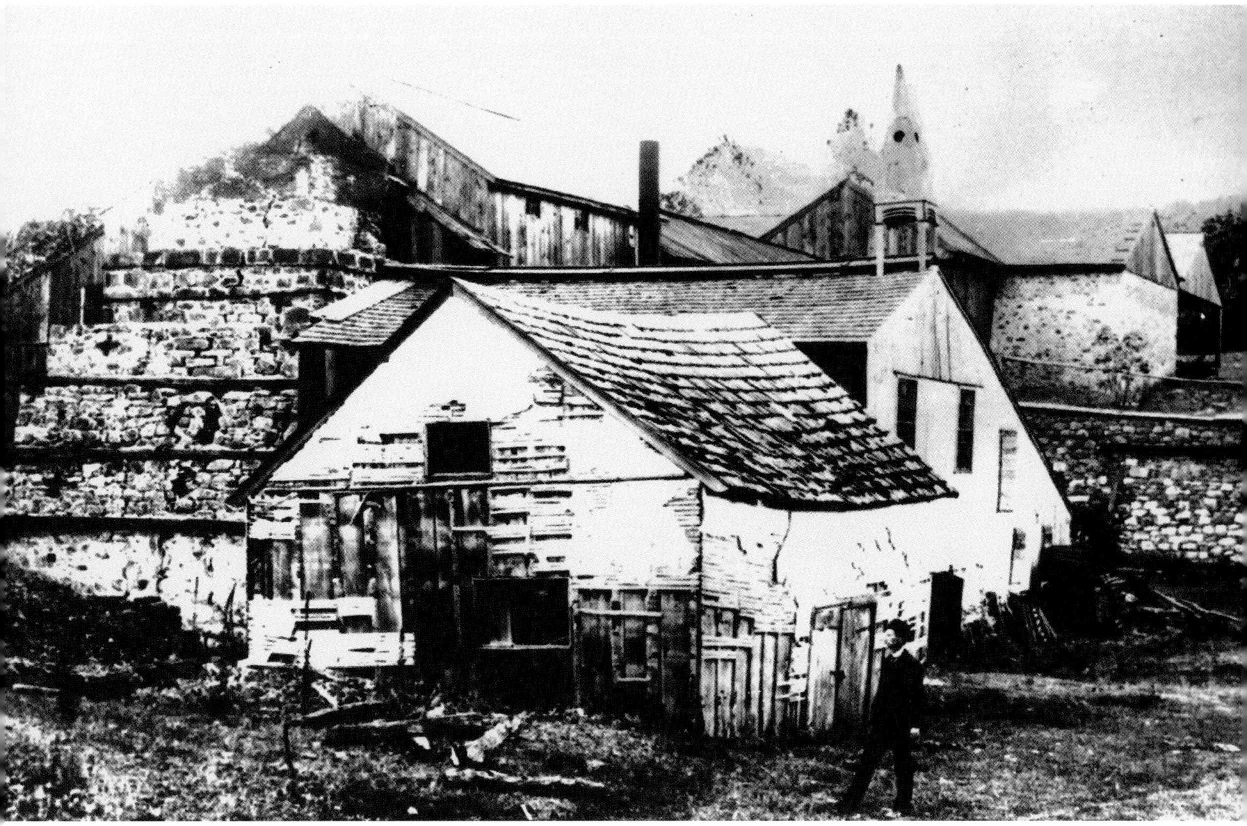

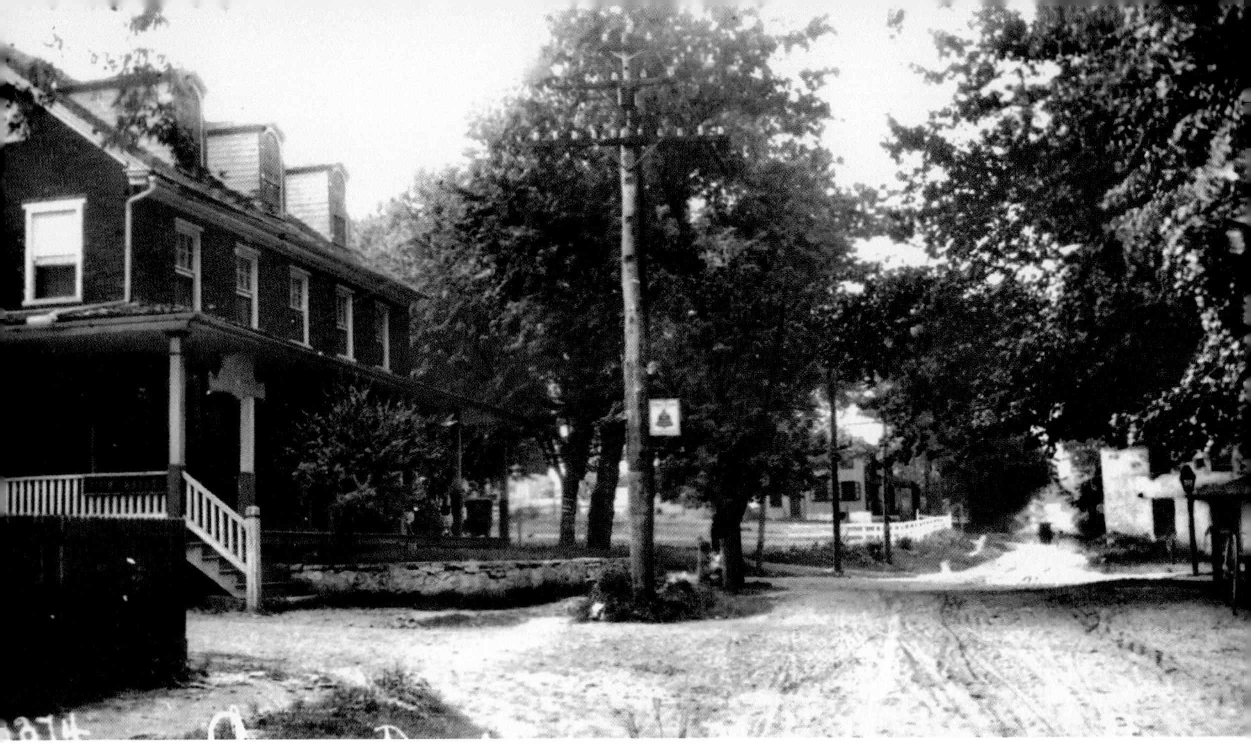

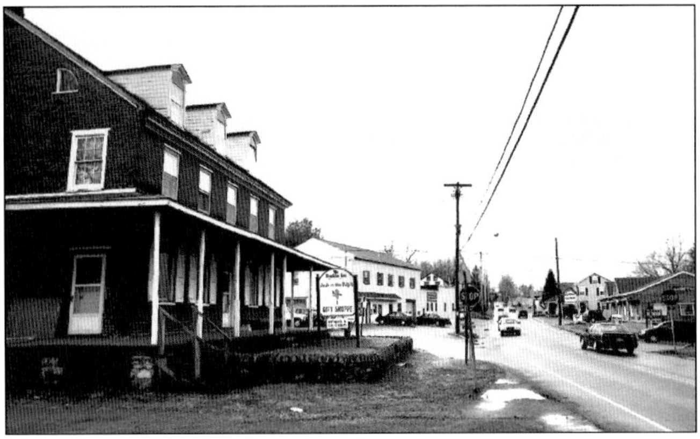

New London village was an important crossroads in the pre-Revolutionary period. It was a connecting point for stage lines from Philadelphia to Lancaster and south to Baltimore. The New London Hotel, built in 1818, shown on the left of the 1910 photograph above, hosted important guests such as Daniel Webster. During its heyday, New London featured a Presbyterian church, the New London Academy, and a nearby iron foundry. The village's development ceased when the railroad was built elsewhere. Today, the village, on Route 896, still retains much of its early architecture.

Moore Hall, a mid-18th-century home in Schuylkill Township, retains many of its original architectural details. In 1729, William Moore, a prominent Chester County judge, received the property from his father. He originally erected a frame house that he replaced with the current stone structure in 1750. An outspoken Tory, he lived in a baronial style made possible by slaves and indentured servants. The house was briefly owned in 1900 by Samuel W. Pennypacker, president judge of the Philadelphia Court of Common Pleas and governor of Pennsylvania from 1903 to 1907. The house underwent extensive renovation in the 1950s. It is still a private residence.

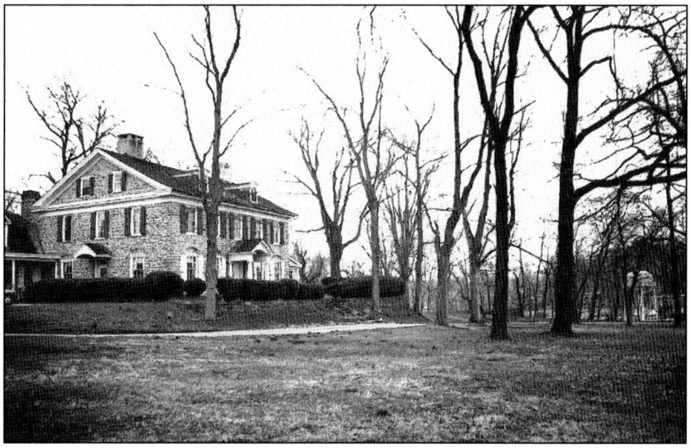

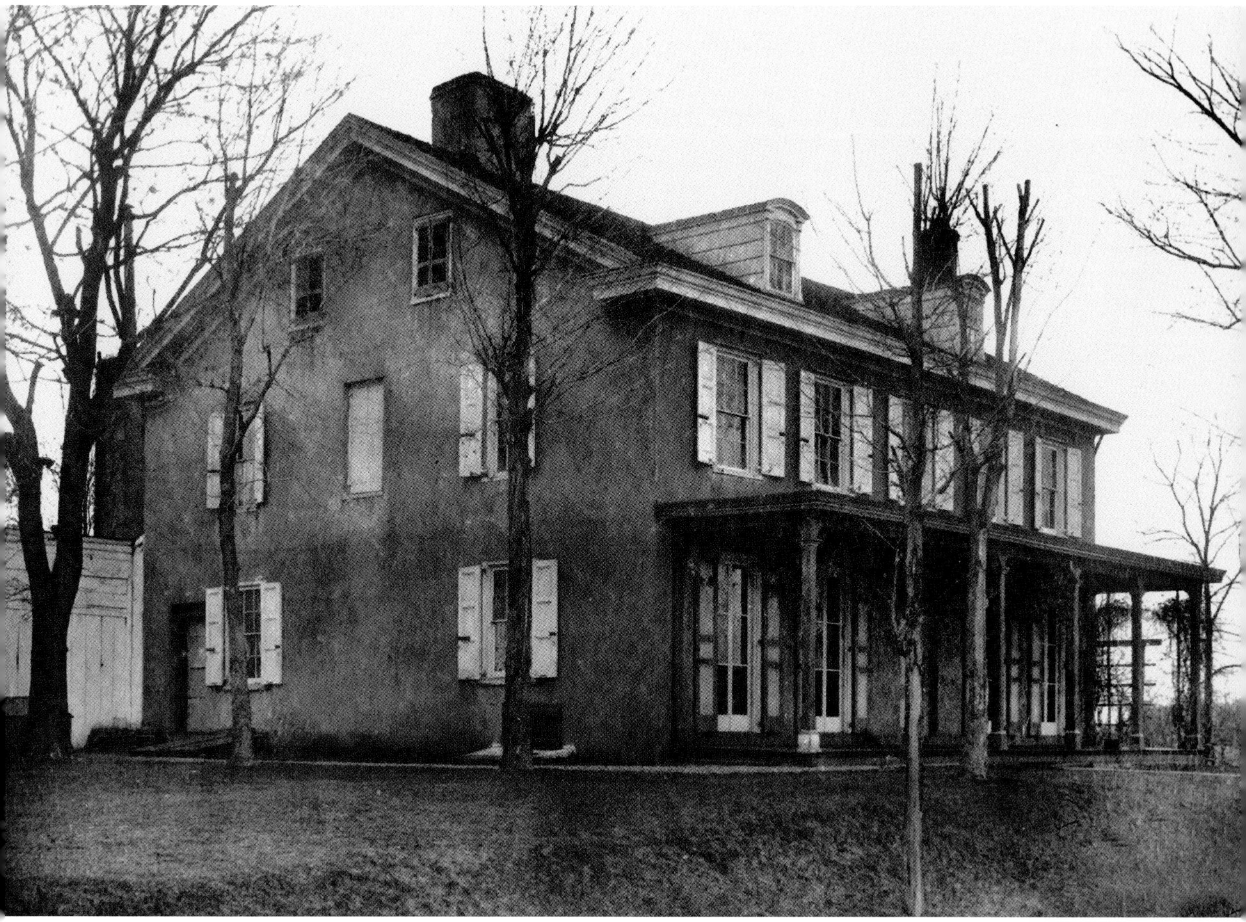

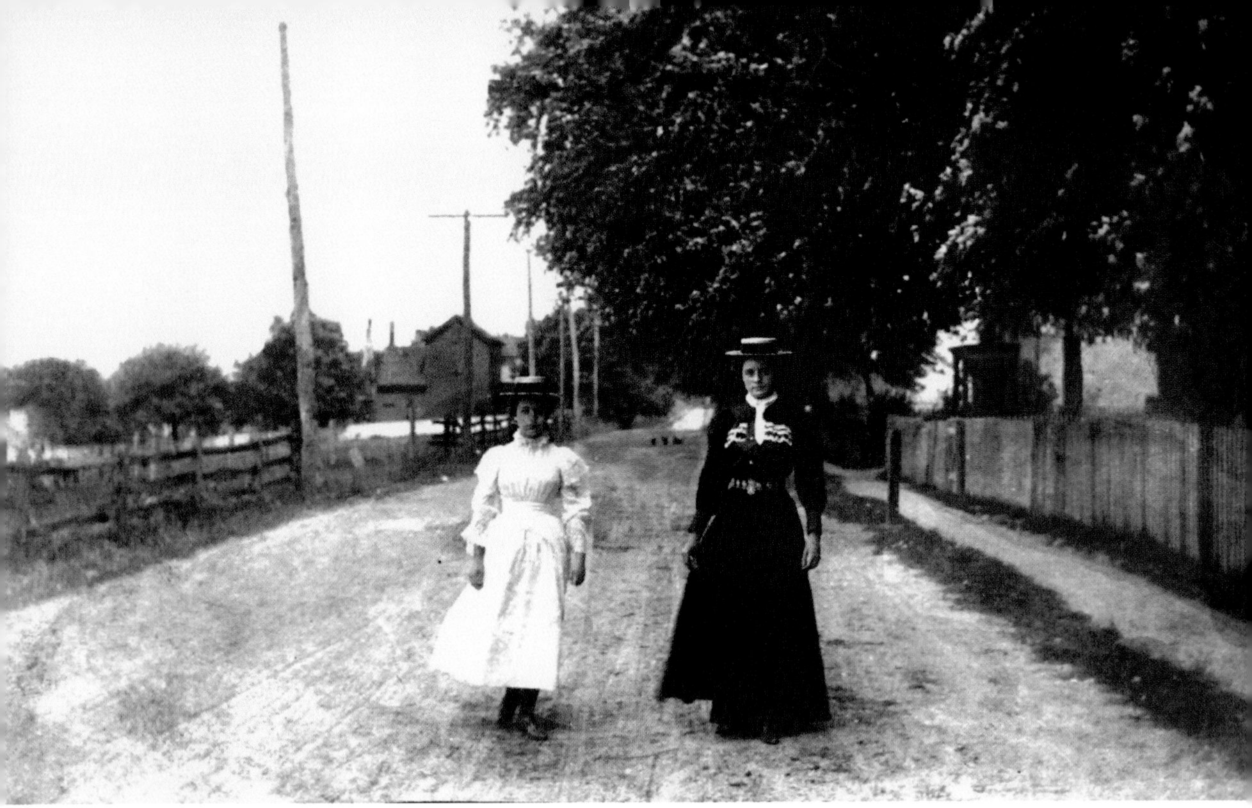

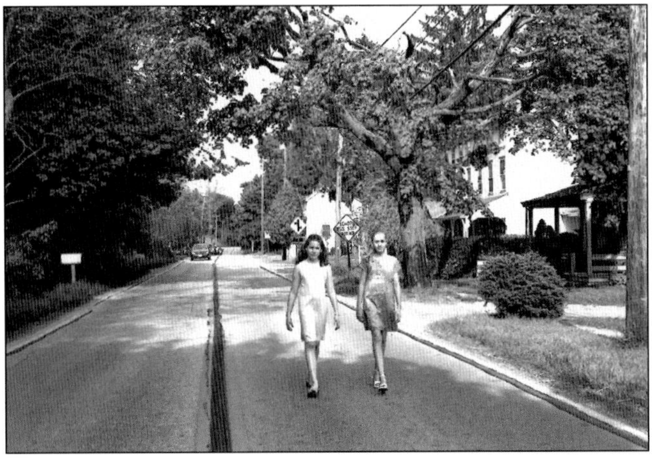

When E. Jane Worrall and Ada DuBois walked along Strasburg Road *c.* 1900, Marshallton was a typical Chester County country town. It consisted of a Friends meetinghouse, Methodist church, blacksmith shop, general stores, cigar store, taverns, town hall, schoolhouse, and a line of comfortable homes along the road. It was originally known as Bradford Meeting, but the town changed the name to Marshallton to honor botanist Humphry Marshall when the post office was established in 1805. In the 2004 view to the left, Alexandra Gasho and Gillian Hutton walk through a village that is little changed by time. The current residents take great pride in maintaining the original ambiance of the fieldstone and stucco buildings in Marshallton. Many of the old shops are now used as private homes.

Built by Joseph Cope *c.* 1850, Highland Home was a prosperous farm of 100 acres in East Bradford Township. Here Cope raised Southdown sheep that produced 100 pounds of wool, according to the 1860 agricultural census. Cope also grew wheat, corn, rye, oats, hay, and potatoes. Herman Hoopes purchased the property in 1896 and made massive alterations, raising the roof, adding a wraparound porch, building a 40-foot-long servant's quarters, and changing the woodwork in the interior. He made it into a gentleman's country retreat suitable for entertaining. So extensive was the 1896 redesign of the house that the current owners could not return the house to its original appearance. They have restored it to the 1896 appearance through information supplied by the Hoopes family. Gardens, furnishings, and the architecture of the house are all consistent with the *fin-de-siècle* era.

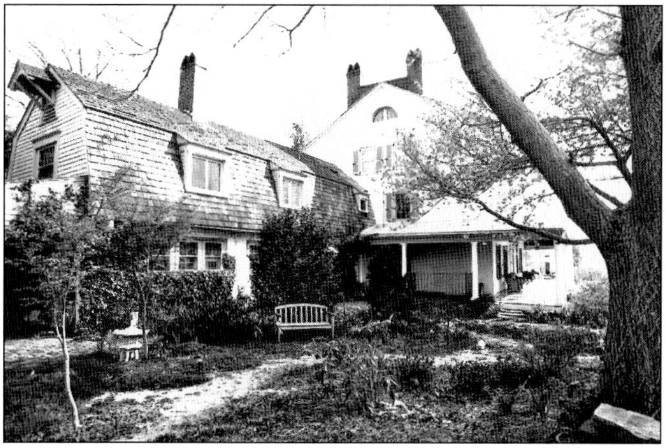

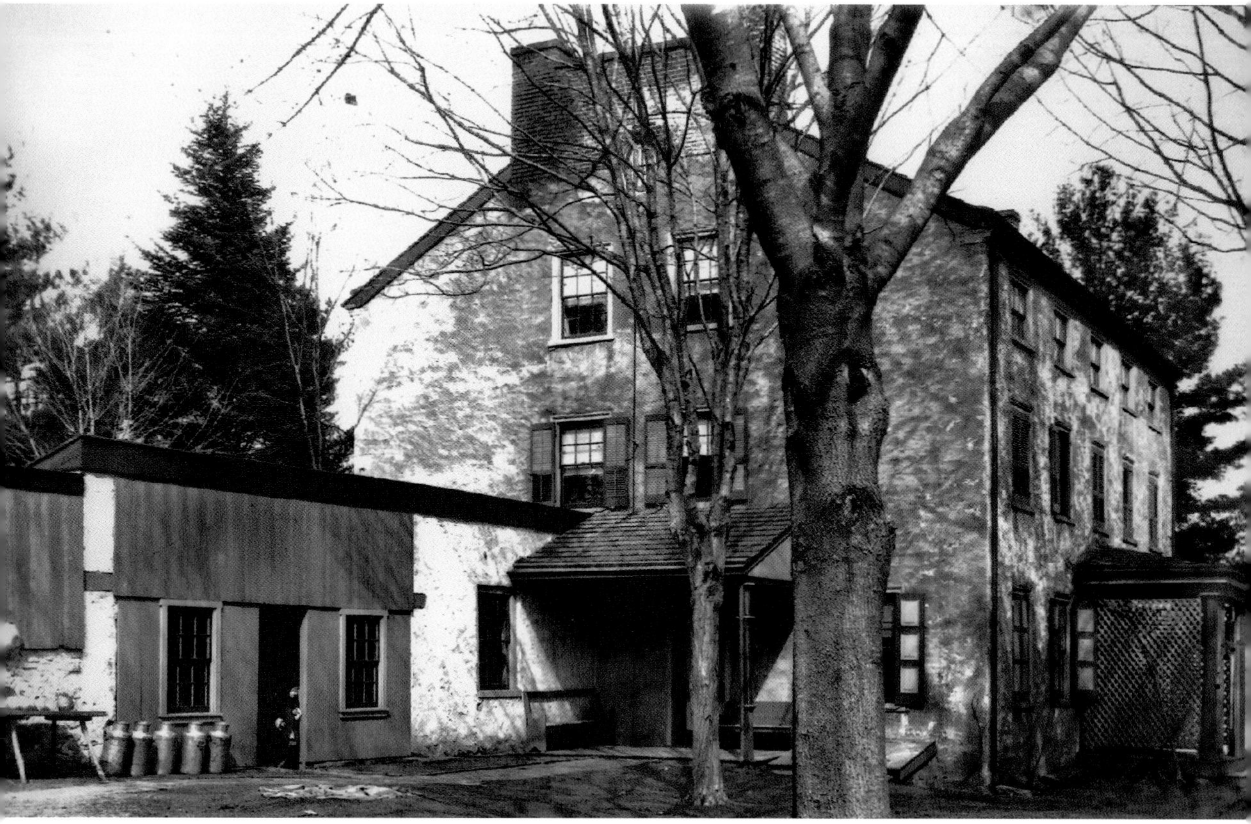

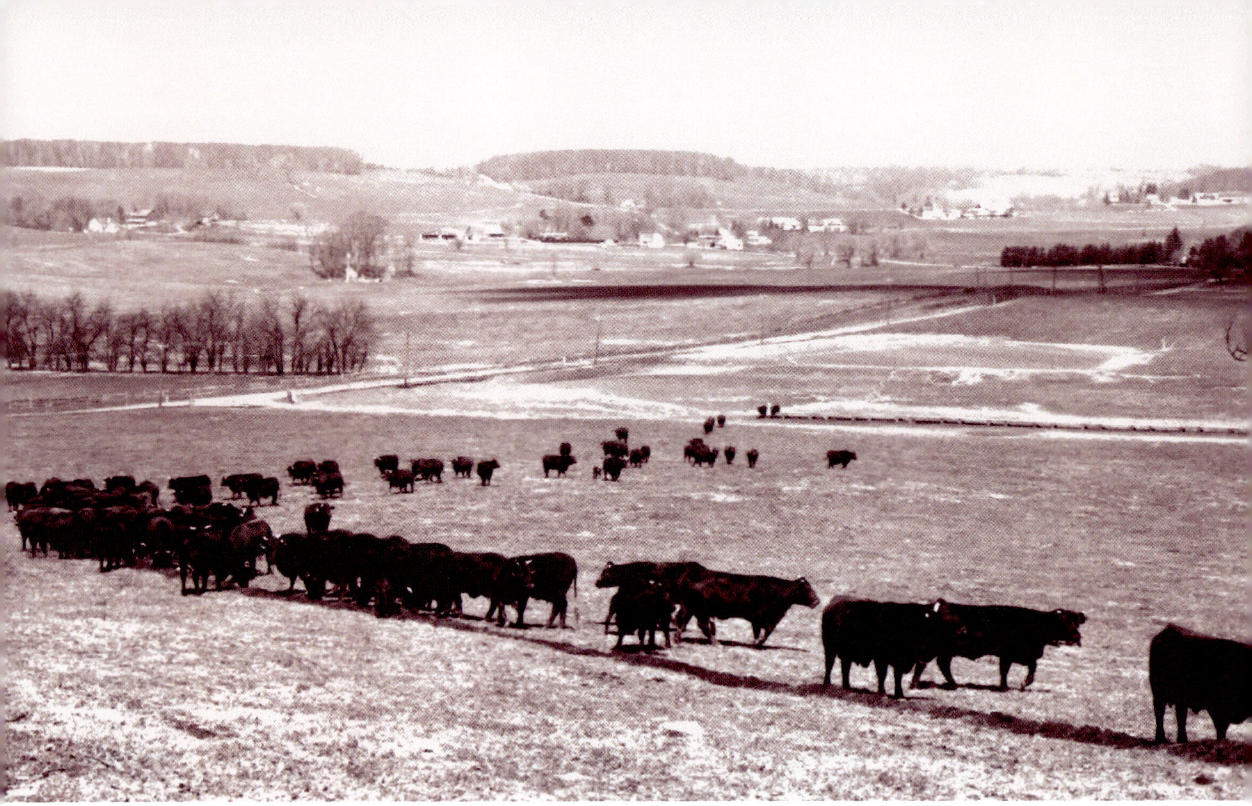

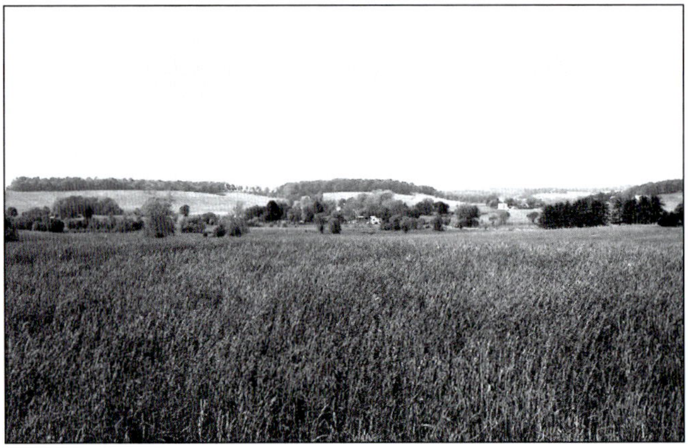

In 1946, when Robert Kleberg Jr. purchased 8,000 acres from Lammont du Pont in Chester County, King Ranch was established. Santa Gertrudis cattle were shipped from Texas in the spring to fatten on the rich meadowland on the way to market. During the 1970s, King Ranch created a prime herd of breeding stock, as this historical photograph shows. When the farm was disbanded in 1984, the Brandywine Conservancy, along with Buck and Doe Associates L.P., purchased 5,380 acres for the purpose of preserving their natural, scenic, historic, and agricultural resources. They preserved the agricultural use of the land and the natural resources of the Buck and Doe Run Creeks through conservation easements. These tributaries supply half of the water in the west branch of the Brandywine Creek.

People's Hall, Ercildoun, was erected in 1845 as a free hall in which to discuss various subjects regardless of color, sex, religion, or political party. Abolitionists seeking a place to freely discuss antislavery issues were instrumental in the building of the hall. Temperance was also a favorite topic. The motto of the hall was "Let truth and error grapple." Over the years, various churches used the building. It has been a polling place and was used for revival meetings, Grange meetings and Girl Scout meetings. The opening and closing ceremonies for the Ercildoun Academy and many other functions have been held here. Now restored, it houses the very active East Fallowfield Historical Society, which uses it for public events.

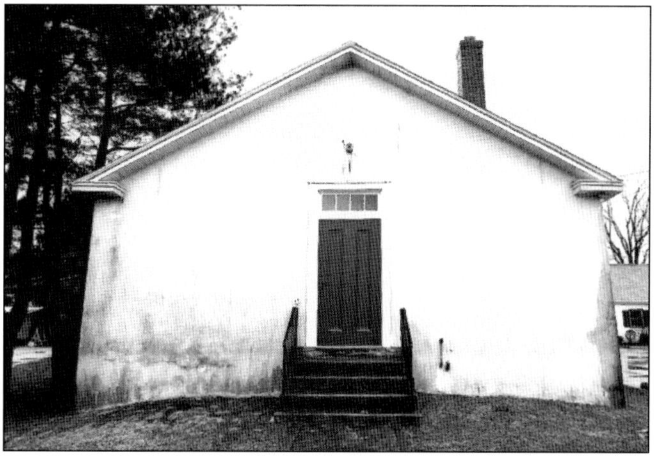

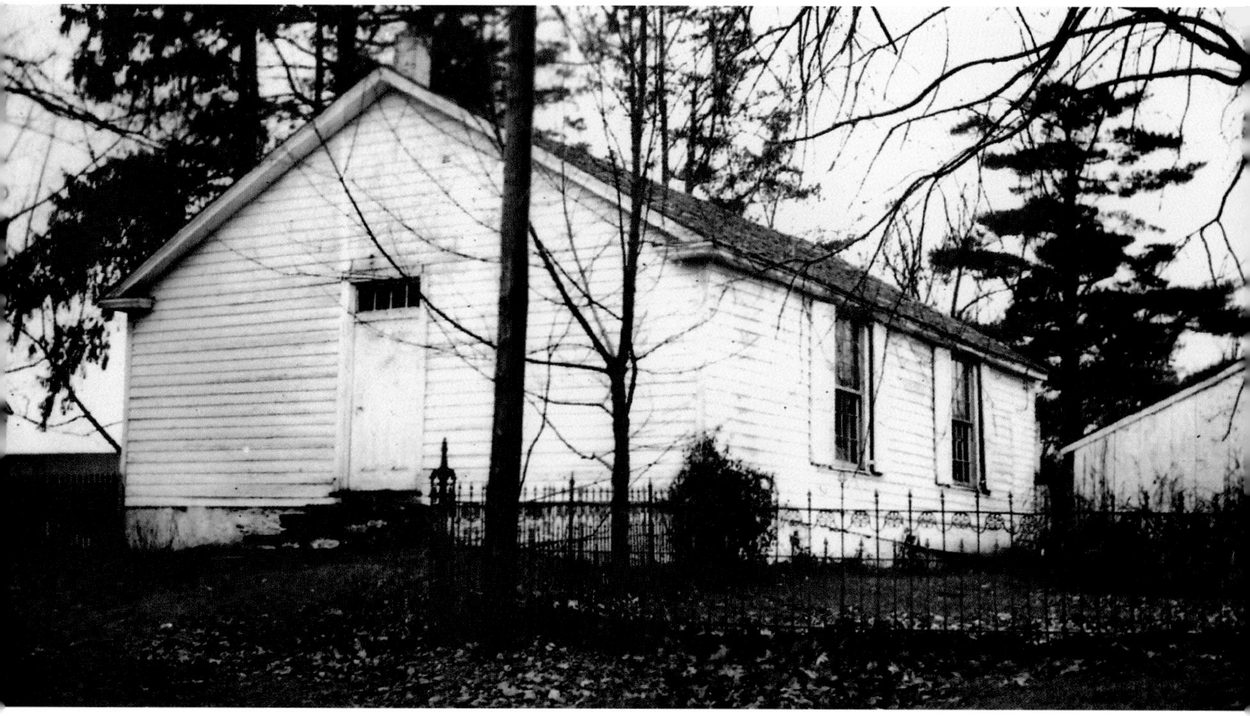

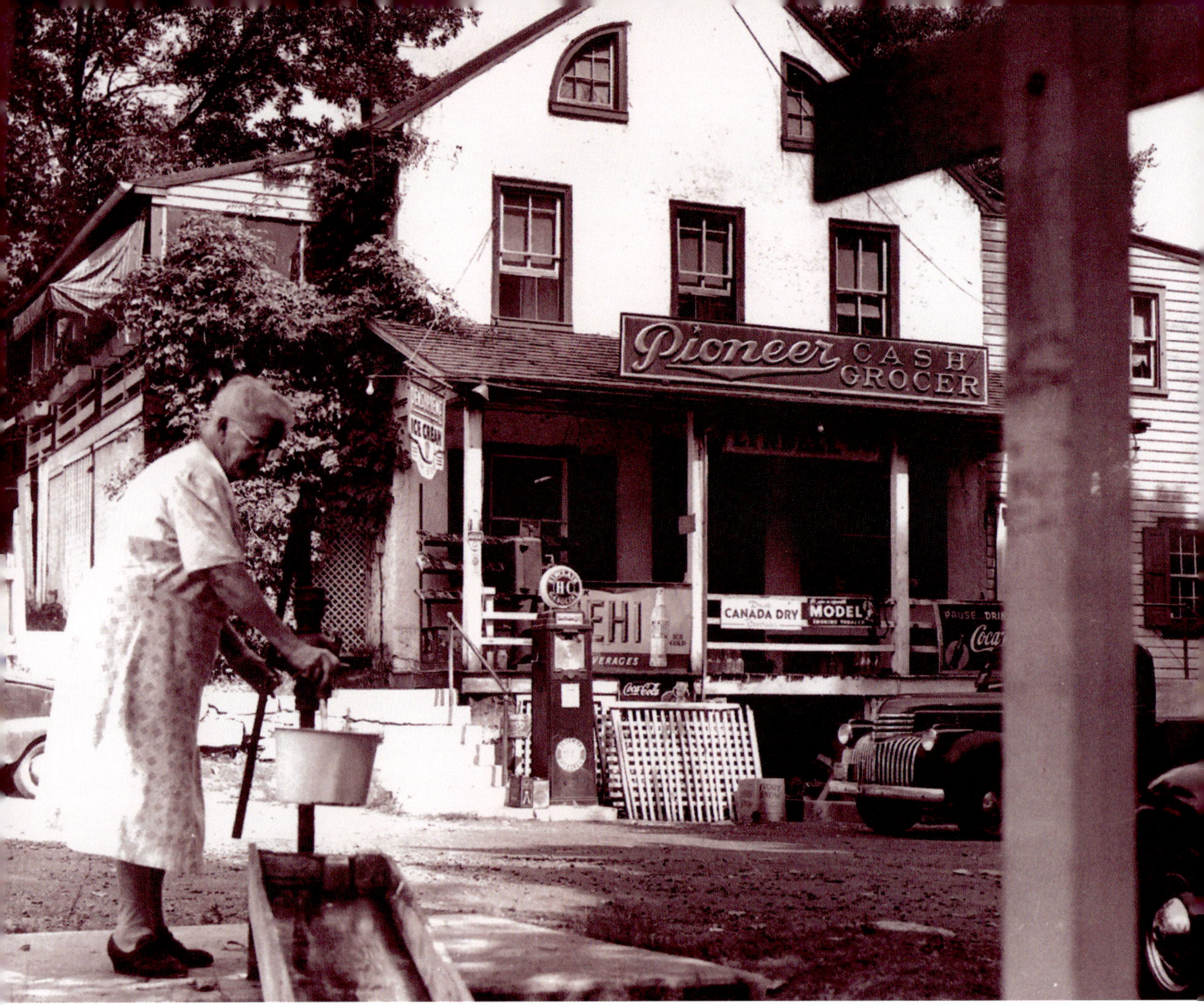

This structure dates from 1835, when the village was known as Brooklyn. A post office was established there in 1880, and the name was changed to Lyndell. Throughout the years, the general store supplied customers with groceries, hardware, feed, coal, farm implements, tires, and auto accessories. Regular deliveries were made to customers in Downingtown, Thorndale, Reeceville, and Guthriesville. Cora Shock, shown in this photograph, served as postmistress from 1944 to 1949, when Frank Sinex purchased the business and ran it until 1976. Still a post office and country store, the property has changed hands many times in recent years.

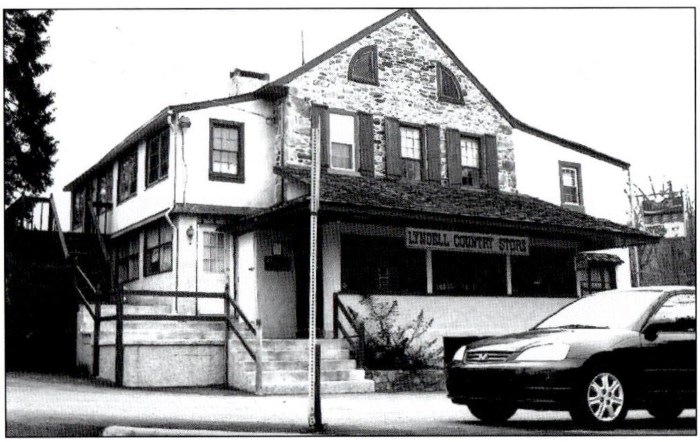

Walter P. Reynolds was one of 10 Oxford area farmers to volunteer to participate in the sanitary milk movement instituted by Dr. Charles E. North in 1914. His farm, seen *c.* 1900, is one of the birthplaces of the movement that led to the production of grade A milk. The process, which met considerable resistance by some, included cleaning the cows' udders and flanks, washing the farmer's hands, and cooling the milk until delivery to the milk receiving station. Abbott's Dairy was a key supporter of the movement, which greatly improved the quality of milk sold to the public. The original barn was destroyed by fire and has been replaced by the larger one seen today on this currently productive farm.

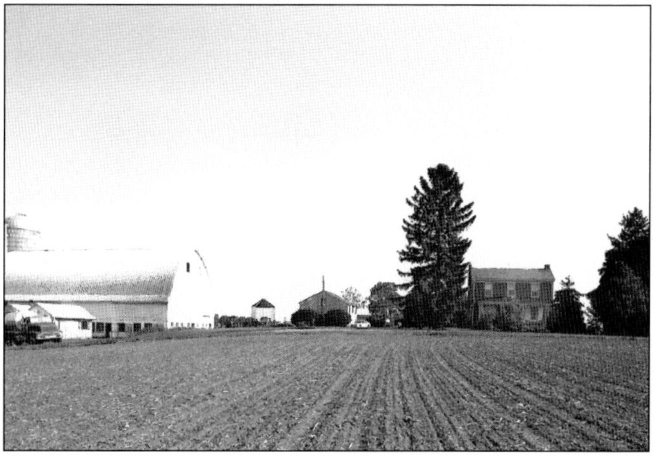

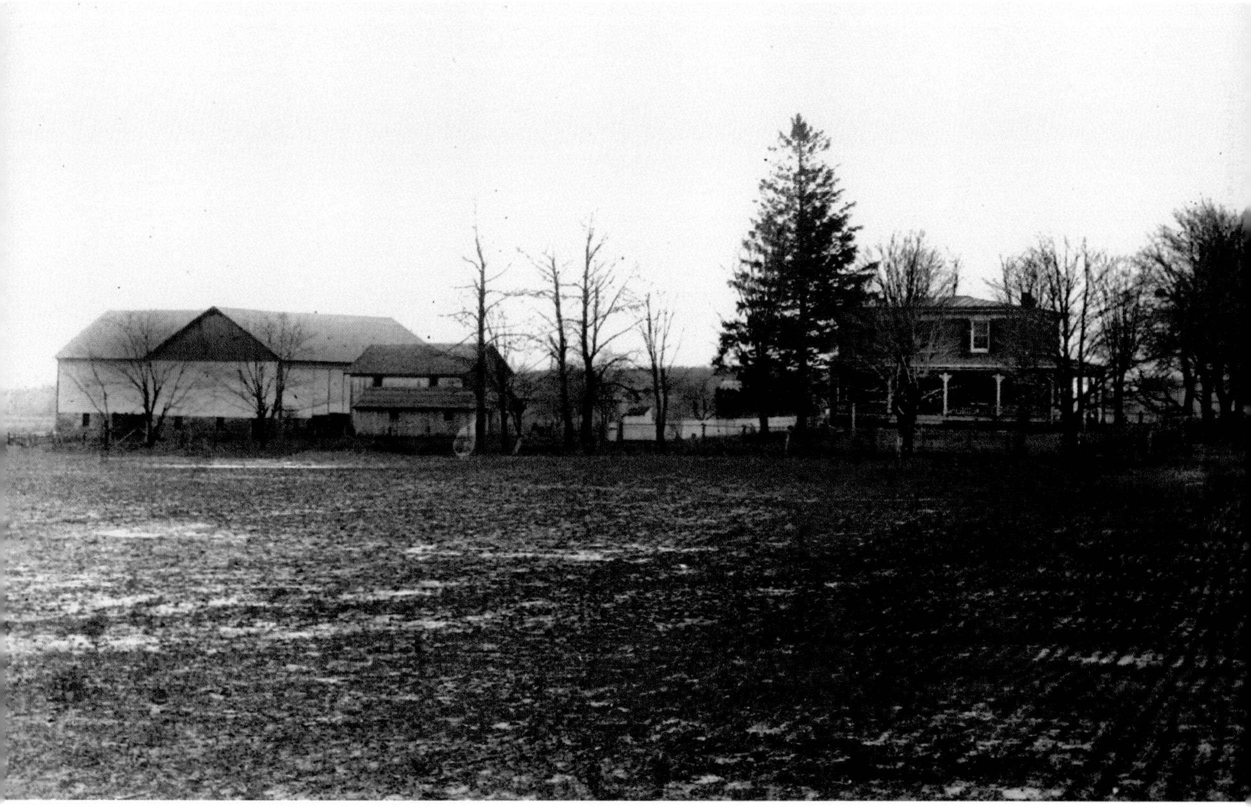

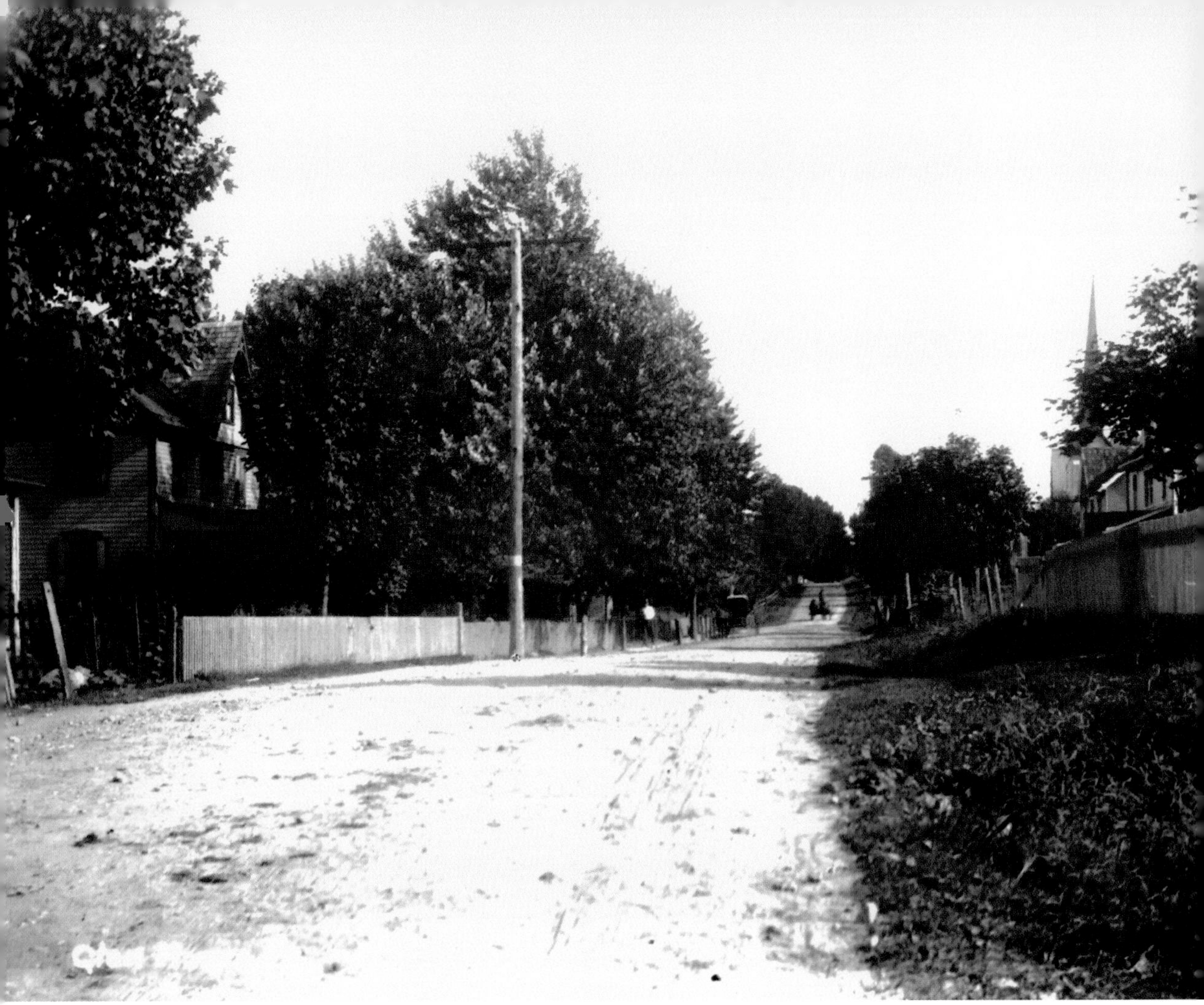

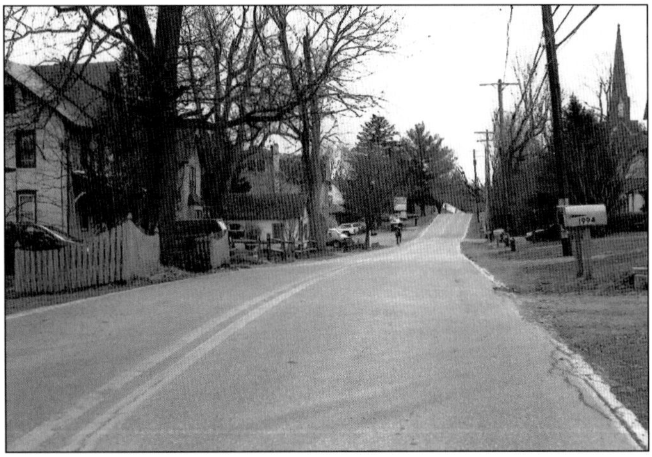

Originally called Indiantown, Glenmoore was also known as Moorestown and Norwood until the name was changed to Glen Moore in 1874. James Moore was credited in developing the area when he purchased an old gristmill in 1848 and built stores and homes along Creek Road (Route 282) in Wallace Township. Today, Glen Moore is a little village that time has passed by. Once a farming community, Glen Moore is now largely residential. Most of the industry left with the discontinuation of the railroad during the 1960s. Now in the planning stage is a new residential community on a 600-acre tract nearby.

Bryn Coed Farm in West Vincent Township was the summer home of Owen J. Roberts, the noted Philadelphia lawyer who was appointed an associate justice of the Supreme Court by Pres. Herbert Hoover in 1930. Roberts served on the court until 1945. After retiring from the court, he made Bryn Coed his permanent home and lived there until his death in 1955. Roberts raised purebred Guernsey cattle on the farm with the herd frequently exceeding 100. The photograph below shows the dairy barn and other buildings in the late 1930s. The farm is still in active use today.

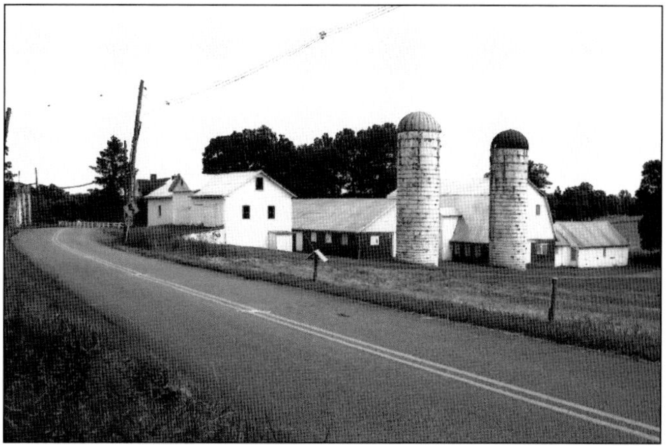

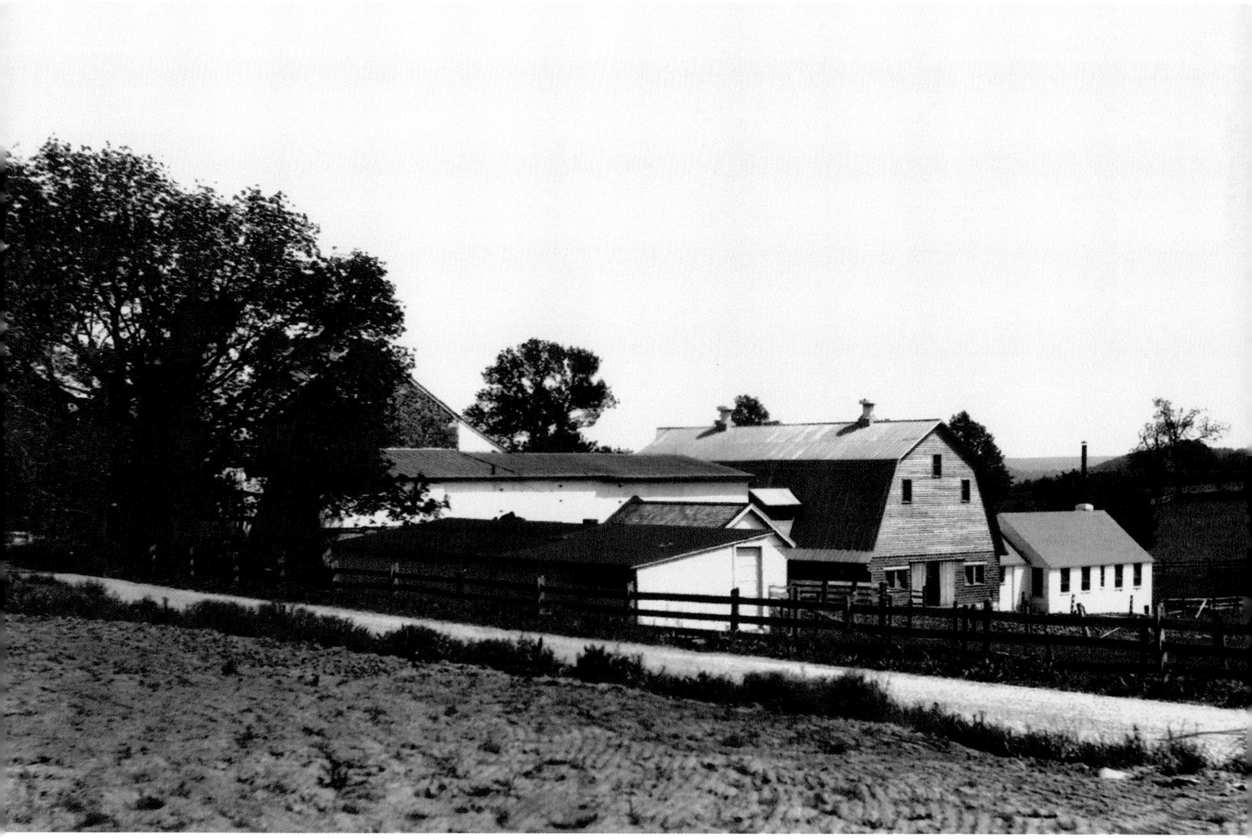

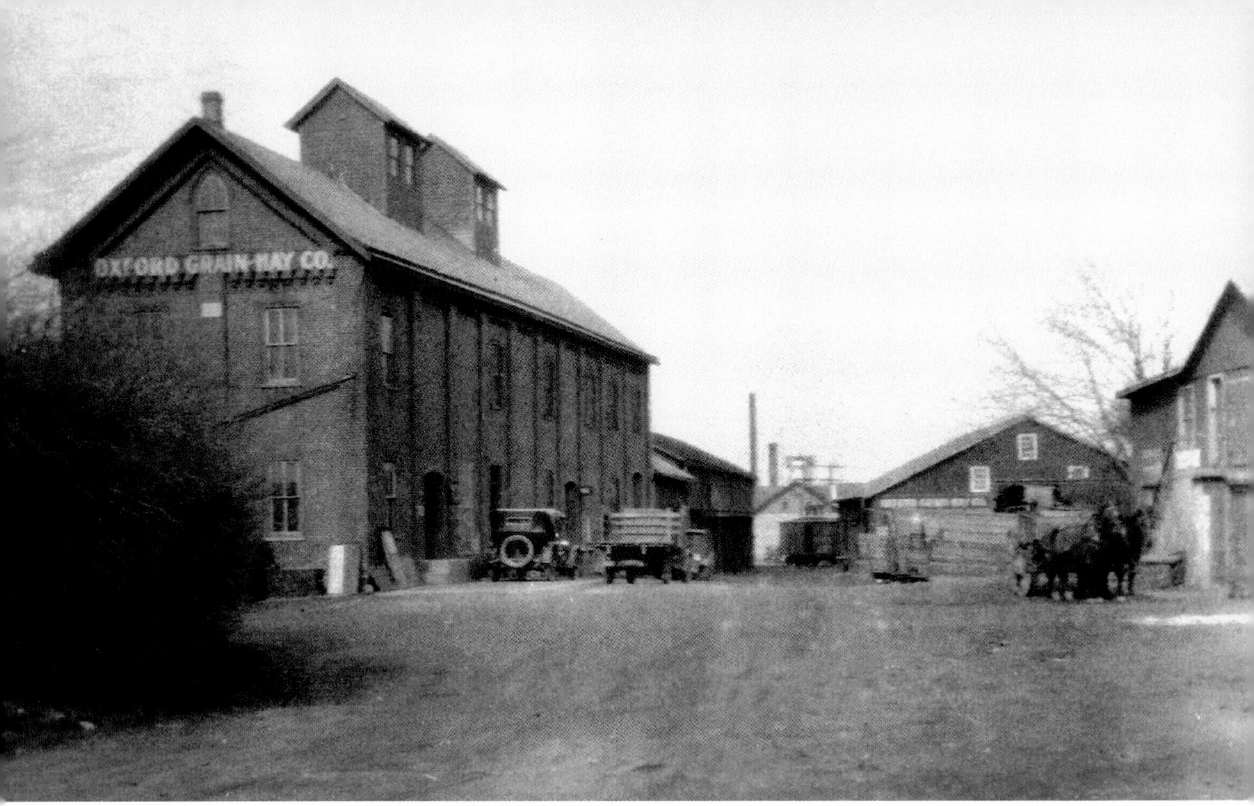

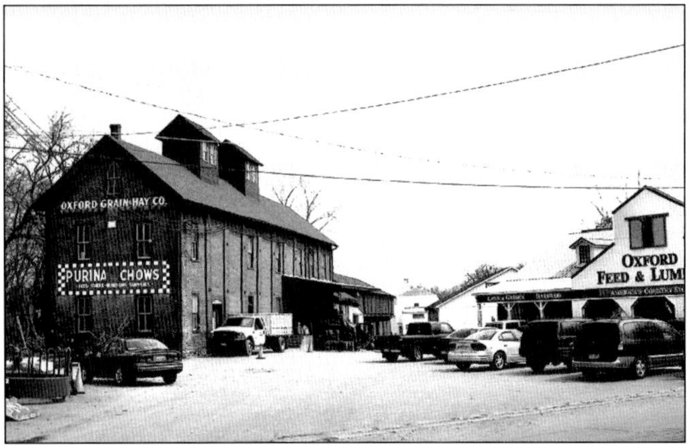

The Oxford Feed and Hay Company was begun by S. R. Dickey in 1865. He sold seeds, lumber, and agricultural supplies to the surrounding farmers and purchased grain and hay from them to sell in city markets. The company prospered, changing hands several times. The red-brick grain elevator was built in 1880. In 1919, Lawrence C. Drennen was hired as bookkeeper, and by 1946 he joined L. E. Shoemaker as a partner. Since then, five generations of the Drennen family have operated the business. Today, a new retail store, built in 2000, provides products to a new generation of Oxford residents. America's Country Store sells horse, pet, and wild bird food, lawn and garden supplies, lumber and building hardware, as well as cards and gifts.

The Edison Electric Illuminating Company, as seen on the corner of Chestnut and Walnut Streets, West Chester, in this 1899 photograph, is telling of the changes electricity brought to our landscape. Beginning in 1885, electricity was sold by subscription to customers between the hours of 7 p.m. and 5 a.m., when daylight was not available. Demand grew for around-the-clock service. When this power plant was torn down in 1971, it was operated by the Philadelphia Electric Company.

Chapter 4
Places That Have Changed

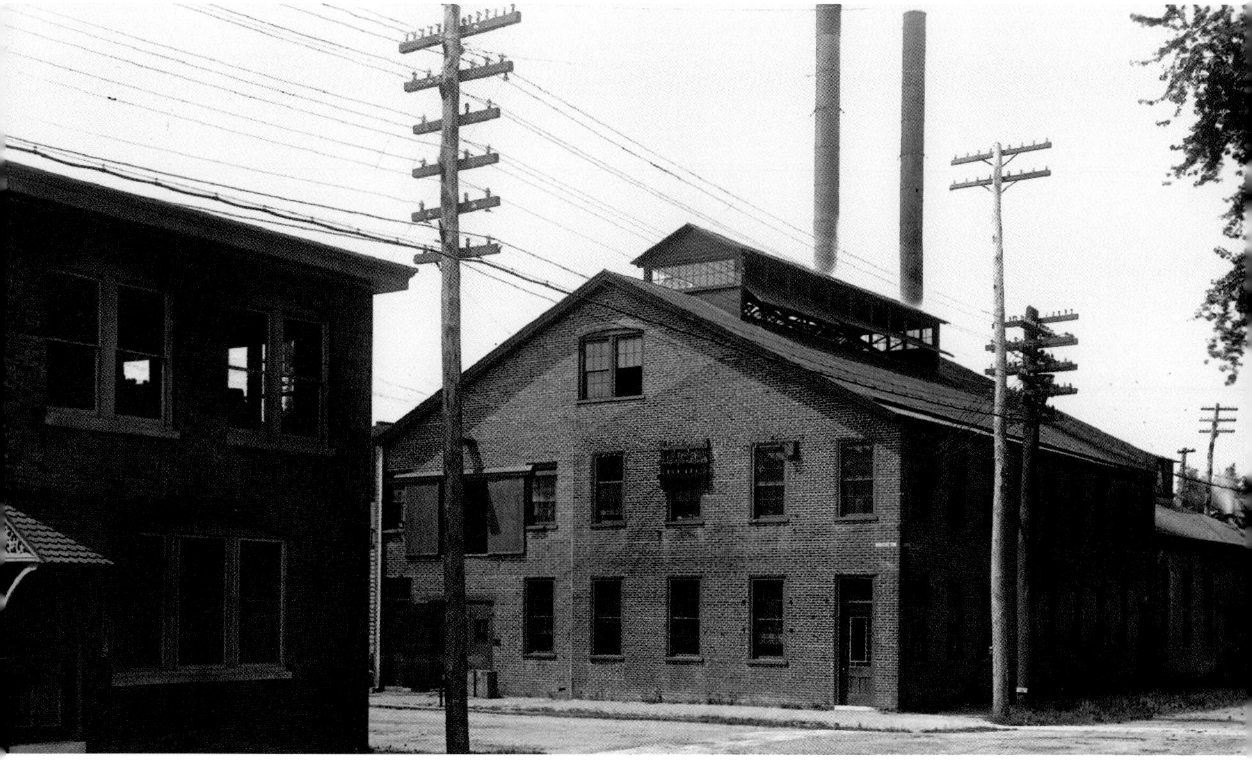

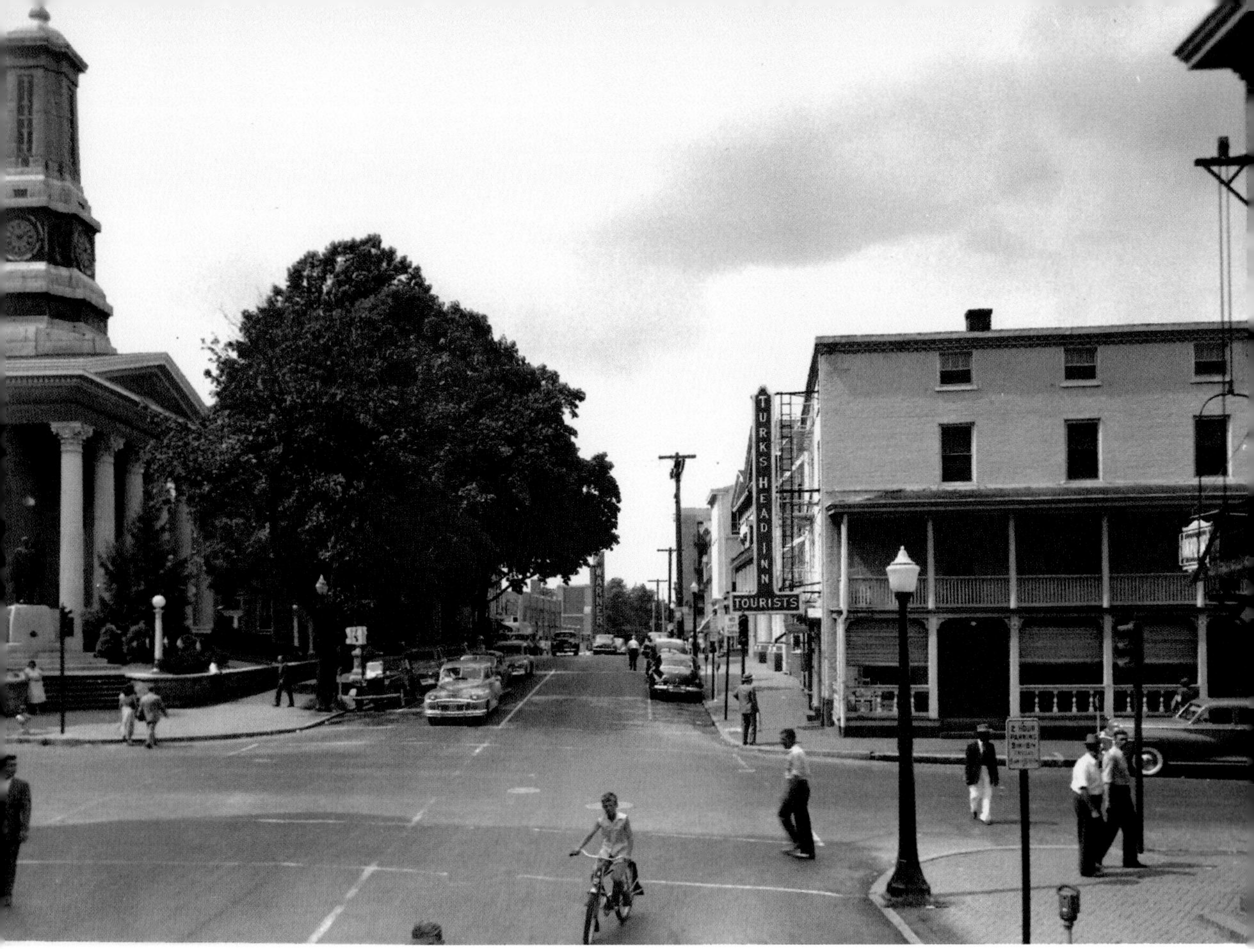

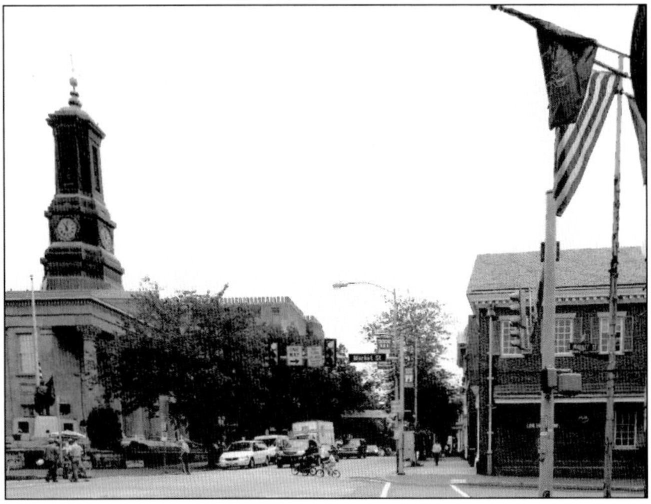

The crossroads of High and Market Streets in West Chester has witnessed many changes. By 1768, a building called the Turk's Head Inn was granted a license at the crossroads. The original brick building was enlarged several times. It was torn down in 1964 and replaced by a neo-Colonial-style bank building. The original courthouse was built on the west side of the street in 1784 along with a jail and hall of records. It was razed to make way for the 1846 courthouse designed by Thomas U. Walter, best known as the architect of the U.S. Capitol dome. An annex was added in 1891, and the North Wing replaced the Assembly Building in 1964. The courthouse was extensively restored between 2003 and 2004.

West Chester had its heyday as a shopping center throughout the 19th century and through the 1950s, when it boasted three department stores: Grant's, Mosteller's, and Kauffman's. On Friday and Saturday nights, people packed the town for dining, shopping, and the movies. West Chester's three movie theaters—the Warner, the Garden, and the Harrison—showed cartoons, newsreels, and feature films to town dwellers eager for relaxation. Malls, with big box stores and multiplex theaters, took business away from towns during the suburban development that occurred after World War II. West Chester has enjoyed a renaissance, as

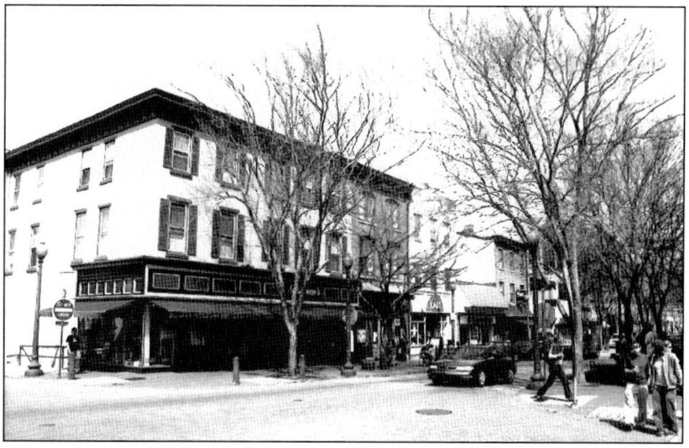

restaurants, art galleries, and specialty shops now find their place beside the courthouse offices.

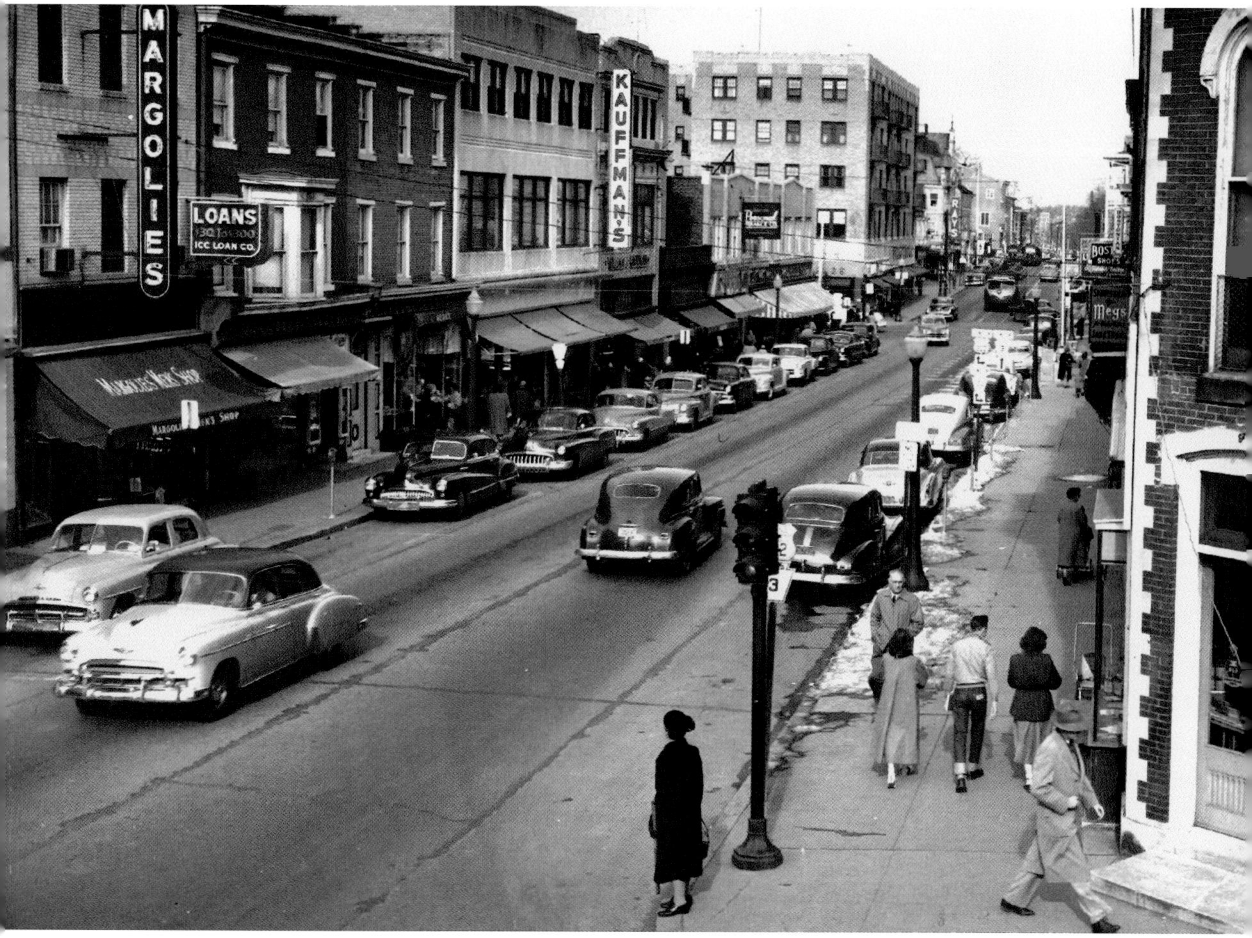

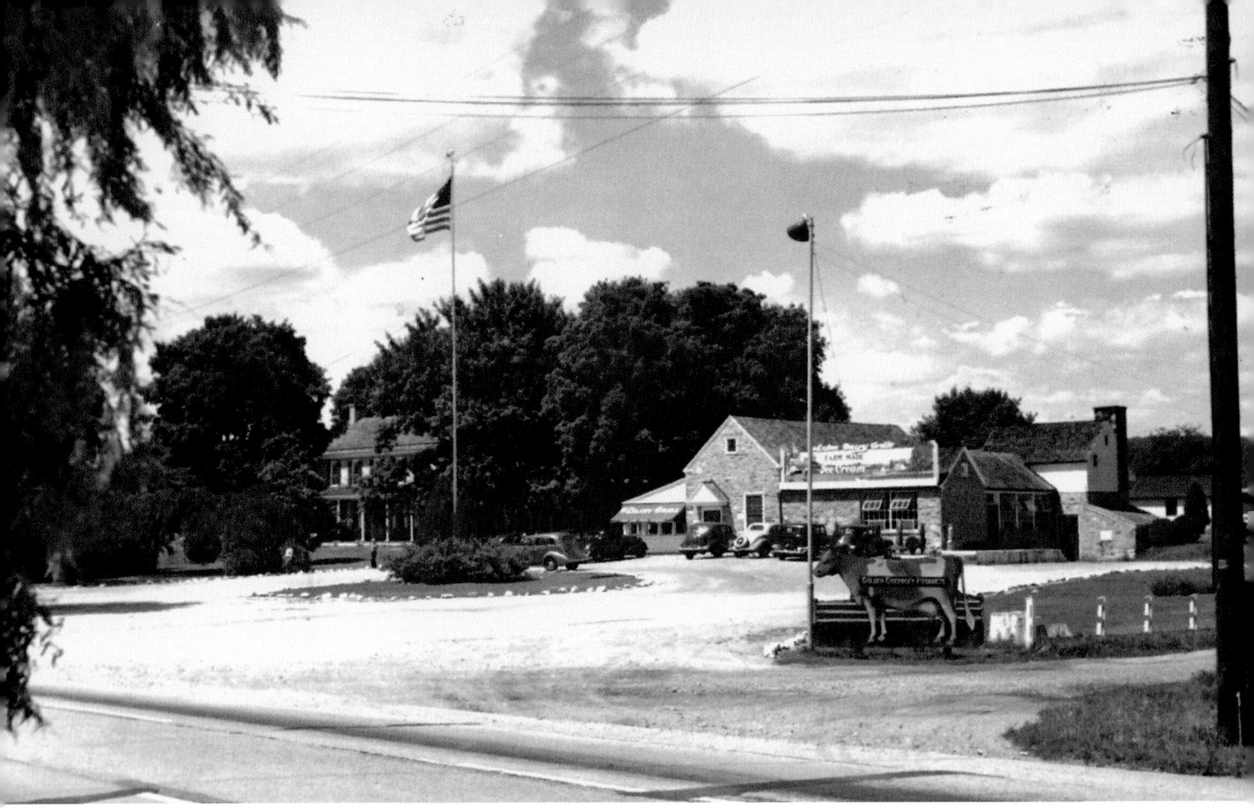

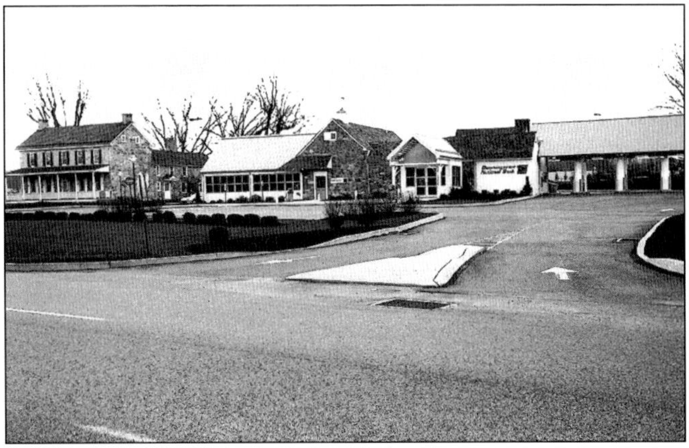

Sleepy Hollow Hall in Exton, built in 1717 with additions until 1820, was the home of wealthy Quaker tanner George Massey from 1791 to 1848. There is a strong tradition that Massey helped fugitives along the Underground Railroad. A large tannery was in business there. The Dairy Grille, opened in 1931 by Ilario (Larry) Polite, was renamed the Guernsey Cow in 1941 for its large colorful cow sign. The business evolved from a produce stand and dairy. "Meet you at the Cow" was a phrase familiar to most Chester Countians. Many enjoyed a Brown Cow (root-beer float), or one of the many original ice-cream flavors, such as Blue Moon. Cream caramels, also made there, were another favorite. Today, a branch of the Downingtown National Bank occupies the site.

Ludwig's Corner in West Vincent Township has long been a major intersection on the Conestoga Turnpike with the road from Downingtown to Pottstown. The photograph below, from the 1920s, shows the view facing east along unpaved Route 401 as it crosses Route 100. The building on the right has a long history as both a general store and country inn. Seen here as Mosteller's General Store, it later became Ludwig's Corner Inn, the Black Angus, and (currently) Ludwig's Inn and Oyster Bar. Extensive renovations have been made over the years. A small shopping center is now adjacent to it. Currently, an estimated 25,000 vehicles pass through the intersection each day.

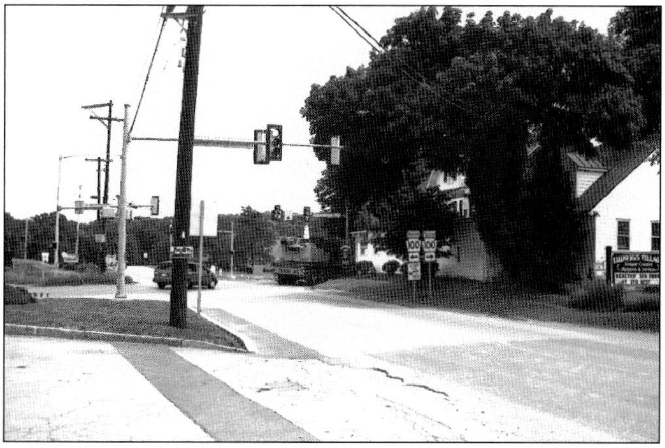

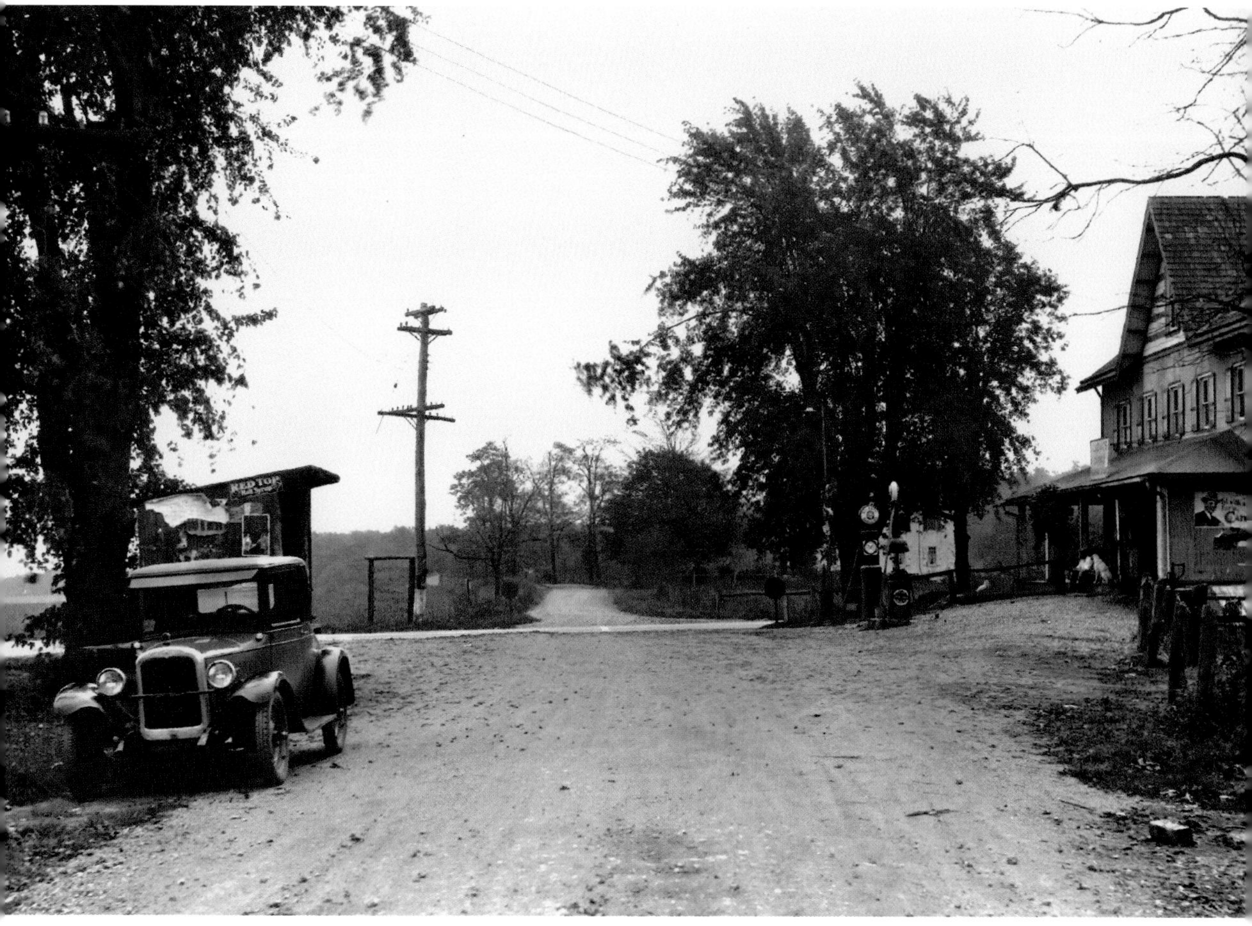

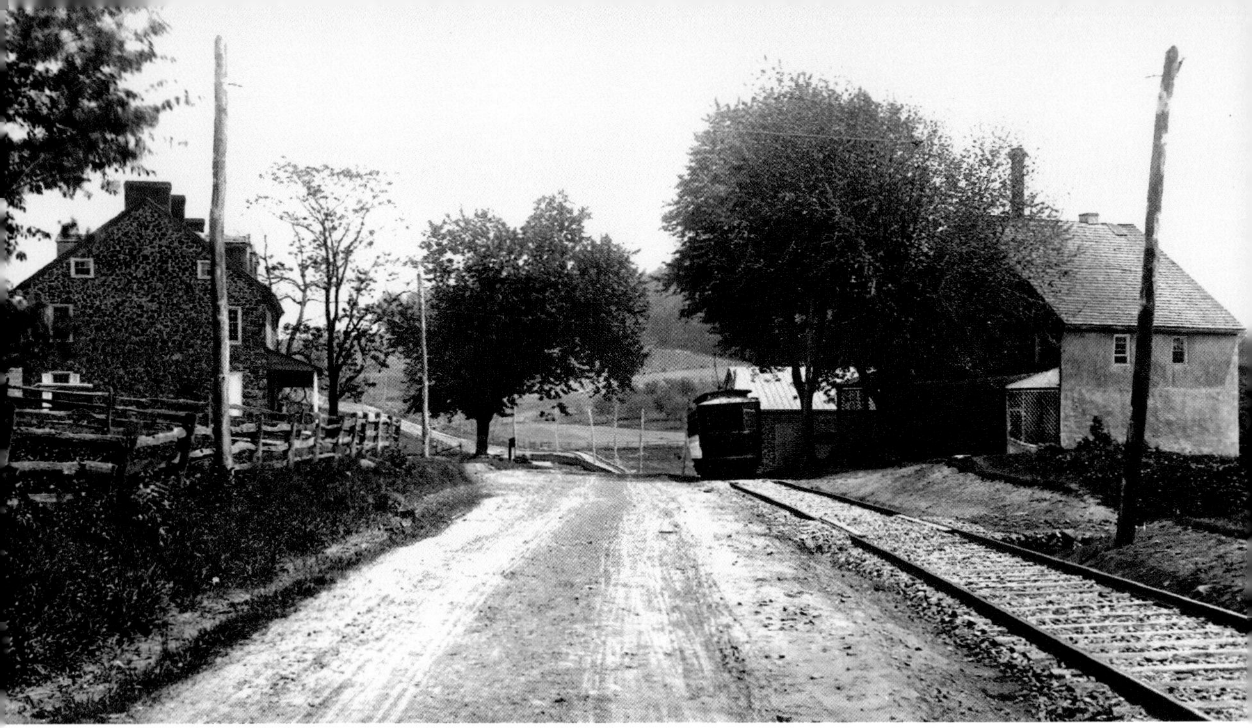

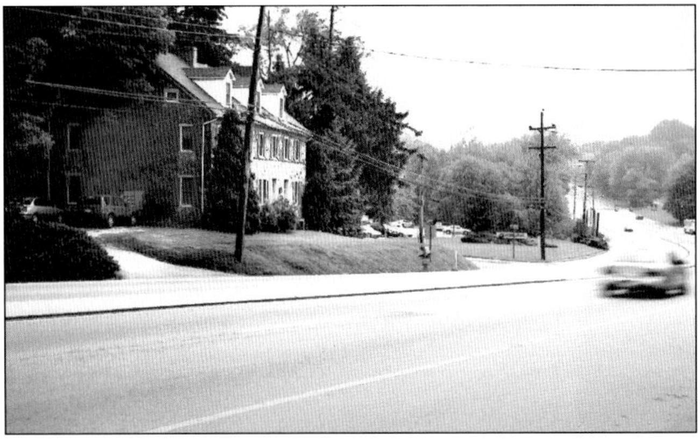

This village along West Chester Pike in East Goshen Township, settled during the early 18th century, was originally called Milltown. The name came from the busy gristmill powered by Chester Creek. The Sheaf of Wheat Hotel is seen on the left in the 1899 photograph above. The Philadelphia and West Chester Traction Company built the trolley line along West Chester Pike from Newtown Square to West Chester. The trolley line was a great convenience for people to connect with 69th Street in Upper Darby. In 1952, a project was undertaken to widen West Chester Pike to four lanes. The trolley line considered adding a second rail and more cars to its popular line but instead opted to remove the trolley line and replace it with bus service.

Lenape Park on the Brandywine has long been a favorite picnic and camping ground. The Wilmington and Northern Railroad line built a station at Lenape and promoted it as a destination. They built a boardwalk, refreshment stand, and dance floor early in the 1890s. Boats were available for hire. The West Chester Street Railroad soon added a trolley line to the grounds that were rented out for Sunday school, organizational, and company picnics. During the 1920s and 1930s, amusements such as roller coasters, bumper cars, Venetian swings, and a carousel were added much to the delight of the community. Today, the updated Brandywine Picnic Park is still a favorite place for picnics. Good old-fashioned fun like horseshoes and boating go alongside the rock climbing and the super slide.

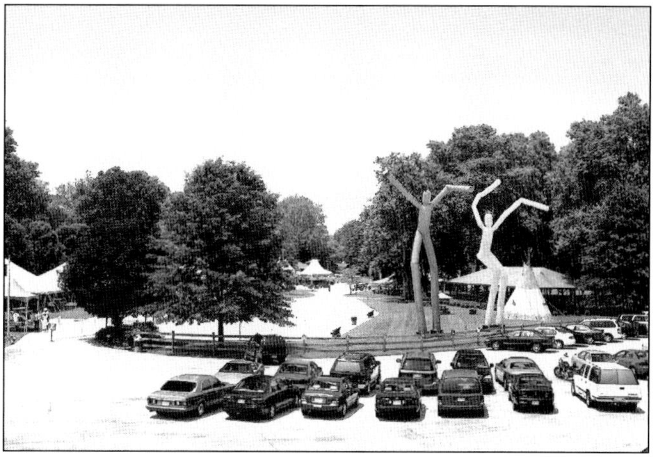

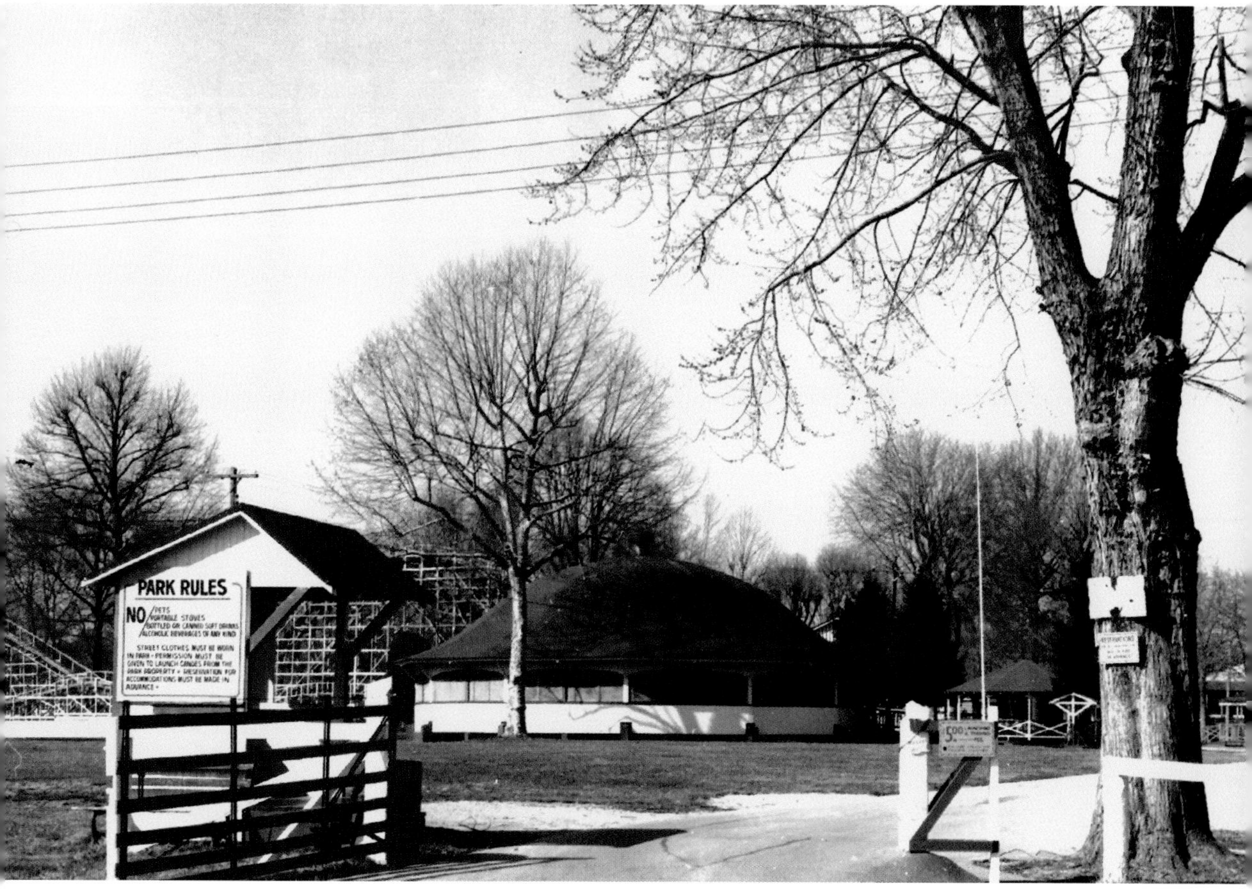

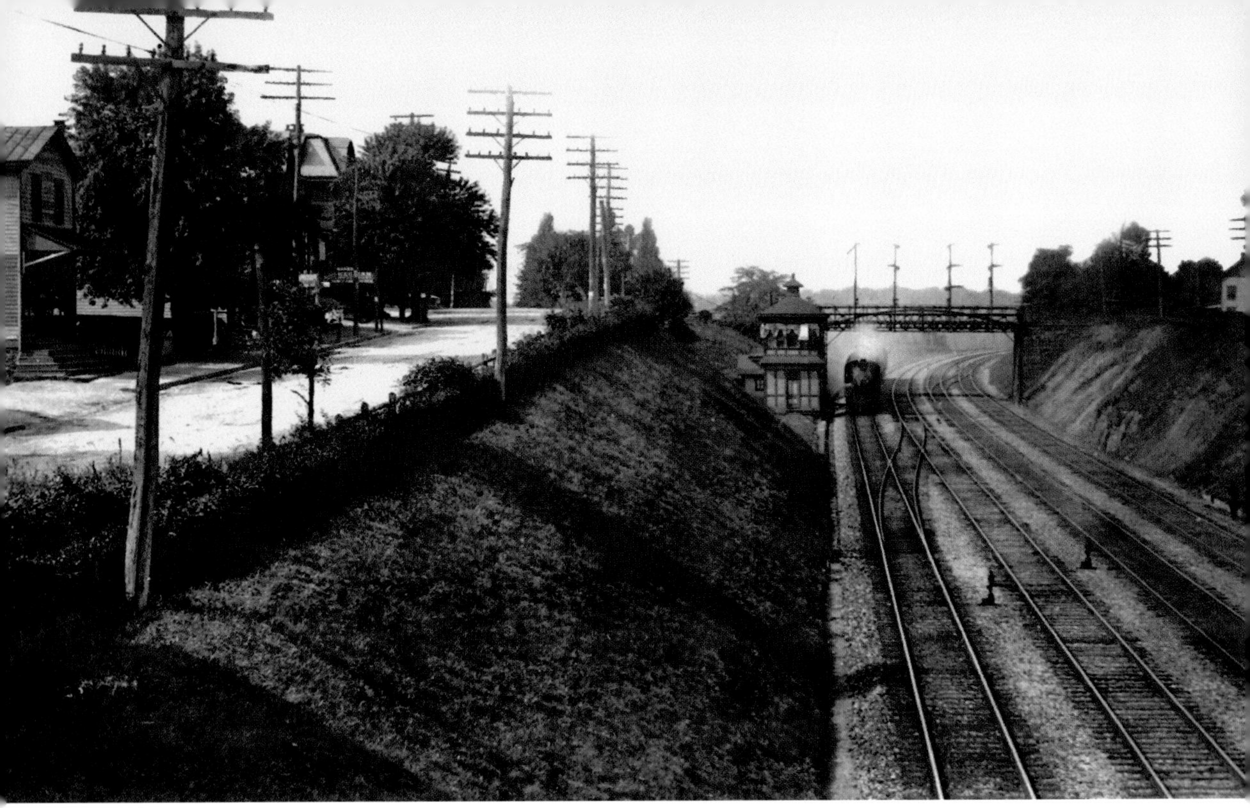

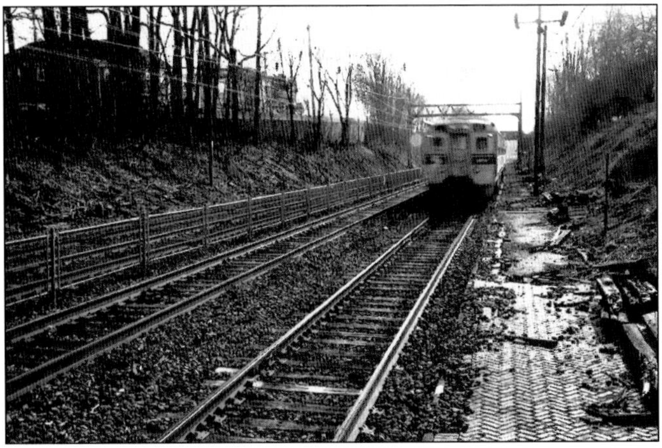

A Pennsylvania Railroad locomotive, heading east toward Philadelphia, crosses under the Bridge Street Bridge as it approaches Berwyn in the 1905 photograph by Lucy Sampson above. Sampson was one of the few professional female photographers in Chester County. Originally, this stop on the railroad was named Reeseville, but area residents changed the name to Berwyn in 1877, and the railroad renamed the station the following spring. The route from Philadelphia through Paoli and westward was known as the "Main Line" and was responsible for much of the development of the area. Starting in the 1880s, many wealthy Philadelphians began moving to homes along the line. There were 22 stops in Chester County in 1909, stretching from Strafford to Atglen. Today, the tracks are shared by Amtrak and SEPTA.

When the Lancaster Turnpike was constructed in 1795, it was the first turnpike in the United States with a hard surface of crushed stone. On this toll road, freight was hauled to market and stage lines brought passengers between Philadelphia and Lancaster. Wayside inns and taverns were dotted along the 62-mile turnpike. When the photograph below was taken in the 1930s, Swayne's Tourist Camp in Glen Loch, on the left, offered rest and refreshment to the growing number of Americans who were traveling by automobile. Today, more than 18,000 automobiles per day travel down this section of Route 30 headed for connections with Route 202 and other roadways.

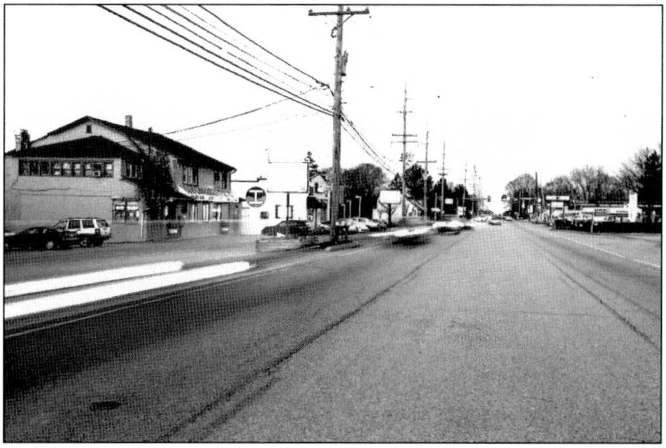

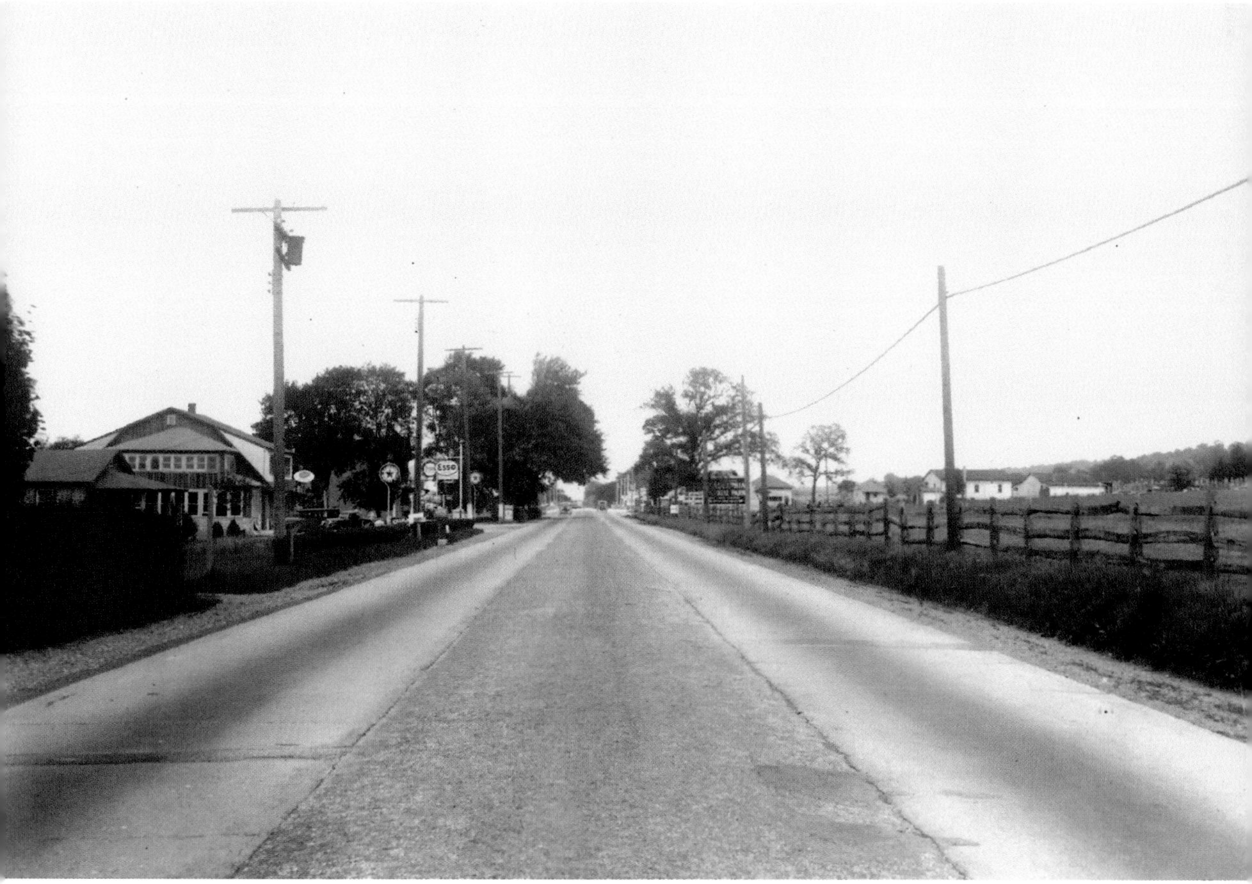

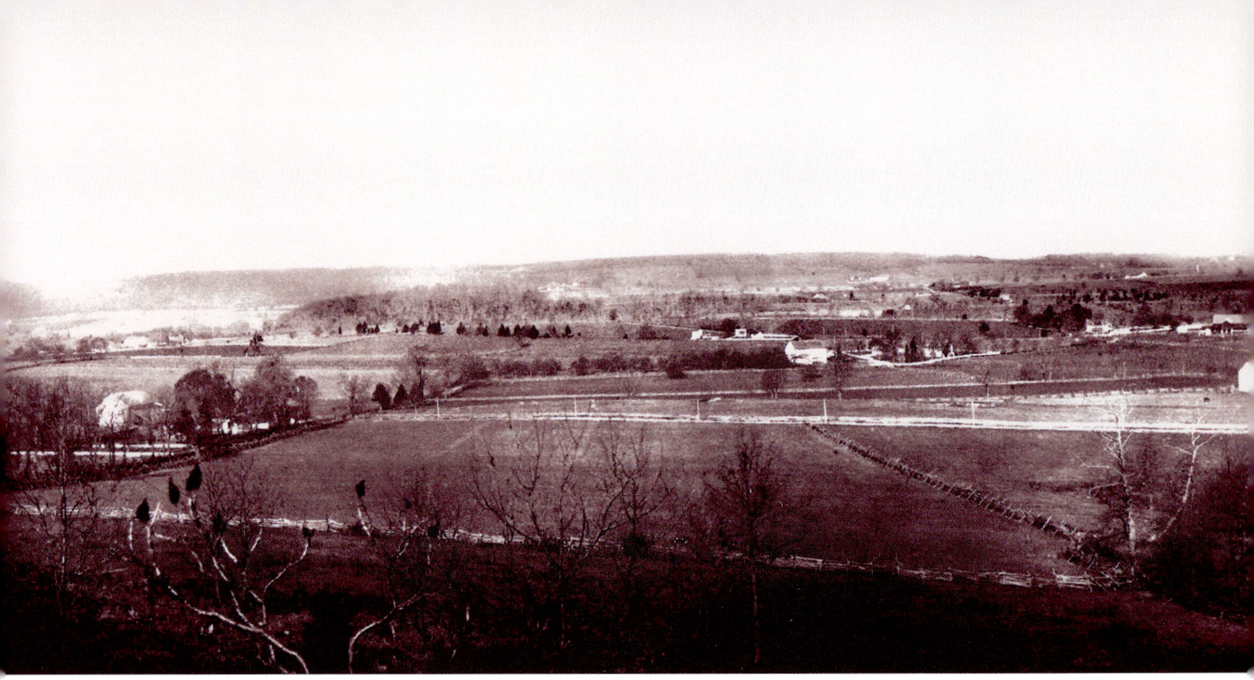

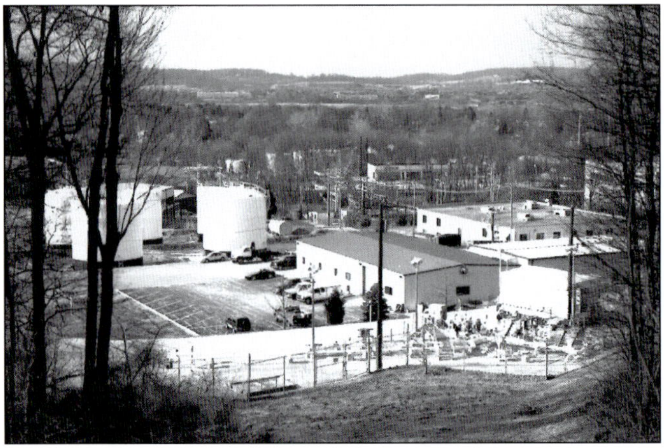

The Great Valley, as seen in the 1890 photograph above, shows a broad valley dotted with farms and small towns. Lancaster Avenue runs horizontally across the center of the picture parallel with the fence. The Whiteland Friends Meeting is visible on the left. In the 1960s, Route 202 was constructed along the path of the defunct Philadelphia and Chester Valley Railroad. This ushered in an era of development of corporate parks, shopping centers, and housing developments.

Loch Aerie was the home of William E. Lockwood, a wealthy manufacturer of paper products, who also had an interest in the Pennsylvania Railroad as the representative of a number of British stockholders. Owner of the Shaw locomotive, he spent much time on various railroad affairs, sometimes lecturing on topics related to railroad activities. In 1865, Lockwood had the Victorian Gothic–style home built. Addison Hutton, who was the architect of Old Main at the West Chester Normal School, designed the building and constructed it of serpentine stone. The cost was a princely $250,000, and it took four years to complete the work on what became one of the finest mansions in the Chester Valley. Currently, the mansion can be seen from the parking lot of the Home Depot in Frazer.

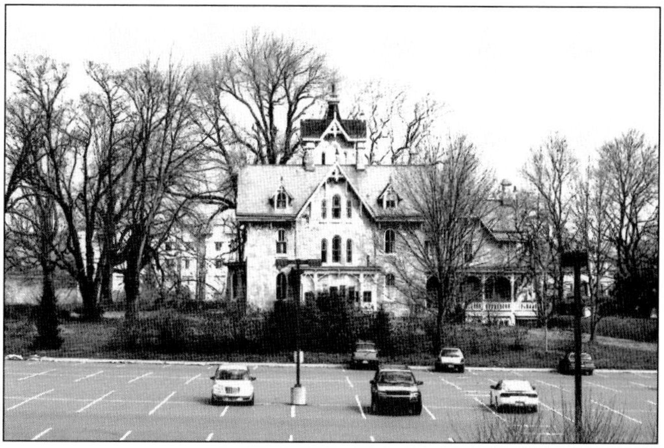

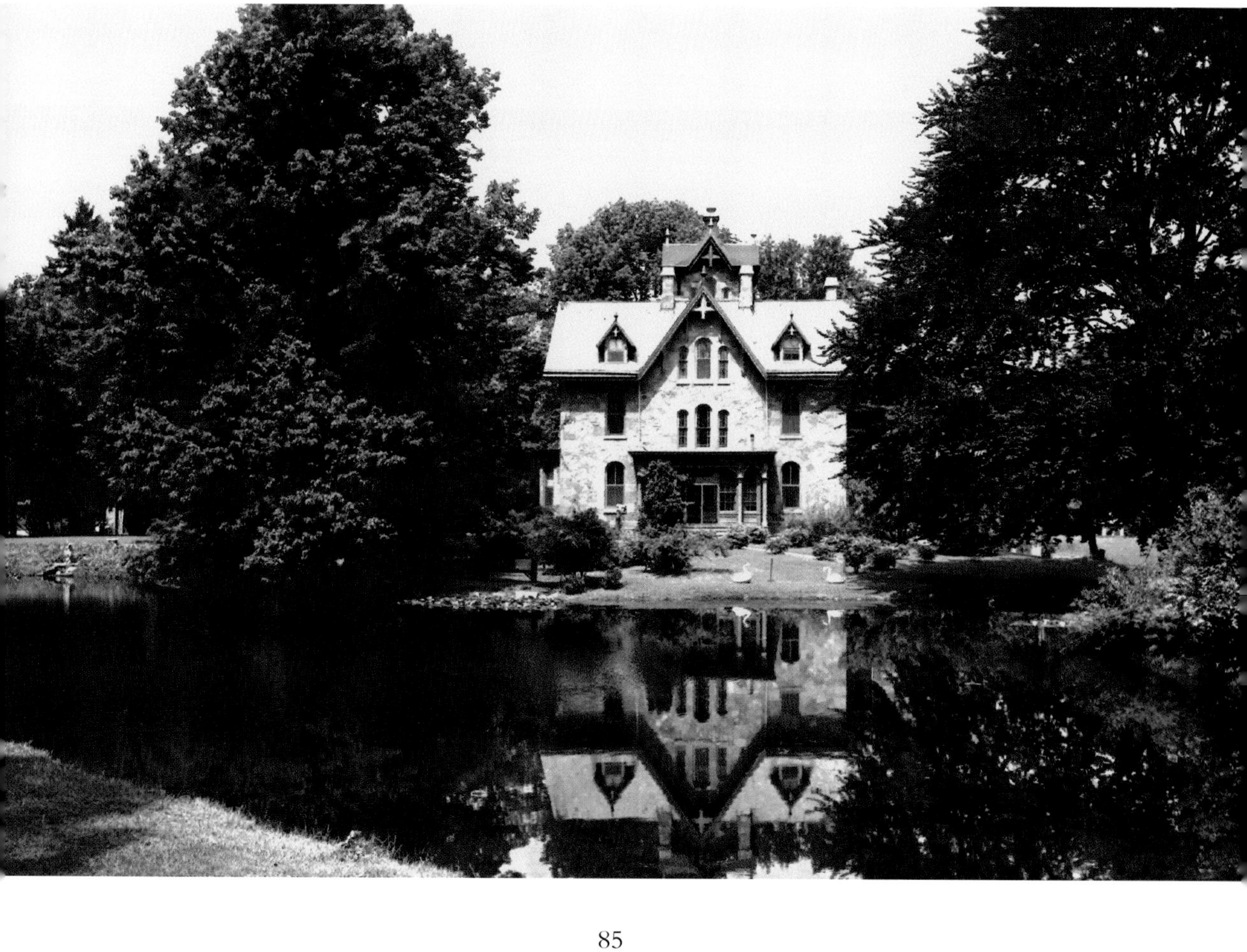

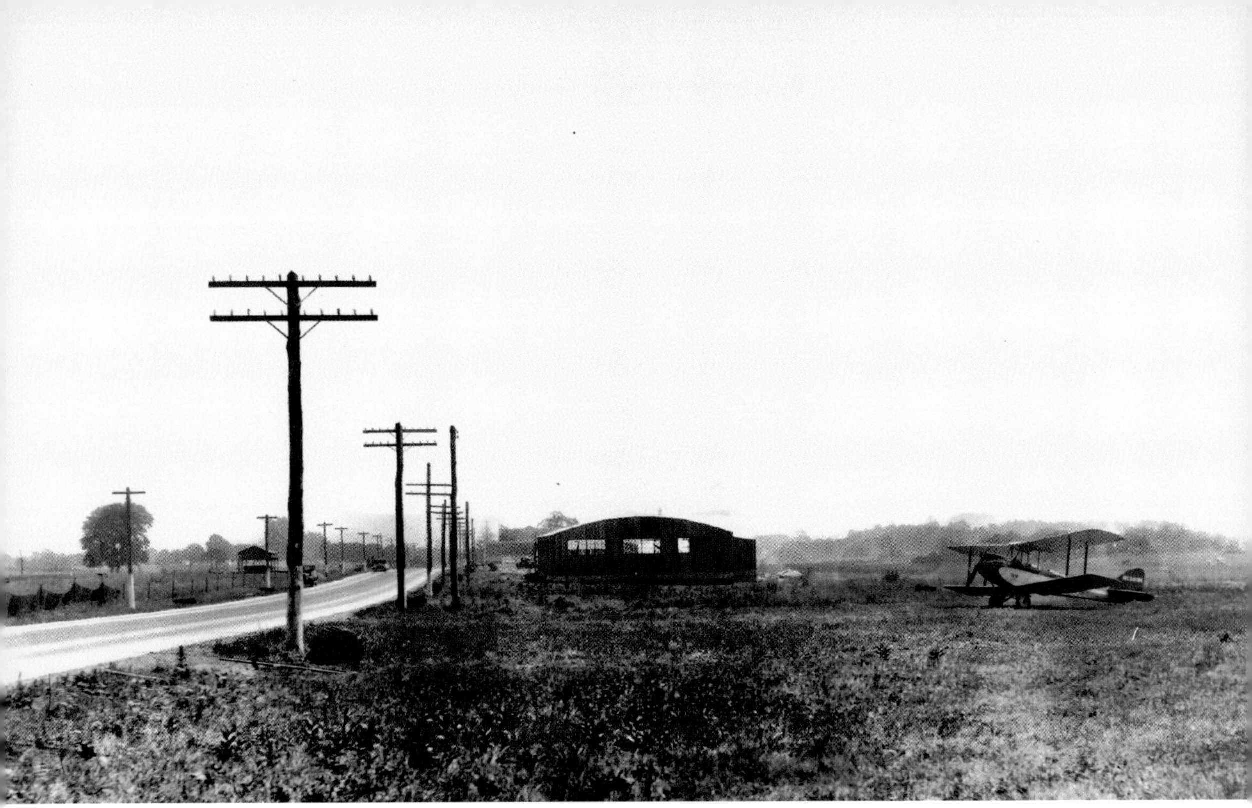

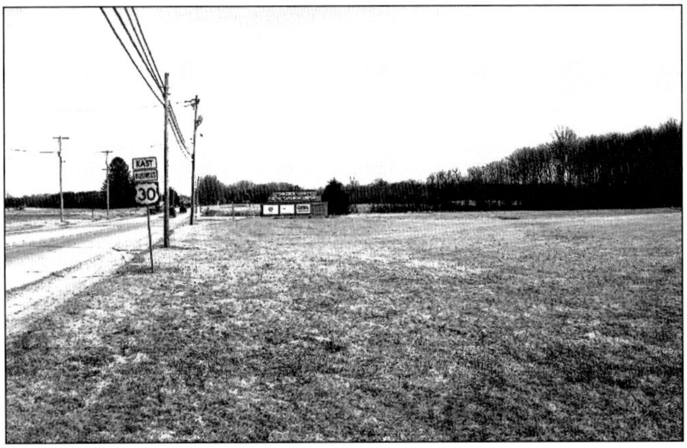

The Coatesville Airport opened in 1930. During the Great Depression, Civil Works Administration funds were used for improvements. Pilots were trained in ground schools at the airport prior to World War II. During the war, activity was severely curtailed by government restrictions on civilian flying along the Atlantic seaboard. Following the war, pilots trained under the GI Bill. In 1958, the airport was purchased by the newly organized Chester County Airport Authority. Today, the Chester County Airport is a major business airport in the western part of the county, and the projections are for continued growth.

Lukens Steel dates from 1810, when Isaac Pennock began an iron and nail factory on the banks of the Brandywine River. In 1813, his daughter Rebecca married Dr. Charles Lukens, who quit his medical practice in 1817 to take over operation of her father's business. Lukens died in 1825, and Rebecca took over the operation of the steel mill. She managed the business until 1849 and turned it into the top producer of boilerplate in the country. For most of its history, Lukens Steel flourished and was a Fortune 500 company as late as 1985. Recent years have seen a decline. In 1998, Bethlehem Steel completed its acquisition of Lukens. International Steel Group purchased all Bethlehem holdings in 2003 and continues to produce steel plate.

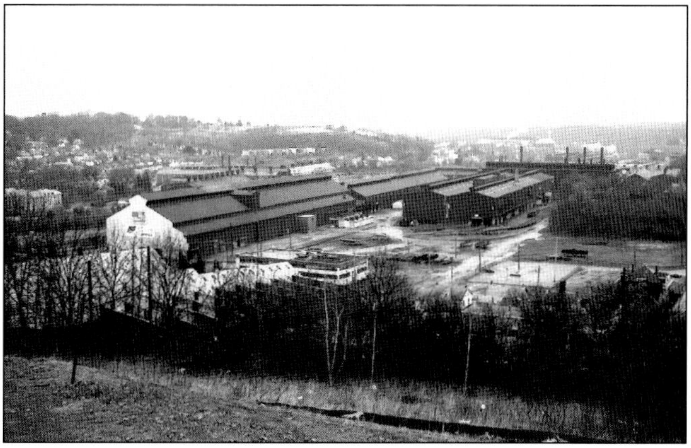

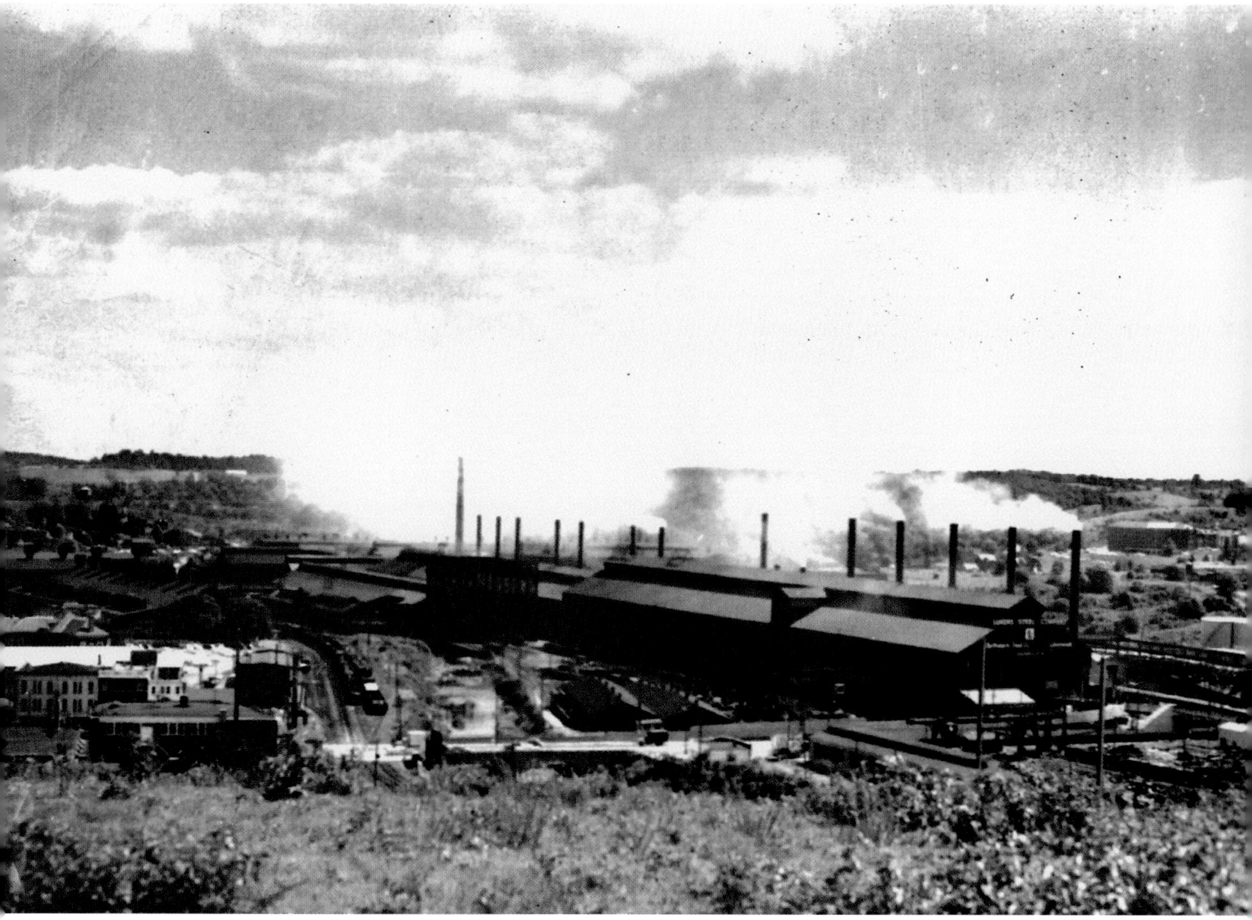

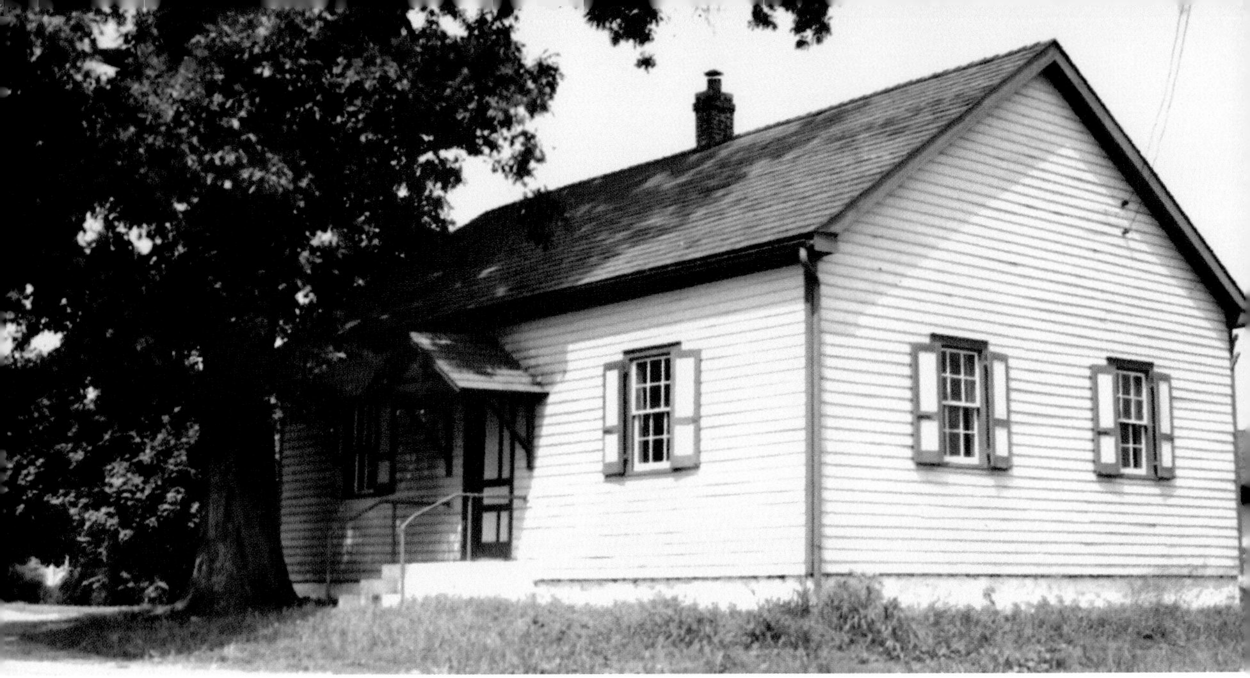

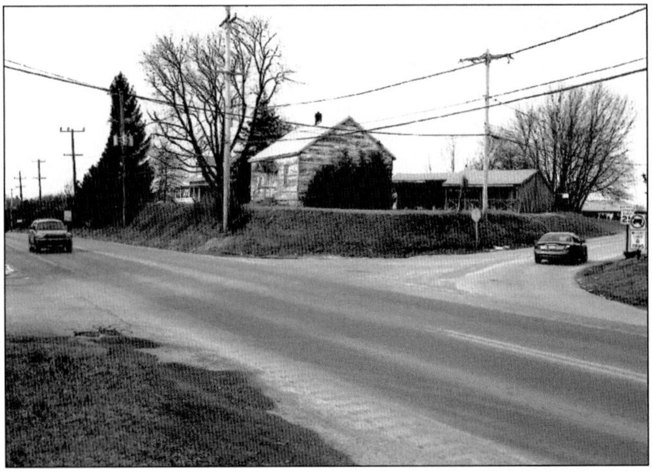

During the 1850s, lively discussions on temperance, woman's rights, and abolition were held at the New Garden Lyceum on Route 41 in New Garden Township. In 1856, a meeting to support John C. Frémont, the first presidential candidate of the newly formed Republican Party, was held there. In 1887, the building was deeded to the township by George Thompson, a trustee for the Lyceum House Company. It then served as a school meeting place for community groups and as a center for lectures and entertainment. The township supervisors used it to meet and also as a storage area. It is privately owned today and is used as a storage facility.

In the 1750s, when the Gap Newport Turnpike was first laid out, Thomas McKean built the William Pitt Hotel for his father, William McKean. When McKean read a copy of a speech made before British Parliament in opposition to the Stamp Act of 1766, he was so impressed that he honored the Earl of Chatham by naming the inn after him. A sign made with the Earl's portrait was hung in front of the inn. Thomas McKean later served three terms as governor of Pennsylvania. Today, the high volume of traffic on Route 41 has caused many problems. When the road was widened, part of the historic inn had to be torn down to accommodate the changes. Kauffman's Furniture now occupies the building.

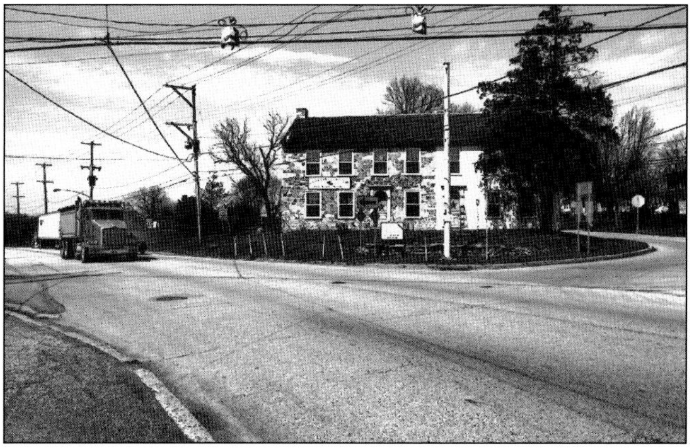

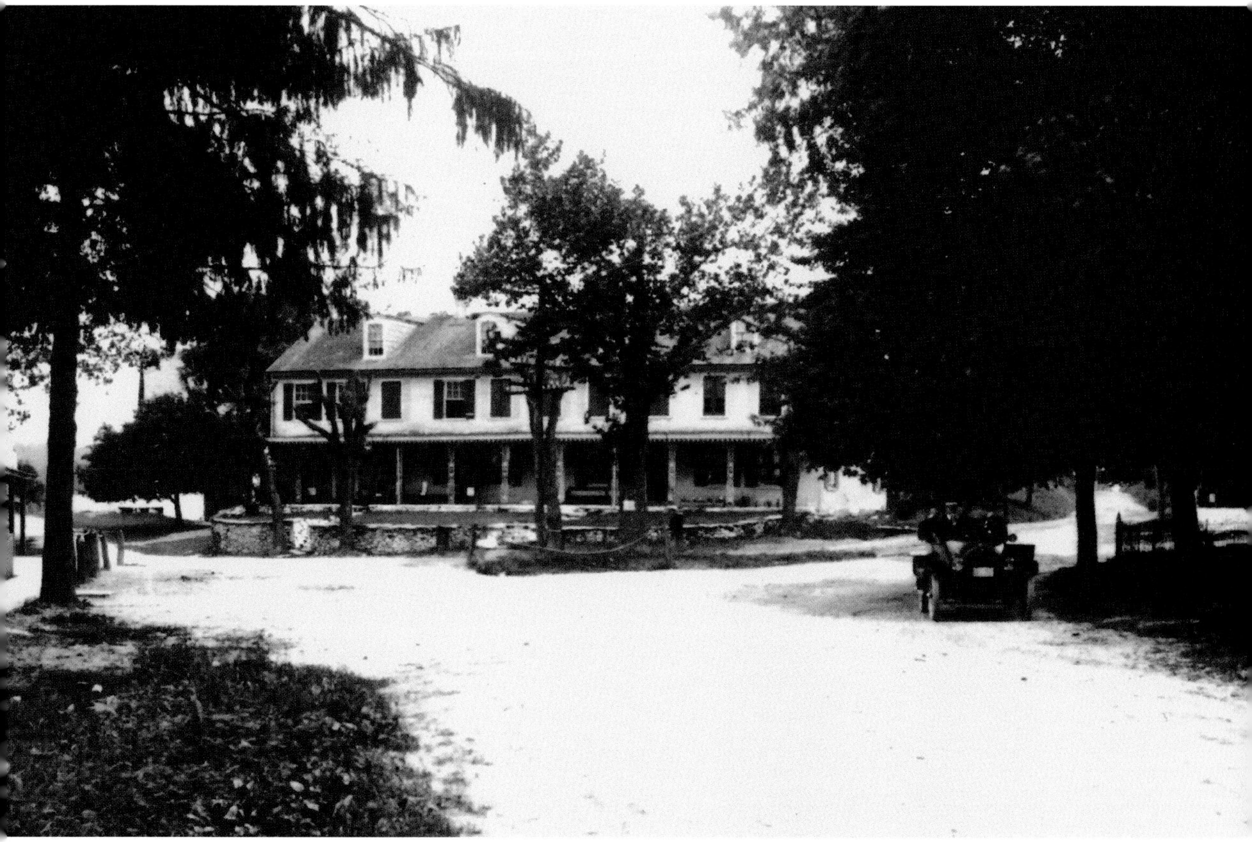

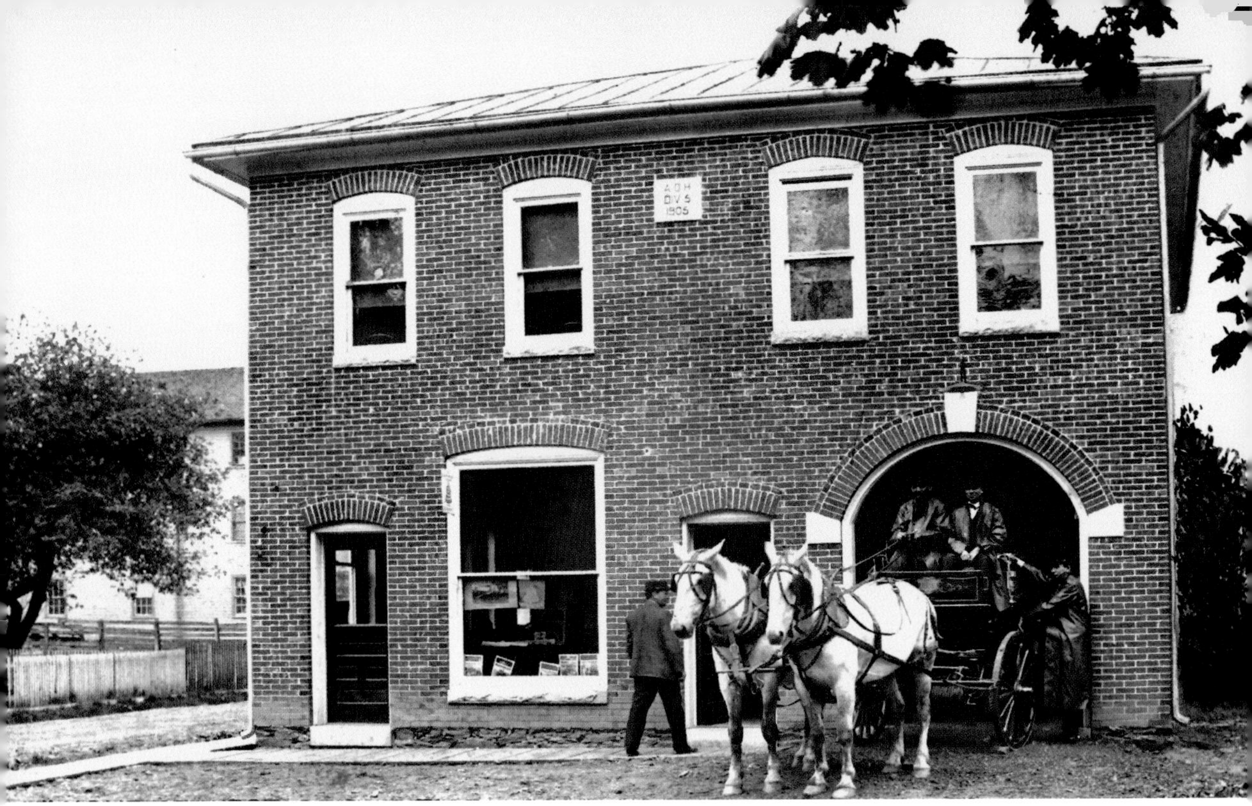

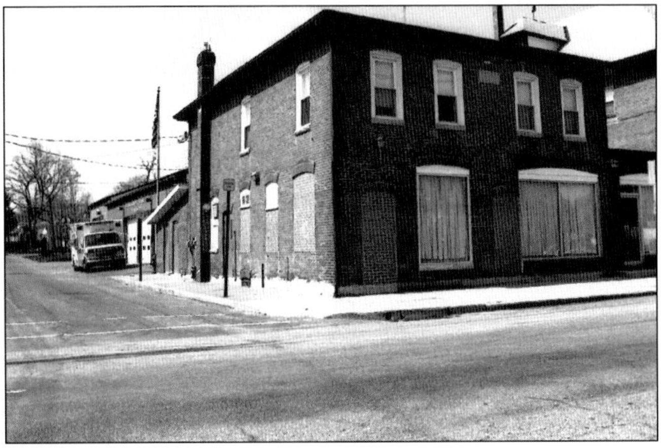

After two serious fires in 1904, the residents of West Grove organized the West Grove Fire Company. Their first chemical fire engine, as seen in the historical photograph, was purchased in 1905 at a cost of $1,500. After renting the space on Walnut Street, the fire company purchased the Hibernian Hall lodge building in 1928. A new firehouse was constructed around the corner from this building in 1952. The firefighters donated their time and talent to aid in the building of the new firehouse.

Charlton Forest Farm in Penn Township was owned by a succession of Charlton family members since it was purchased from Gulielma Penn in the early 1700s. Clara E. Nelson, niece of then farm owner Thomas Charlton, took the 1903 photograph below. Thomas M. Charlton was a Chester County commissioner from 1865 to 1868. He and his wife, Mary Ann Kelso, had six children. They grew corn, oats, wheat, potatoes, apples, and peaches and raised cows and sheep on the 197-acre farm. Currently, the original Charlton family homestead is a private home, although the barn and outbuildings have been replaced by a housing development. The location is convenient for commuting to jobs in Delaware and Maryland. A working dairy farm borders the property.

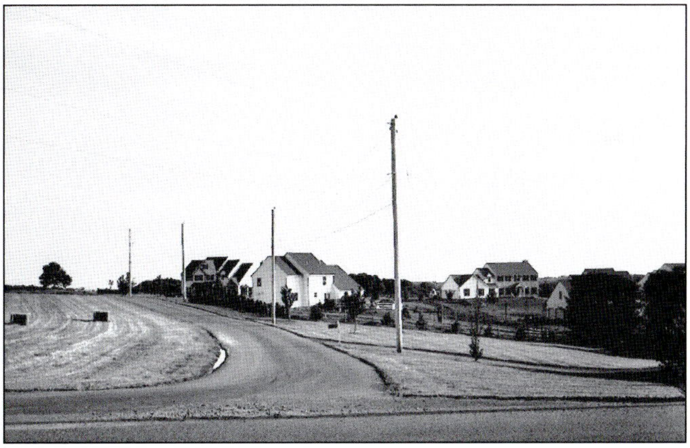

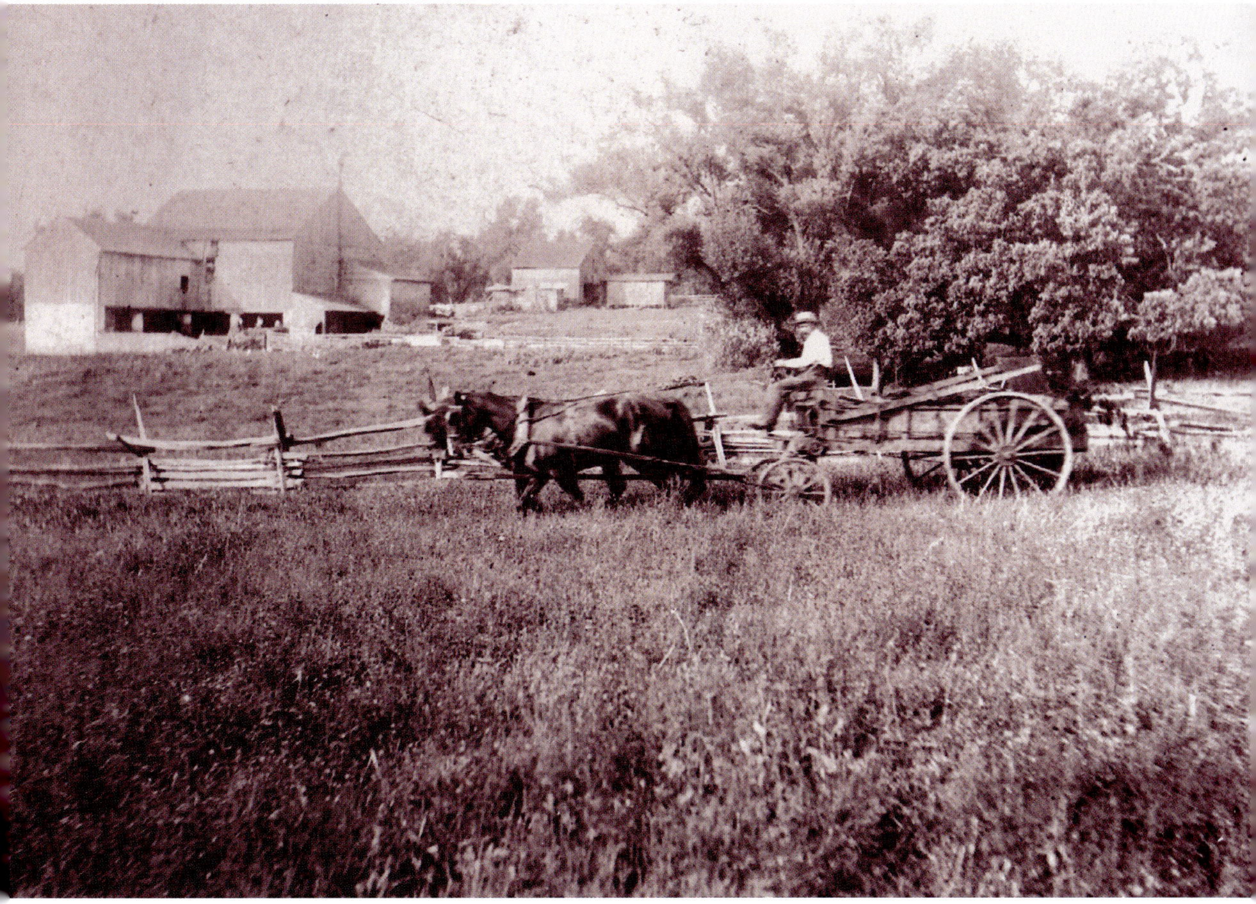

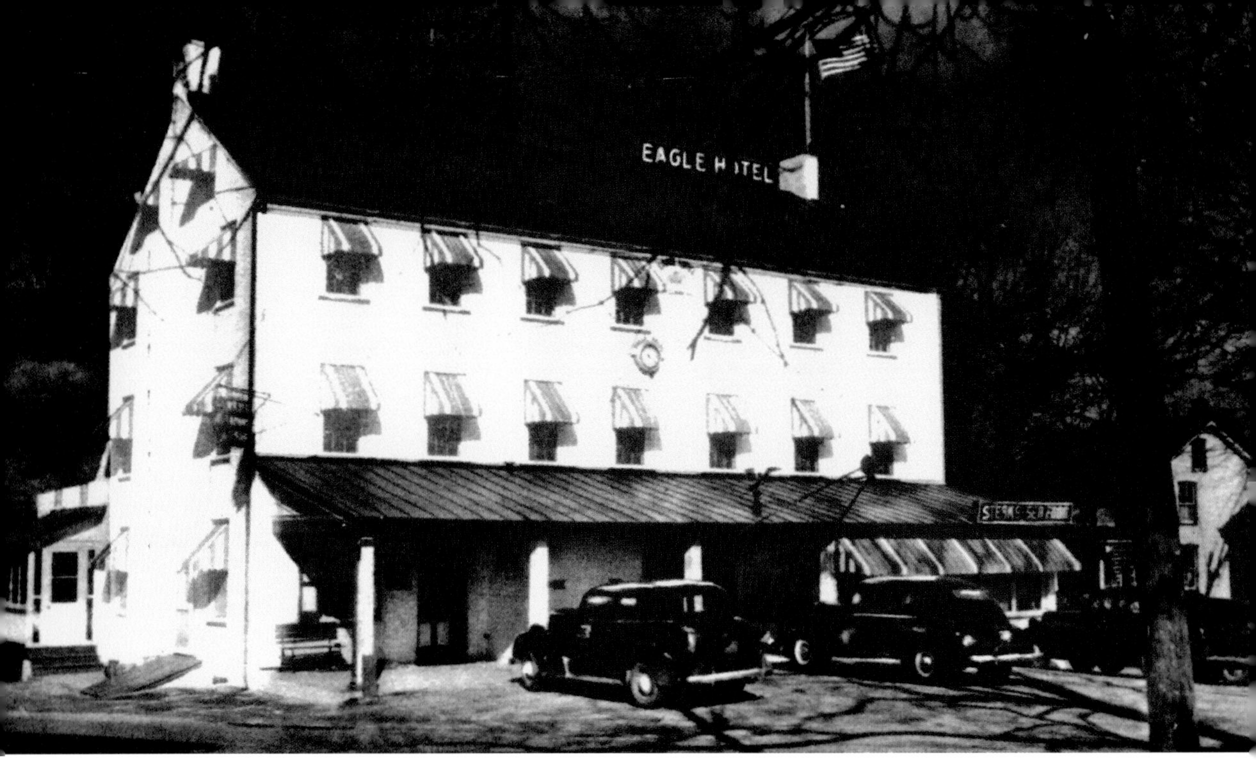

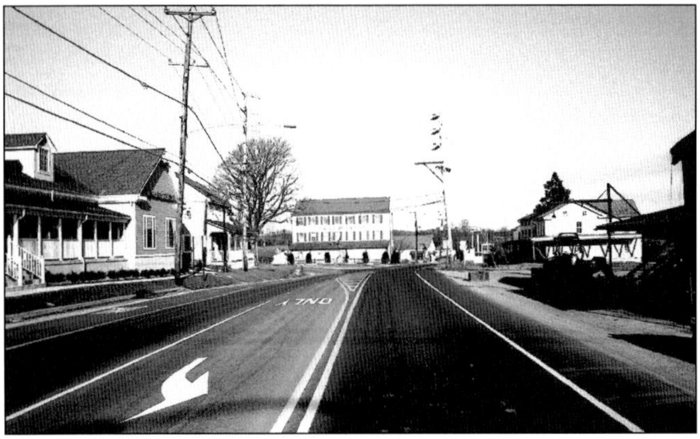

The Eagle Hotel, seen above, dates from 1859. Several inns had previously occupied the site located on Route 100 in Upper Uwchlan Township. In 1727, James Pugh opened the first inn to serve travelers. In 1799, it was renamed the President Adams. James Beerbower tore down the old stone tavern and erected the current building. He served as innkeeper for 44 years. Fire damaged the structure in December 1958, but the building was saved, as a stone partition prevented the fire from spreading throughout the entire attic. The Eagle Tavern still caters to those who journey along the much expanded Route 100 corridor.

The road that became Route 100 in Uwchlan Township was surveyed and laid out in 1726. The village of Lionville grew up around the Red Lion Tavern and Uwchlan Friends Meeting. By the 1890s, when this photograph was taken, it was a quiet village consisting of a general store, blacksmith shop, tannery and butcher shop, tailor, hat maker, Lutheran church, and schoolhouse. A cement roadway replaced the dirt road in 1922. By the early 1950s, PennDOT bypassed Route 100 around the little town, preserving its village ambiance. Today, 48,000 cars daily travel past Lionville on Route 100 to access the Pennsylvania Turnpike nearby.

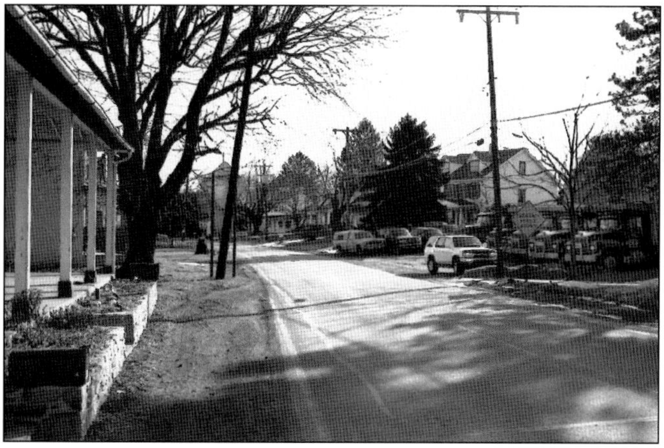

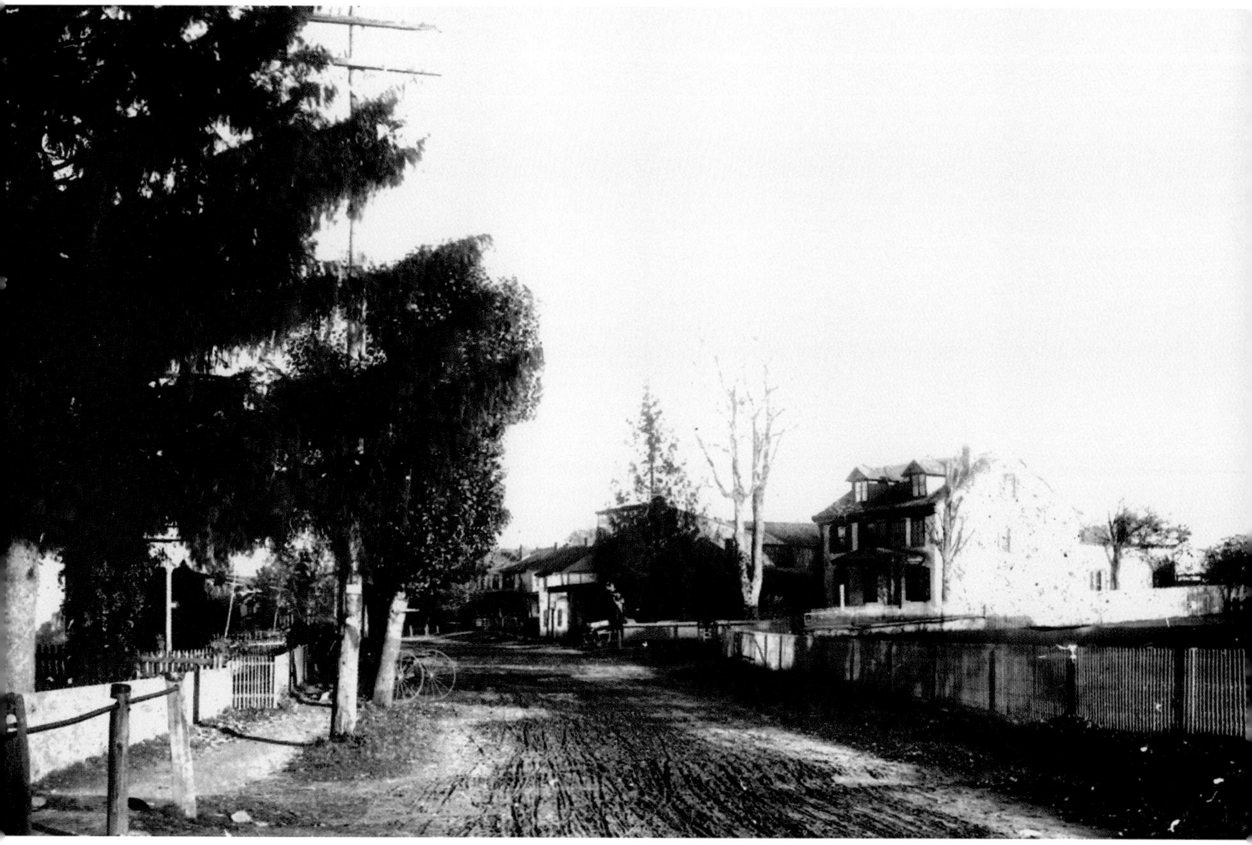

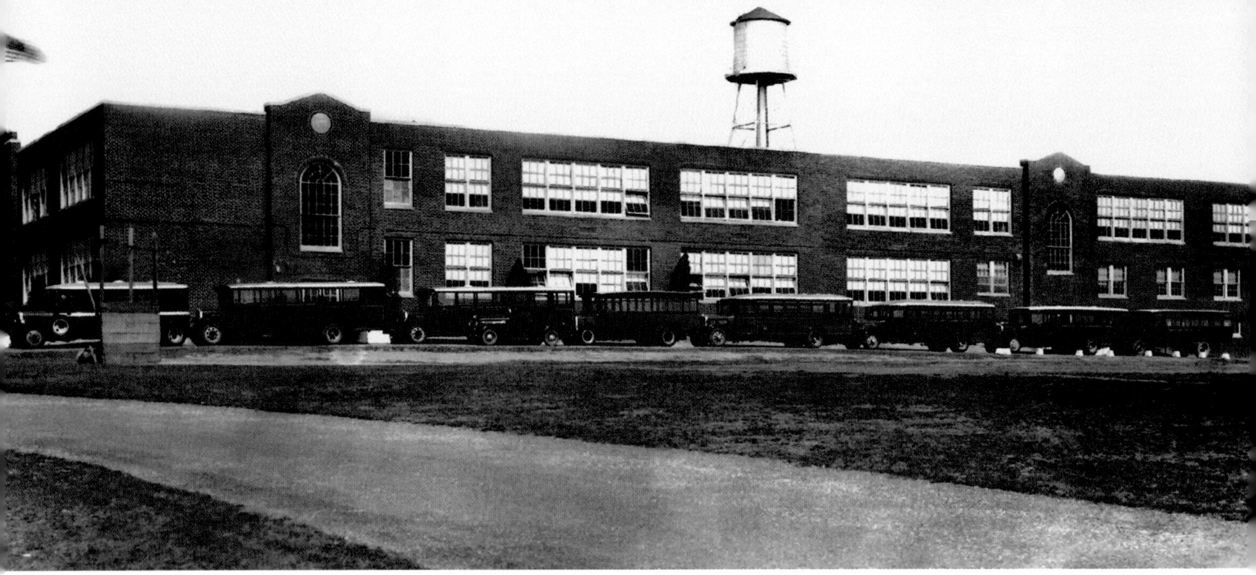

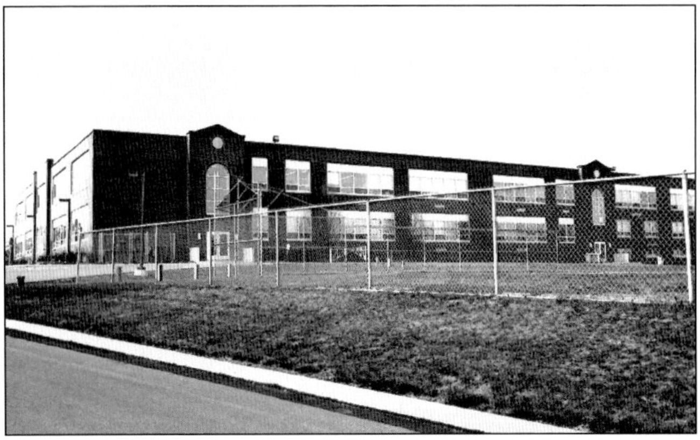

In 1921, the school districts of East Marlborough, Newlin, Pocopson, and West Marlborough joined to form the Unionville Joint Consolidated School District. When the consolidated building opened in 1923, 22 rural schools closed. The school operated as a combined elementary and secondary vocational school until the close of the 1940–1941 school year. Beginning in the 1941–1942 school year, the secondary school was changed from a vocational to an academic high school. That year there were 761 students in all grades, with 16 elementary and 16 secondary teachers. The enrollment of the Unionville-Chadds Ford District is now more than 3,800, and the faculty and staff exceed 250.

Lincoln University was chartered in the spring of 1854 as Ashmun Institute. It was renamed after Pres. Abraham Lincoln in 1866. It was the first institution of higher learning to offer instruction in the arts and sciences to males of African descent. It remained an all-male school until 1952, when women were first admitted. Among its many prestigious graduates are world-renowned author Langston Hughes '29; first African American U.S. Supreme Court justice Thurgood Marshall '30; first president of Nigeria Kwame Nkrumah '39; and Philadelphia judge Jacqueline Allen '74. At present, more than 2,000 students are enrolled in undergraduate and graduate programs. The photograph below shows the campus *c.* 1930.

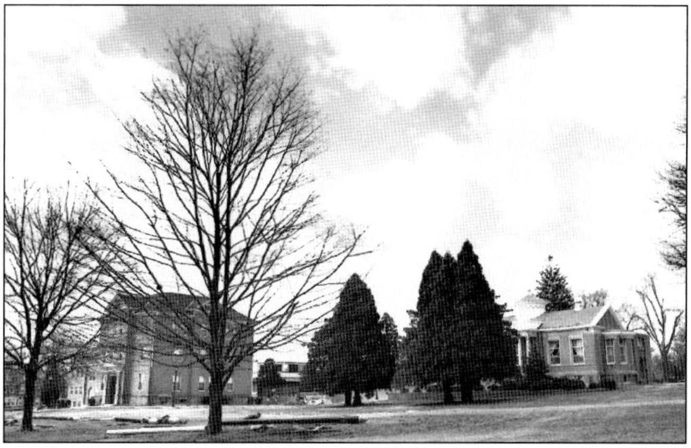

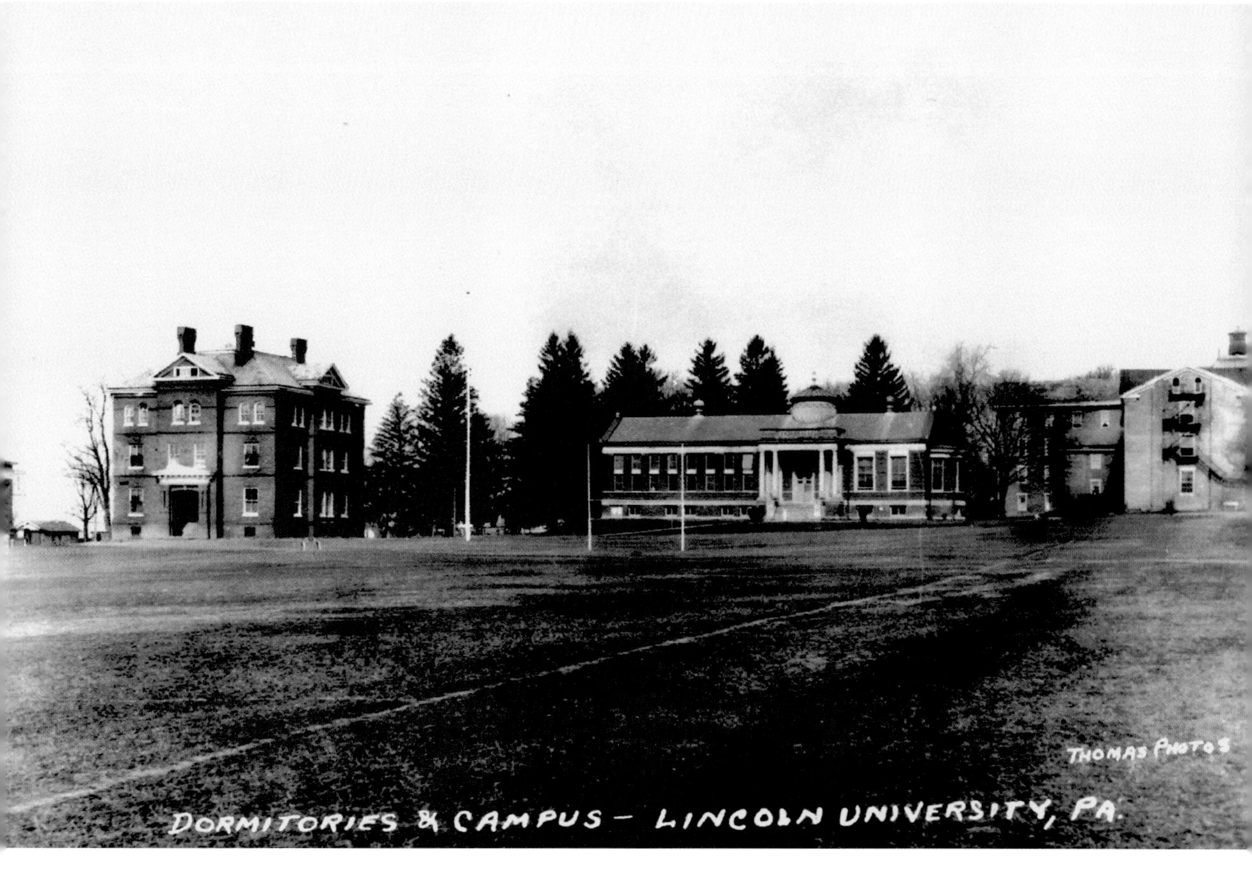

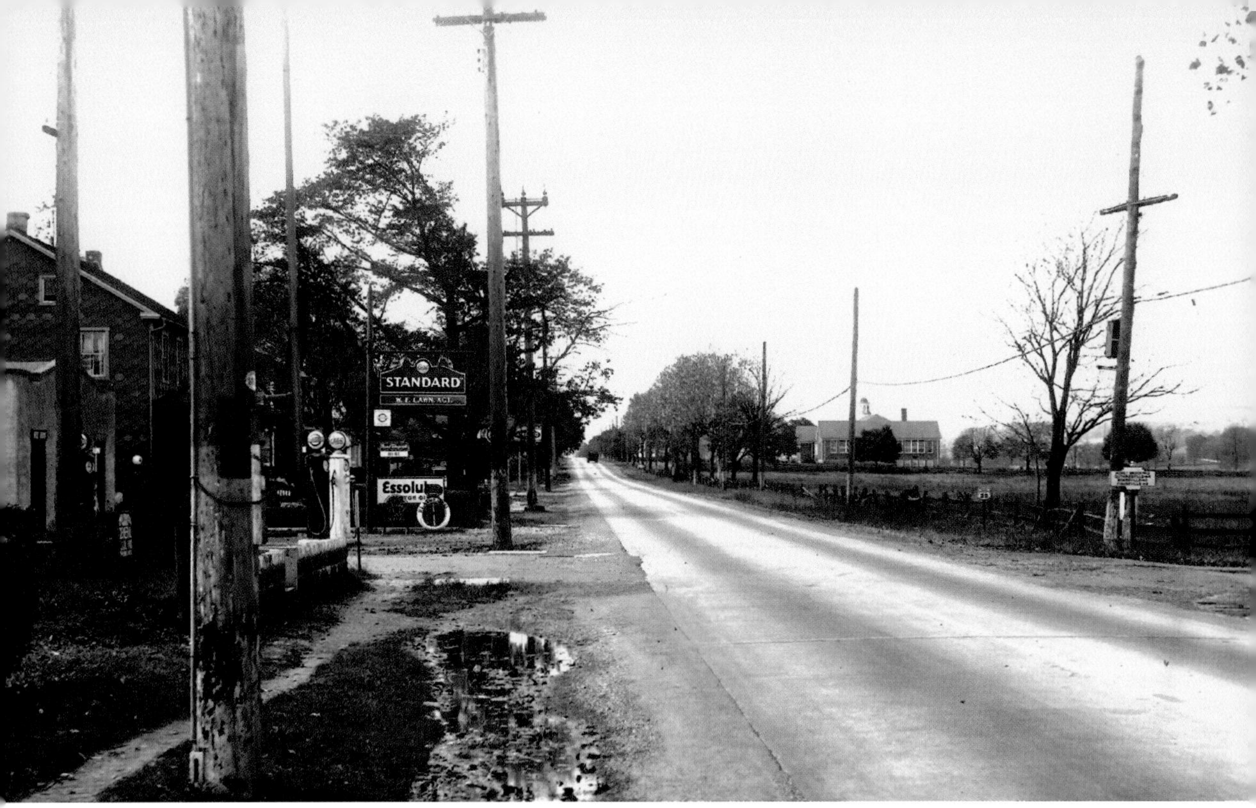

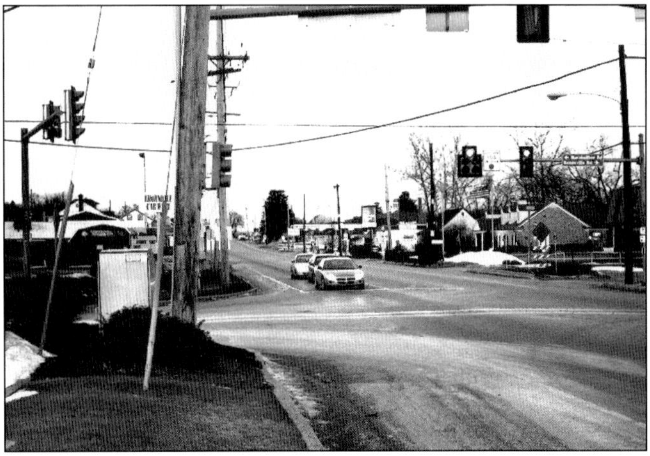

Route 30, which paralleled the Main Line of the Pennsylvania Railroad, has long been a major thoroughfare through Chester County. The 1932 photograph above portrays the road running through Thorndale, some three miles east of Coatesville. Thorndale was founded in 1847 around a rolling mill erected by James and John Forsythe. The Caln Elementary School, seen in the distance on the right, has been serving district students since it opened in January 1928. A portion of the gas station on the left remains, but the houses have been torn down and have been replaced by a McDonald's, a radiator-repair shop, and a car wash. Overall open space has succumbed to strip malls and other business establishments along the congested highway.